PENGUIN BOOKS

THE ROAD TO SOMEWHERE

David Goodhart is the founding editor of *Prospect* magazine and one of the most distinctive voices in British politics today. He is currently head of the Demography, Immigration and Integration Unit at the think tank Policy Exchange, and was previously director of the centre-left think tank Demos. His last book *The British Dream: Successes and Failures of Post-War Immigration* (2013) was runner-up for the Orwell Prize in 2014 and was a finalist for Political Book of the Year in the Paddy Power Political Book Awards. David voted remain in the EU referendum and has been a mainly inactive member of the Labour Party since he was a student.

D0444815

DAVID GOODHART

The Road to Somewhere

The New Tribes Shaping British Politics

PENGUIN BOOKS

PENGUIN BOOKS

UK | USA | Canada | Ireland | Australia
India | New Zealand | South Africa

Penguin Books is part of the Penguin Random House group of companies
whose addresses can be found at global.penguinrandomhouse.com.

First published in Great Britain by C. Hurst & Co. (Publishers) Ltd., 2017
Published in Penguin Books 2017
005

Printed in Great Britain by Clays Ltd, St Ives plc

A CIP catalogue record for this book is available from the British Library

ISBN: 978-0-141-98697-5

www.greenpenguin.co.uk

MIX
Paper from
responsible sources
FSC
www.fsc.org
FSC® C018179

Penguin Random House is committed to a
sustainable future for our business, our readers
and our planet. This book is made from Forest
Stewardship Council® certified paper.

CONTENTS

Introduction   vii
Acknowledgements   xxi

1. The Great Divide   1
   A Journey from Anywhere   14

2. Anywheres and Somewheres   19
   The Decline (but Survival) of Traditional Values   27
   Higher Education and Mobility   33
   The Great Liberalisation   38
   The Outriders   44

3. European Populism and the Crisis of the Left   49
   Populism Goes Mainstream   54
   America and Europe: The Populist Convergence   64
   Populist Parties: The Necessary, the Weird and the Ugly   69
   Why Populists Damage the Left Most   75

4. Globalisation, Europe and the Persistence of the National   81
   A World on the Move?   81
   The Globalisation Overshoot   85
   The European Tragedy   91
   The Persistence of the National   104

5. A Foreign Country?   117
   The Immigration Story   122
   What About Integration?   127
   The London Conceit   134

CONTENTS

6. The Knowledge Economy and Economic Demoralisation   147
   The Disappearing Middle   149
   A Short History of Education and Training   154
   Living Standards and Inequality   167
   Short-Termism and Foreign Ownership   172

7. The Achievement Society   179
   What is Actually Happening on Mobility?   183
   Making it into the Elite   187

8. What About the Family?   193
   More State, Less Family   199
   What do Women Want?   205
   Supporting Partnerships in an Age of Male-Female Equality   210

9. A New Settlement   215
   Somewheres are not going Anywhere   221
   Giving Somewheres a Voice   225

Notes   235
Select Bibliography   261
Index   265

INTRODUCTION

There were many and varied reactions to this book when it was first published at the end of March 2017 but all agreed on *one* thing: the timing was impeccable. It was one of the first books to offer a general explanation for the two upsets of 2016—Brexit and Trump—in terms of the new value divisions in developed democracies.

My explanation in miniature ran like this. A large minority group of the highly educated and mobile—the Anywheres—who tend to value autonomy and openness and comfortably surf social change have recently come to dominate our society and politics. There is also a larger but less influential group—the Somewheres—who are more rooted and less well educated, who value security and familiarity and are more connected to group identities than Anywheres. Somewheres feel that their more socially conservative intuitions have been excluded from the public space in recent decades, which has destabilised our politics and led to the Brexit and Trump backlashes.

Several things have happened since first publication in early 2017—above all elections in the UK, France and the Netherlands—to suggest that we may now be experiencing an Anywhere fight-back against that 2016 advance of Somewheres—or at least the forward march of Somewhere priorities may have been halted for now.

Somewheres do not only vote for populist parties but almost all populist voters are drawn from Somewhere ranks. The main populist party performed strongly in both the French and Netherlands elections (the Front National scoring almost 34 per cent in the final round of the presidential election and the PVV scoring 13 per cent and putting it in second place in the Netherlands general election) but, as widely expected, fell well short of victory and may have reached the high-water mark for that kind of 'hard' populist party. Moreover, Emmanuel Macron in France campaigned as 'Anywhere and proud' and achieved a remarkable result in the presidential election, albeit one which did not seem able to provide any kind of new settlement of French divisions.

And what of the unexpected UK election result in 2017? Some people argued that the relative success of the Corbyn Labour party—followed swiftly by the Grenfell Tower tragedy—marked a return to two-party, left–right, socio-economic politics, rendering redundant Anywhere–Somewhere type value analysis with its greater stress on socio-cultural factors.

On the contrary, the voting patterns vindicated an Anywhere–Somewhere analysis even if the result itself seems to have damaged one possible centre-right solution to the value divide in the form of 'Mayism'. And Grenfell, with a mainly ethnic minority and often foreign born population, was as much a symbol of Britain's new openness and cultural diversity as of its older class divide.

Nevertheless, the Corbyn team managed to appear principled while displaying a high level of pragmatism that united the left, squeezed the smaller parties and disarmed their critics. They revived, albeit only temporarily, a new version of the old professional middle class–blue-collar Labour coalition based on a hard Remainer resentment of Theresa May's version of Brexit and a student-led youth protest vote. This was in part an Anywhere *middle class* left populism, exemplified by Labour's policy of abolishing student tuition fees but keeping the freeze on welfare benefits for the poor. Both parties addressed intergenerational fairness, the Conservatives by cutting subsidies to the affluent old, Labour by increasing subsidies to the affluent young.

Labour's support for Brexit, albeit somewhat more ambiguous than the Conservative's, helped to downplay Corbyn's long stated 'global villager' preferences on immigration and national identity. This, combined with an attractive anti-austerity argument, helped the party to, at least temporarily, reverse its haemorrhaging of working class voters, especially those working in the public sector.

But class cross-dressing between the two main parties continued, underlining one of the main arguments of the book that we are seeing greater political *con*vergence between classes and value groups on economic issues and greater *di*vergence on 'security and identity' cultural issues. (It was striking how unfavourable to business both main party manifestos were.)

Overall, better-off voters still tended to back the Tories but, according to the most comprehensive post-election YouGov survey, the Tory working class (C2DE) vote rose dramatically from 32 per cent in 2015 to 44 per cent in 2017 which was higher than Labour's share (42 per cent) and exactly the same as the party's share of the middle class (ABC1) vote. The Tories picked up almost 60 per cent of the former UKIP vote, compared with Labour's 18 per cent, as well as some traditional Labour seats like Mansfield, while the swing to Labour was highest in middle class/student seats like Bristol West, Hove and Hampstead and the party scored almost 40 per cent among the professional and managerial groups (AB).

The Corbyn 'effect' that bequeathed the post-election political stalemate by narrowing the vote gap between the two big parties to less than three percentage points was summed up by John Gray, writing just after the election in the *New Statesman*: 'Corbyn has brought together some of the most vital forces on the contemporary scene: the anti-capitalist radicalism of young people who are innocent of history, a bourgeois cult of personal authenticity and naked self-interest expressed as self-admiring virtue.'

The parliamentary stalemate may also reflect a deeper stalemate between the Anywhere and Somewhere value blocs, a socio-cultural version of the economic deadlock between the middle class and the organised working class in the 1960s and 1970s—finally broken by the arrival of Margaret Thatcher in 1979.

The final chapter of this book argues that the central task of politics is now to find a new settlement between Anywhere and Somewhere priorities in our society and culture. What the last election has shown is just what a difficult task that is likely to be for both main parties. It seemed to me, writing at the end of 2016, that the most likely source of a solution would come from 'admonished Anywheres' like Theresa May who realised that politicians had not been listening enough to the decent populist instincts of the Somewheres.

May, with her adviser Nick Timothy, did indeed come up with a plausible new settlement that took Somewhere preferences seriously over Brexit and immigration and then took off in a novel, leftish direction (for Conservatives) on public housing, executive pay, workers on boards, beefing up technical education and paying for social care through tapping into housing wealth. The problem was that this radical centrist politics had been imposed from the top down and the traditional Tory rank and file were not ready for it, at least the social care part.

It is hard to see how a Corbyn-led Labour party ever more entrenched in the Anywhere values of the younger, graduate middle class can construct, or would even want to construct, a new settlement between Anywheres and Somewheres. If the propertied middle class of middle England has in effect vetoed a tilt to working class Somewhere Britain on the part of the Tory party, the young zealous Anywheres in the university seats would surely similarly veto any shift in a more nationalist or socially conservative direction for Labour, in the unlikely event of a leadership emerging that wanted to take that path.

Incidentally, my description of the large, and largely unexamined, cultural, economic and political power of higher education in Britain—with its often militant Anywhere ideology—was borne out in the last election with the student dominated seats and the radical Remainers playing such a big role in Labour's success. (Ironically, however, one of the long term changes that is likely to follow recent elections in Britain and America, where the abolition of tuition fees has played such a galvanising role for the student vote, is that fees will, indeed, decline and the power and wealth of the higher education sector with them.)

So, British politics entered the first phase of the Brexit negotiations in a state of confusion, suspended between a Somewhere Brexit and an

Anywhere Brexit. The quest remained for a politician or political party able to give voice and shape to a new Anywhere–Somewhere settlement.

* * *

I learnt many things from the public debate about this book. Many of my critics wanted to change the subject to technology (the next technological revolution may do to Anywhere jobs what the last one did to Somewhere ones) or to economics (no financial crash, no wage stagnation, no populism).

Others objected to what they saw as the simplifying, binary Anywhere–Somewhere divide. It was certainly a useful simplification when it came to attracting attention to the book. But there is, in fact, plenty of light and shade in my more detailed description of the main value groups inside and I also describe a large Inbetweener group (though, as one reviewer pointed out, with no embellishment).

I emphasised to such critics two points which perhaps do not come across strongly enough in the book. First, that both of these loose worldviews are decent and legitimate, they just happen to conflict in certain fundamental ways. Second, I invented the labels but not the value groups themselves that are, as the academics say 'in the data' (meaning sources like the British Social Attitudes surveys) if you interrogate them appropriately.

It is true that I am making the common-sense assumption that the people who are taking a restrictive view on, say, immigration are *the same people* who are strongly concerned about national citizenship and common norms and so on. You could also argue with some of the proportions that I allocate to the different groups and sub-groups (including the proportion of decent populists), which are certainly fuzzy at the edges, but these would be only minor differences.

Friendly critics pointed, rightly, to the absence of religion in the book and its potential importance as a bridge between the localism of particular religious communities and the universal connectedness of many faiths.

Several readers pointed out that I had failed to note how the culture of art and architecture has become overwhelmingly Anywhere dominated. David Lucas argued that so much Anywhere architecture is faceless and devoid of the ornamentation that was a traditional form of visual storytelling. (Similarly, Roger Scruton has written well about how often modern art is at war with ideas of home.)

Another point that I was rightly picked up on was not stressing enough that Anywhere is a metaphor. Obviously, Anywhere people come from somewhere but the majority who are 'leavers,' in the sense of leaving their home town for university and/or career and not returning, can still be quite rooted in *new* places and networks. Indeed, they are often connected to strong 'chosen' communities in liberal Anywhere hot-spots like Brighton or Stoke Newington and can also express a 'group think' as binding and blinding as Somewheres.

* * *

There are three themes in the book that I have become more absorbed in since writing it and that I want to touch on briefly here: the family, the achievement society and free trade.

I expected the family chapter of the book to be the most controversial and was pleasantly surprised when it did not seem to attract the wrong kind of polemical, polarising attention. This is not an area of politics or policy I had thought much about until writing the book—my own mother was a pre-feminist woman, but women's equality has been part of the common sense of my liberal, professional social circles throughout my adult life. But when I considered the drift of recent policy for the book I was surprised to find how narrowly it reflected the priorities of a relatively small group of women who focus heavily on career.

During the 2017 general election the family was repeatedly invoked by all parties but the actual family got almost no attention in the party manifestos, including the Conservative one. Yet you do not have to be an old-school traditionalist to wonder whether many of our contemporary problems do not have at least some root in a neglect of the private realm.

Consider this list: the crisis in social care, thanks in part to the decline in family obligation; the housing crisis, exacerbated by the decline of the stable two-parent family; the over-dependence on immigration, because of the economic and cultural bias against larger families; the rise of stress and mental illness, especially among young people; the curse of loneliness for millions of older people; the persistence of gender pay inequality, and the difficulty of recruiting people to caring jobs because they are so undervalued and underpaid.

A central challenge of modern politics is how to restore dignity and prestige to the domestic realm—which means one parent, usually but not always a mother, being able to afford to stay at home for longer—without reversing the advances in women's equality and autonomy of the past generations.

Yet all the water is still flowing against domesticity despite the continuing attachment to it revealed in the opinion surveys. At the higher end, policy is about equality at work and minimising the impact of motherhood on professional women's careers, and at the lower income and single mother end it is about providing the support to enable women to work as much as possible, so contributing to household income and Treasury coffers. The main points in the Conservative manifesto on the family were about parity for women in public appointments, helping men and women to share parenting more easily and another increase in childcare subsidy (but only if you hand your child to a stranger to care for while you work).

The broader ambivalence about the family reflects the decline of religious feeling and traditional female altruism, and a more individualistic Anywhere way of life for both men and women. (As of June 2017 more than one third of current EU leaders were childless through either choice or misfortune.) It also reflects the increasing economisation of public life.

Moreover, policy is increasingly driven by the assumption that the gender division of labour should not merely be modified but transcended altogether: men and women are not only equal, it is assumed, but have exactly the same priorities. And the decline of the mainstream, two-parent family is seen as an unalterable part of the modern world, the result of choices that individuals make when less constrained by tradition.

Affluent professional families often stick to conventional marriage arrangements for themselves but do not preach what they practice, and they are happy to turn a blind eye to the less stable social and marriage norms for less well educated, low earners (a pattern also detected in the US by the conservative Charles Murray and liberal Robert Putnam).

Nobody in mainstream politics wants to 'return to the 1950s'. Yet there has been so much stress on greater autonomy for women, and the central importance of work outside the home, that we have lost sight of two equally important goals: how to respect the choices of many different kinds of women, especially those who put family first, and how to preserve the two-parent family in an era of greater moral freedom.

There is no need to continue fighting the last war for equality— my two daughters face no more obstacles to professional success than my two sons (at least until motherhood). In the interests of genuine pluralism, society can now support both the egalitarian-androgynous way of life—in which men and women share all tasks equally—and a modified version of the gender division of labour, and even the stay-at-home mother (and occasionally father).

There is surely a big political win for any party that really does listen to mainstream Somewhere Britain on this subject. Ending the bias against domesticity would be fair, popular and might even save the state money. It would be modern social conservatism with a purpose.

* * *

The second area in which I felt I was just scratching the surface of something much bigger was the achievement society/social mobility theme. Underlying so many of the changes that have made life more uncomfortable for many Somewheres in recent decades is one bigger change: the elevation of educational qualifications and cognitive ability into the gold standard of social esteem.

Only a couple of generations ago, a large number of people

performed skilled jobs that required little cognitive ability but required a lot of experience to do well and thus protected the status of those doing them. And those middling, often manufacturing, jobs also offered achievable incremental progression. Now the majority of jobs in Britain either require a university degree or virtually no training at all.

And thanks to residential universities and the dominance of London, cognitive ability and social achievement is associated with *leaving*, separating oneself from one's roots and becoming an Anywhere. (Leavers, meaning people who leave their home town and never return to live there, tended to be Remainers in the EU referendum and remainers tended to be Leavers.)

Today, about three in five Britons still live within twenty miles of where they lived when aged 14—but few of those people are Russell Group university graduates. David Morris has noted a growing divergence within the graduate population itself between those at more and less prestigious institutions. Russell Group university students are more likely to have the full Anywhere experience, travelling long distances from home and being surrounded by many international students. Students at former polytechnics travel shorter distances and might even still live at home, and such universities are now less likely to have many overseas students.

Social mobility is the mantra of all political parties yet the main tool to achieve it has been expanding higher education, disproportionately benefitting the middle class and southern England—according to Allen Simpson, London and the south-east account for nearly 70 per cent of the UK's top 20 per cent of socially mobile areas, while Yorkshire and Humberside, the north-east and the west Midlands between them count for none. We have created in recent decades what feels like a hereditary meritocracy.

Everyone is in favour of getting the best-qualified people into the right jobs and most people want bright people from whatever background to travel as far as their talents will take them. Yet there is only so much room at Oxbridge or in the top professions and, in any case, it presents a very narrow vision of what a good and successful life entails.

Should it not be possible to lead such a life in Rotherham? Justine Greening, the secretary of state for education, is doubtful. In a March 2017 speech about social mobility she said this: 'I just had a flashback to all the years I spent growing up in Rotherham where I was aiming for something better—many of the things we have been talking about; a better job, owning my own home, an interesting career, a life that I found really challenging... I knew there was something better out there.' I'm sure I would have wanted to leave Rotherham too. But the unselfconscious way in which a cabinet minister doubts whether it is possible to lead a fulfilled life in a town of 120,000 people reveals something topsy-turvy about our country.

There can also be social virtue in staying put, indeed the contribution to the cohesion of neighbourhoods of people staying loyal to a place should be acknowledged more by local councils. One reader wrote to me with the sad story of a neighbour of his in east London who is in his late 60s and still lives in the house he was born in. He used to be known as the local 'sheriff' because he knew everyone, and was a conduit for all the local gossip, in his ethnically mixed street. But now with the pace of population churn much faster many residents don't know him or know that it is 'his' street.

As Joan Williams pointed out in her book *White Working Class: Overcoming Class Cluelessness in America*: 'For many perfectly able working class people their dream is not to join the upper middle class with its different culture but to stay true to their own values in their own communities, just with more money.'

So this is, surely, the new 'third way' of our times: how to achieve an open, mobile society—and elite—while continuing to value meaningful (in other words, stable) communities? How to encourage success and upward mobility without casting a shadow of failure over those who do not (or cannot) move up and out?

The new settlement is not about a lurch into illiberalism—large majorities have accepted the great liberalisation of recent decades on race, gender and sexuality—it is finding ways of redistributing status and social honour as much as money.

And what about free trade? The vast majority of people in Britain and America work in the non-traded service sector. But arguments about trade have a broader relevance to questions of national control and sovereignty.

It is clear, as Michael Lind and others have argued, that economists tend to over-estimate the benefits and under-estimate the costs of free trade especially when you take employment into account and do not take the interests of the consumer as decisive.

Technology is a big factor in manufacturing job losses but so too is trade; a paper by David Autor, David Dorn and Gordon Hanson found that 55 per cent of job losses in US manufacturing between 2000 and 2007 was caused by the surge in Chinese manufacturing exports. Keynes famously argued: 'Free trade assumes that if you throw men out of work in one direction you re-employ them in another. As soon as that link is broken the whole of the free trade argument breaks down.'

Global growth has fallen in every decade since the 1960s from over 5 per cent a year in that decade to under three per cent in the 2000s despite the fact that economic integration has increased substantially and trade has become far freer.

Similarly with free trade deals like NAFTA. Robert Wade argues it has brought great gains to shareholders and top executives in the US and Canada and to their Mexican counterparts, yet Mexico's growth has been sluggish in recent years and average real wages are lower in Mexico City than Shanghai.

At the very least this evidence suggests that the free trade argument should not be left unchallenged especially as it tends to go hand in hand with a loosening of the national corporate citizen rules that companies once felt obliged to follow—labour is now just a global factor of production. And of course labour is usually Somewhere industrial labour. The trade in high-end services is much weaker around the world in part because the professional Anywheres are in a stronger political position to protect themselves from global competition.

INTRODUCTION

Some forms of mild protection that take account of entrenched national preferences and allow for things like local sourcing rules should not be ruled out *a priori* by the international economic institutions.

Nations collaborating together to increase their collective muscle in the global economy is often the rational path but sometimes the cure is worse than the disease, as the Italian and Greek governments discovered when the EU effectively dictated how their governments should behave, and even who should be in them, during the Euro crisis.

The rise of the technocratic state and highly collaborative structures like the EU seems like an increase in control over global forces to political elites but is often perceived as a loss of power by non-elites. Decisions are being made at a more remote level by institutions with which Somewheres feel little identification or loyalty. Moreover, as Iain Martin has pointed out, international bodies are often impotent to negotiate because of the competing national interests of their members. There has, for example, so far been very little effective regulation from Brussels of the tech giants like Apple, Amazon, Facebook and Google (though the latter is now facing a big EU fine for breaching competition rules) from Brussels in part because the leading countries often have different priorities: Germany's is privacy, France's is preserving the national culture and the UK's is security.

* * *

Where does the Anywhere–Somewhere settlement work best? Smaller European countries like Ireland or Denmark have preserved a national intimacy that prevents Anywheres pulling away too far. Scotland under the SNP, too, perhaps deserves greater credit for its attempt at a new Anywhere–Somewhere settlement north of the border within the framework of moderate Scottish nationalism.

But it is Germany that seems to have got a better balance than most big developed countries. (Austria and Switzerland are similar, though much smaller.) There is no London, nor global universities to upset the balance and a much greater focus on the middling and the local.

There is also an institutionalized voice for employees in business and the three-year apprenticeship system continues to confer respect on even basic jobs in retail. The Länder system gives many people a strong regional identity and even a local dialect to go with it.

It is true that German Anywheres in politics and the media remain wary of normal national feeling and tend towards post-national political correctness, as we saw in the 2015 refugee crisis. But there is one part of Germany that has partially insulated itself from this trend—conservative, Catholic Bavaria is perhaps the place that gets it most right in all of Europe with its combination of social conservatism and economic dynamism. It has been said that Anywheres regard society as a shop, while Somewheres regard it as a home. Bavaria is a home with some very good shops.

Finally, I have often been asked in the past few months whether I have come to save or to bury liberalism. I usually answer neither but I do wish it would practise what it preaches on pluralism by not imposing Anywhere priorities on Somewheres who have different ones. An emotionally intelligent Anywhere politics must be able to combine individual liberty and minority rights on the one hand and a strong sense of belonging and group attachment on the other.

The American sociologist Daniel Bell used to say that he was a social democrat in economics, a liberal in politics, and on social and cultural matters somewhat conservative. This is the 'hidden majority' that remains unspoken for in developed democracies. It is my hope that the recent value conflicts represented by Brexit and Trump and the current political stalemate in Britain and elsewhere are stations on the way to that majority finding a voice.

ACKNOWLEDGEMENTS

This book is in part a response to recent events. It also grew out of my earlier writing on immigration and multiculturalism (in *The British Dream*) and is an attempt to provide a broader critique of contemporary liberalism from the radical centre. I had planned something more abstract and timeless with Postliberal in the title. Then those events intervened and I have instead written something swifter and more specific. It draws on several things I have written in the three years since *British Dream*, above all the *Demos Quarterly* essay 'A Postliberal Future?' This book is certainly informed by Postliberal (and Blue Labour) thinking but I have not used the word Postliberal in the title, or in the book at all, as it is too opaque and open to misinterpretation.

There are many people I would like to thank for various kinds of assistance or insight in the writing of this book and the more general evolution of my thinking (see also the Select Bibliography at the end). Special thanks to: Andrew Adonis, Katharine Birbalsingh, Belinda Brown, Geoff Dench, Eric Kaufmann, Michael Lind, Paul Morland, Toby Mundy, Bob Rowthorn, Allen Simpson plus Michael Dwyer, Jon de Peyer, Alison Alexanian and the team at Hurst. I would also like to thank: Michelle Bannister, Jamie Bartlett, Hannah Beard, Phillip Blond, Sam Bright, Alex Brummer, Andrew Cahn, Samantha Callan, Daisy Christodoulou, Jon Cruddas, René Cuperus, William Davies, Swati Dhingra, Stephen Driver, Bobby Duffy, Daniel Finkelstein, Janan Ganesh, Maurice Glasman, Dean Godson, Maud Goodhart, Matthew Goodwin, Charles Grant, Andrew Green, Francis Green, Kathy Gyngell, Jonathan Haidt, Daphne Halikiopoulou, Ernst Hillebrand, Nick Hillman, Sunder Katwala,

ACKNOWLEDGEMENTS

Inara Khan, Shiria Khatun, Ivan Krastev, David Landsman, Tim Leunig, Warwick Lightfoot, Alexander Linklater, John Lloyd, Rebecca Lowe Coulson, Pam Meadows, Anand Menon, David Metcalf, Jasper McMahon, Richard Norrie, Liav Orgad, Geoff Owen, Marie Peacock, Trevor Phillips, John Philpott, Avi Posen, Rachel Reeves, Christopher Roberts, Shamit Saggar, Paul Scheffer, Tom Schuller, Roger Scruton, Jonathan Simons, Jon Simmons, David Soskice, Philippa Stockley, Nick Timothy, David Willetts, Max Wind-Cowie, Alison Wolf, Philip Wood, Michela Wrong.

THE GREAT DIVIDE

Brexit and the election of Donald Trump—the two biggest protest votes in modern democratic history—marked not so much the arrival of the populist era in western politics but its coming of age.

Looking back from the future, the first few years of the twenty-first century, culminating in those two votes, will come to be seen as the moment when the politics of culture and identity rose to challenge the politics of left and right. Socio-cultural politics took its place at the top table alongside traditional socio-economic politics—meaning as much as money.

This book, conceived at the beginning of 2016, was originally intended to, among other things, warn against the coming backlash against the political status quo—and in particular against the 'double liberalism', both economic and social, that has dominated politics, particularly in Britain and America, for more than a generation.

The backlash came earlier than I expected, but it did not come out of the blue. In fact it was widely predicted and has been several decades in the making. Britain has been catching up with more established trends in continental Europe and the US. The spirit of the new political era can be found in solid support for populist parties across Europe (many of which have been part of governing coalitions), in persistent opposition to large scale immigration, in Trump's election in the US, in Brexit, in the success of the Scottish National Party, in the

Jeremy Corbyn left populism of the 2017 U.K. election and the electoral collapse of much of the European centre-left. This book will focus on Britain but will consider related trends in Europe and the US.

Both Brexit and Trump's election were unexpected victories given a decisive tilt by unhappy white working class voters—motivated, it seems, more by cultural loss, related to immigration and ethnic change, than by economic calculation. But they are also very different phenomena. Trump's 'strongman' appeal marked a more radical departure in both tone and content from what has gone before in western politics and will, of course, have more far-reaching consequences than Brexit. If Trump keeps his isolationist election promises the world may slide towards a trade war and global economic depression, not to mention a free hand for Russia in her near abroad; if he jettisons them his core supporters may not take it well.

Liberal democracy is unlikely to be toppled, even in the US. The habits of compromise and civic order are too ingrained, and America will remain a land of plenty for the vast majority. And in Britain large parts of politics will remain either technocratic or marked by left-right priorities—how best to combine state and private funding in social care or infrastructure spending, for example, or how to rein in inequality. But since the turn of the century western politics has had to make room for a new set of voices pre-occupied with national borders and pace of change, appealing to people who feel displaced by a more open, ethnically fluid, graduate-favouring economy and society, designed by and for the new elites.

Many liberal-minded people in Britain and elsewhere have been uncomfortable about granting space to these political forces and regard hostility to the openness required by European integration and a more global economy as simply irrational, if not xenophobic.

Some of those core Remainers reported waking up the day after the Brexit vote feeling, at least briefly, that they were living in a foreign country. If that was, indeed, the case they were merely experiencing, in political reverse, what a majority of people apparently feel every day.

For several years now more than half of British people have agreed with this statement (and similar ones): 'Britain has changed in recent times beyond recognition, it sometimes feels like a foreign country and this makes me feel uncomfortable.' Older people, the least well educated and the least affluent are most likely to assent, but there is quite widespread support from other groups too.[1]

Even allowing for the querulous spirit that opinion polls often seem to inspire, this is an astonishing thing for the majority of the population to agree to in a country as stable, peaceful, rich and successful as today's Britain. It is a similar story in the US where 81 per cent of Trump supporters said life was better fifty years ago.[2] What is going on?

Much of the British commentariat see an 'open v closed' divide as the new political fault-line. Tony Blair dedicated a speech to the distinction in 2007 just before he left office: 'Modern politics has less to do with traditional positions of right versus left, more to do today, with what I would call the modern choice, which is open versus closed.'[3]

He was partly right, but he failed to grasp why so many people find his version of open so unappealing. To understand that we have to consider the great value divide in British society, echoed to varying extents in other developed societies. The old distinctions of class and economic interest have not disappeared but are increasingly over-laid by a larger and looser one—between the people who see the world from Anywhere and the people who see it from Somewhere.

Anywheres dominate our culture and society. They tend to do well at school—Vernon Bogdanor calls them the 'exam-passing classes'—then usually move from home to a residential university in their late teens and on to a career in the professions that might take them to London or even abroad for a year or two. Such people have portable 'achieved' identities, based on educational and career success which makes them generally comfortable and confident with new places and people.

Somewheres are more rooted and usually have 'ascribed' identities—Scottish farmer, working class Geordie, Cornish housewife—based on group belonging and particular places, which is why they often find rapid change more unsettling. One core group of Somewheres have been called the 'left behind'—mainly older white working class men with little education.[4] They have lost economically with the decline of well-paid jobs for people without qualifications and culturally, too, with the disappearance of a distinct working-class culture and the marginalisation of their views in the public conversation. However, Somewhere ambivalence about recent social trends spreads far beyond this group and is shared by many in all social classes, especially the least mobile. Despite recent increases in geographical mobility, about 60 per cent of British people still live within 20 miles of where they lived when they were fourteen.[5]

Of course, few of us belong completely to either group—we all have a mix of achieved and ascribed identities—and there is a large minority of Inbetweeners. Even the most cosmopolitan and mobile members of the Anywhere group retain some connection with their roots and even the most small town Somewhere might go on holiday abroad with EasyJet or talk on Skype to a relative in Australia.

Moreover, a large section of Britain's traditional elite remains very rooted in south east England and London, in a few old public schools and universities. Indeed they are more southern-based than in the past as the dominant families of the great northern and midland towns have gravitated south. But even if this part of the elite has not moved very far physically they are much less likely than in earlier generations to remain connected to Somewheres through land ownership, the church, the armed forces or as an employer. They are, however, connected to the new elites. As has happened before in British history, the old elite has absorbed the new one—the rising 'cognitive' elite of meritocrats, from lower social class and sometimes immigrant backgrounds. In doing so it has often exchanged traditional conservatism for a more liberal Anywhere ideology—consider George Osborne in whom the economic liberalism of the right and social liberalism of the left is said to combine.

In any case Anywheres and Somewheres do not overlap precisely with more conventional social categories. Rather, they are looser alignments of sentiment and worldview. Both groups include a huge variety of people and social types—Somewheres range from northern working class pensioners to Home Counties market town *Daily Mail* readers; Anywheres from polished business executives to radical academics.

Although I have invented the labels, I have not invented the two value clusters that are clearly visible in a host of opinion and value surveys— with Anywheres making up 20 to 25 per cent of the population, compared to around half for Somewheres (and the rest Inbetweeners).

This book and the Anywhere/Somewhere categorisation is both a frame for understanding what is going on in contemporary politics and a plea for a less headstrong Anywhere liberalism. The Anywheres have counted for too much in the past generation—their sense of political entitlement startlingly revealed after the Brexit and Trump votes—and populism, in its many shapes and sizes, has arisen as a counter-balance to their dominance throughout the developed world. It can be a destructive counter-balance, but if we are to be tough on populism we must be tough on the causes of populism too—and one of those causes has been Anywhere over-reach.

Extrapolating from opinion surveys, and adding my own judgments and observations, I have assembled a loose Anywhere ideology that I call 'progressive individualism'. This is a worldview for more or less successful individuals who also care about society. It places a high value on autonomy, mobility and novelty and a much lower value on group identity, tradition and national social contracts (faith, flag and family). Most Anywheres are comfortable with immigration, European integration and the spread of human rights legislation, all of which tend to dilute the claims of national citizenship. They are not in the main anti-national, indeed they can be quite patriotic, but they also see themselves as citizens of the world. Work, and in fact life itself, is about individual self-realisation. Anywheres are comfortable with the achievement society; meritocracy and most forms of equality (though not necessarily economic) are second nature to them. Where the interests of Anywheres are at stake—in everything from reform of higher education to gay marriage—things happen. Where they are not, the wheels grind more slowly, if at all.

By contrast, the Somewheres are more socially conservative and communitarian by instinct. They are not on the whole highly religious, unlike their equivalents in the US, and only a small number on the far-right fringes are hard authoritarians or consistent xenophobes. They are moderately nationalistic and if English quite likely to identify as such. They feel uncomfortable about many aspects of cultural and economic change—such as mass immigration, an achievement society in which they struggle to achieve, the reduced status of non-graduate employment and more fluid gender roles. They do not choose 'closed' over 'open' but want a form of openness that does not disadvantage them. They are also, in the main, modern people for whom women's equality and minority rights, distrust of power, free expression, consumerism and individual choice, are part of the air they breathe. They want some of the same things that Anywheres want, but they want them more slowly and in moderation. Their worldview—as with Anywheres I have assembled it from opinion surveys and my own observations—is best described by a phrase that many would regard as a contradiction in terms: 'decent populism'.

The relative powerlessness of British Somewheres in recent times is shown by, among other things: the miserable state of vocational education and apprenticeship provision in a graduate-dominated society, the double infrastructure failure in housing (in the south east) and transport links (in the north), and the bias against domesticity in family policy.

Both Anywhere and Somewhere worldviews are valid and legitimate and their divergence from each other is neither new nor surprising. What has changed is the balance of power, and numbers, between them. Until thirty or forty years ago the Somewhere worldview remained completely dominant. It was British common sense. Then in the space of two generations another Anywhere common sense has risen to challenge and partly replace it.

This is thanks, above all, to two things—the legacy of baby boomer '1960s' liberalism and the expansion of higher education, which has played a key role in disseminating that legacy. We are now entering a third phase—Brexit followed by an Anywhere fight-back in the 2017 election—in which neither worldview is so clearly dominant.

The helter-skelter expansion of higher education in the past twenty-five years—and the elevation of educational success into the main marker of social esteem—has been one of the most important, and least understood, developments in British society. It has been a liberation for many and for others a symptom of their declining status.

The Anywhere world of geographical, and often social, mobility, of higher education and professional careers was once the preserve of a small elite; it has now become general, though not universal. For Somewheres, meanwhile, post-industrialism has largely abolished manual labour, reduced the status of lower income males and weakened the national social contract—neither the affluent nor employers feel the same obligation towards 'their' working class that they once did.

In a democracy the Somewheres cannot, however, be ignored. And in recent years in Britain and Europe, and in the US through Donald Trump, they have begun to speak through new and established parties and outside party structures altogether. In Britain they helped to win the Brexit referendum and then the vote itself, and by constantly telling pollsters how worried they are about immigration they have kept that issue at the centre of British politics.

The Anywhere ideology is invariably a cheerleader for restless change. Consider this from Tony Blair, again, at the 2005 Labour conference: 'I hear people say we have to stop and debate globalisation. You might as well debate whether autumn should follow summer... The character of this changing world is indifferent to tradition. Unforgiving of frailty. No respecter of past reputations. It has no custom and practice. It is replete with opportunities, but they only go to those swift to adapt, slow to complain, open, willing and able to change.' This from the leader of the party which historically represented the people who benefitted least from capitalist modernisation.

When change seems to benefit everyone—such as broad-based economic growth or improved healthcare—the conflict between the two worldviews recedes. But when change does not seem to benefit everyone—as with the arrival of the two 'masses', a mass immigration society and a mass higher education system for almost half of school leavers—the restrained populism of Somewheres can find a voice.

One of the implicit promises of modern democratic citizenship is some degree of control over one's life. This translates most easily into a right to stop things happening, the right, at its most basic, to some stability and continuity in the place and the way one lives. Given the nature of the modern world even this is not a promise that democratic politicians can easily deliver, especially when committed to an economic liberalism that has exported factories and imported workers. Consider the extraordinary ethnic and physical changes in London and Birmingham in the past thirty years.

Somewheres are often said to be myopic, unable to see that accepting change brings longer-term advantage. Yet it is also the case that the people from Anywhere with more fluid identities and an educational passport to thrive are well equipped to benefit from change, while the people from Somewhere are often not, even in the long run.

Anywheres tend to see Somewhere conservatism as irrational or as a backlash against the advance of liberal social values. It can be that, but it is also to be expected that people who feel buffeted by external events with little political agency, social confidence or control over their destinies will cling all the harder to those spaces where they can exercise some control—in the familiar routines of their daily lives and beliefs. Somewhere conservatism may have shed many of the historical trappings of mid-twentieth century classic working-class conservatism—the protestant faith, jingoism, white supremacy—but the instinct to stick with the familiar and to those small zones of control and esteem means Somewheres are often hostile both to market change and to top-down state paternalism.

Most Somewheres are not bigots and xenophobes. Indeed much of what I call the 'great liberalisation' of the past forty years in attitudes to race, gender and sexuality (see the next chapter) has been absorbed and accepted by the majority of Somewheres. But compared with Anywheres the acceptance has been more selective and tentative and has not extended to enthusiasm for mass immigration or European integration. Somewheres are seldom anti-immigrant but invariably anti-mass immigration. They still believe that there is such a thing as Society.

The 1960s were not just about challenging traditional ideas and hierarchies—they also marked a further dismantling of the stable, ordered society in which roles were clearly ordained. Individuals became freer to win or lose (see chapter seven). That was disorientating to many. Most Somewheres did not share the optimism of baby boomer Anywhere liberalism and instead found that the emerging post-industrial, post-nationalist, post-modern Britain was in many non-material ways a less hospitable place for them.

Eric Kaufmann, a leading authority on nationalism and ethnicity, has shown that the Brexit and Trump backlashes were not only about education and mobility but also about a core values divide, relating to order and authority, that cuts across age, income, education and even political parties in western democracies.[6] There is a cluster of questions that pollsters ask about the importance of children being obedient, support for capital punishment and so on—known as the authoritarian-libertarian axis—and a position closer to the authoritarian end of the axis turns out to be the key predictor of whether someone voted Brexit or not. (Only 11.5 per cent on the axis are actually classified as authoritarian though 52 per cent are described as illiberal.)[7]

Strong authoritarianism is the instinct of only a small minority but the broader desire of Somewheres for a more stable, ordered world, is now being heard in the parliaments and chancelleries of the developed world. And Generation Z, everyone born after 2001, seems to confirm this new tilt towards caution and conservatism.[8]

Kaufmann emphasises the ethnic aspect of this shift: 'As large scale immigration challenges the demographic sway of white majorities, the gap between whites who embrace change and those who resist it is emerging as the key political cleavage across the west. Compared to this cultural chasm, material differences between haves and have nots... are much less important.'[9]

This chimes with the view that at least part of Trump's success came through appealing to a hitherto latent white identity politics. In any case, populist politics is certainly here to stay and, though many of the parties themselves are unstable and often dominated by furious personality clashes, the demand for their product shows no sign of fading. Their appeal is primarily motivated by cultural anxiety and hard to measure psychological loss. Economic loss is a factor too—a significant majority of the 56 per cent of British people who describe themselves as 'have nots' voted Brexit—but if it was primarily about economic loss the populists of the left would surely be stronger.

There is another important aspect to this argument. Anywheres often claim that the trends they support are historically inevitable—whether it is mass immigration, the current form of globalisation or the decline of settled communities. But in reality, rich societies are much less mobile than Anywheres assume and the same is true for humanity as a whole: a little over 3 per cent of the world's 7.3 billion people live outside their country of birth and this percentage has only increased slightly in recent decades. Only twenty-five years ago, net immigration to Britain was zero. It is true that inflows into rich countries have risen quite sharply since then but that has been partly the result of policy choices. Large-scale immigration is not a force of nature.

Also economic globalisation, at least in a technical sense, is less developed than is often assumed. If globalisation is defined as the emergence of a single global economy, with transnational corporations with worldwide production networks and few barriers to the free flow of goods, labour and capital, then it has barely started.

The globalisation story tends to focus on its impact on trade, finance, transport and communications technologies and immigrant diasporas, all of which are either inherently international or easy to internationalise. Even here the impact is much less than usually assumed and all these activitives are governed by national laws or international agreements drawn up between national governments. According to the trans-nationality index of the United Nations Conference on Trade and Development, even the 100 most global corporations still have nearly half of their sales, assets and employment in their home country (where they may still benefit from formal and informal protections).[10]

Moreover, the vast majority of workers in advanced countries work in the service sector serving the domestic market, not in the global economy. And while states have to take account of global market forces, they continue to have a large amount of potential discretion over fiscal, tax and welfare policy. Recent globalisation has in part represented a welcome rebalancing of power and wealth away from rich western states like Britain towards developing countries like China and India. But there is no reason why it should disadvantage poorer people in rich countries nor override entrenched national preferences.

The global openness of the past twenty-five years has been on balance a blessing for most British people, but the blessing becomes more mixed the further down the income and education spectrum you move. The particular forms that globalisation takes are not, however, set in stone—it is a matter of politics and can be adjusted. If the Anywhere technocrats who dominate the World Trade Organisation, the EU, the international human rights courts, and so on, are forced to concede that their version of globalisation is, in part, a choice, not an irresistible force like the seasons, as Tony Blair claimed, then by extension they must persuade us that it is a desirable destination. And that is very much harder. A better globalisation is possible and a world order based on many Somewhere nation states cooperating together is far preferable to one big supranational Anywhere.

This book will show that the people from Anywhere in Britain—including the metropolitan elites of left and right, reflecting the interests of the upper professional class—have dominated the political agenda whichever party has been in power for the past twenty-five years and have too often failed to distinguish their own sectional interests from the general interest.

It is true that the Anywheres have some social trends on their side, what *Economist* journalist Jeremy Cliffe has described as the 'Londonisation' of Britain: increased mobility and immigration, the spread of higher education, the social liberalism of younger generations, the detaching effect of social media and the decline of many traditional allegiances.[11] But many of these liberalising trends are reversible, particularly if automation starts to do to Anywhere jobs what it has partly already done to Somewhere ones, and in any case it is impossible to imagine a world without at least a large minority of people with core Somewhere values—half the population will always be in the bottom half of the income and the ability spectrums.

I use the word 'liberalism' many times in the course of the book so I should say something about it. We are all liberals now—from Nick Clegg to Nigel Farage—in the limited sense that we all believe in the rule of law, individual rights and checks and balances on power.

Then there are the more specific liberalisms that the word is more generally associated with today: the rights and equality revolution starting in the 1960s that we call social liberalism and the market revolution of the 1980s that we call economic liberalism. Social liberals are not necessarily economic liberals and vice versa but the two have partly merged in the past twenty-five years following the conversion of the centre-left to more market friendly economics. This 'double liberalism', I mentioned earlier, has dominated British society since the early 1990s and strongly overlaps with Anywhere progressive individualism.

One might also call it the liberal baby boomer worldview. Think of someone like Richard Branson, the hippy capitalist: individualistic, committed to autonomy and 'doing your own thing', a bit wary of the national, wide but shallow attachments. Such liberals usually care about social justice too but, as the American social psychologist Jonathan Haidt has pointed out, they often don't 'get' other political impulses— loyalty, authority and the sacred.

Compared with traditional societies, modern societies have a low level of moral and political consensus and, to many liberals, therein lies our freedom. John Stuart Mill's famous 'harm principle'—'the only purpose for which power can be rightly exercised over any member of a civilised community, against his will, is to prevent harm to others'—speaks to the individualistic, even libertarian, live and let live ethos of part of modern Britain. (Though harm is an ambiguous concept and is now being extended by student radicals to encompass the idea of offence.)

We should recall, though, that Mill was rebelling against the conformism and authoritarianism of Victorian society. And in our much more liberal and diverse society it is common norms that now need protecting as much as liberty.

The harm caused by a slowly disconnecting society is hard to pinpoint, even if it is real enough. But liberalism does not care much for common norms or rather finds them too arbitrary. Who is David Goodhart to tell you what your norms are? Why not someone else? On what basis do we agree our shared norms? There is no recourse to authority, because liberal modernity has largely undermined religious and moral authority in the name of freedom and individual choice. So we are just left with the liberal agreement to disagree.

But modern liberalism, far from being such a content-less technique for reconciling different points of view, ends up imposing the worldview of the mobile, graduate, upper professional elite—the Anywheres—on the rest of society. Some of that worldview, such as sex equality, has been broadly absorbed into mainstream common sense, but some of it has not: the erosion of national citizen favouritism, for example. That is the point where Anywheres and Somewheres fall out.

This book is mainly about Britain, though many of the issues I discuss are also relevant to other rich democracies. Most of this book is also about white British people, who still constitute around 80 per cent of the British population. But ethnic minority Britons are also an important and growing part of the story. Minorities can be an emblem of the rapid change that makes some of the long settled population anxious. But they also take their various places on the Anywhere/ Somewhere spectrum. Superficially, minorities are often Anywhere inclined in that they are usually less attached to British traditions that may have excluded or humiliated them in the past and are more inclined to support an openness that allowed their families into the country in the first place. Yet they also have a special interest in social stability, tend to be more religious and often have more socially conservative views about the family and gender relations than the white British, which inclines them in a Somewhere direction. (Some of the most ethnically divided parts of Britain, such as the northern 'mill towns', are home to parallel Somewhere groups.)

It is time that Anywheres stopped looking down on Somewheres, white or non-white, and learnt to accept the legitimacy of their 'change is loss' worldview and even accommodate some of their sentiments and intuitions. As Michael Ignatieff, the former leader of the Canadian Liberal party, put it in a review of former British Deputy Prime Minister Nick Clegg's account of the 2010 coalition government: 'Clegg has a bad case of high-minded liberal self-regard and it leaves him perpetually baffled that the people he calls populists stole support from under his nose. Presenting yourself as the voice of reason isn't smart politics. It's elitist condescension. Brexiters had their reasons and their reasons won the argument.'[12]

And in the words of Britain's one UKIP Member of Parliament, Douglas Carswell: 'The crowd is no longer a mob.'[13] Anywheres cannot continue ruling without consent of the crowd, just as Somewheres cannot exercise political power by shouting insults from the side-lines—feeling condescended to is not a good enough reason to vote for an inexperienced demagogue as president.

Brexit and the election of Donald Trump need not mean that the forward march of liberalism is permanently halted. But a liberalism of the future that can appeal to a critical mass of Somewheres needs a less thin and unhistorical understanding of people and societies and a slower, more evolutionary approach to change that tries harder to win the consent of those who benefit least.

Orthodox liberalism's stress on choice and autonomy makes it uncomfortable with forms of identity and experience which are not chosen. It likes the idea of community in theory but does not see that a meaningful one excludes as well as includes. To this kind of liberalism people are rational, self-interested individualists existing apart from strong group attachments or loyalties. Much of modern economics and law are based on this model of human behaviour, which is why both disciplines often fail to properly account for national borders and pref- erences. And if you accept these liberal premises then any defence of tradition or community is likely to appear irrational or, in the case of immigration, racist.

Without a more rooted, emotionally intelligent liberalism that can find the common ground between Anywheres and Somewheres, the possibility of even more unpleasant backlashes cannot be completely ruled out, even in Britain. Brexit may be an early tremor rather like the unexpected populist surge in the Netherlands in the early 2000s. This book is partly about describing the underlying decency of many Somewhere ideas and intuitions and defending them from the disdain of some members of the Anywhere classes. But there are also crude and xenophobic versions of Somewhere politics where populism slides towards the far right or the threatening bombast of a Donald Trump.

* * *

A Journey from Anywhere

For most of my adult life I have been firmly in the Anywhere camp, and by background and life-style remain so. In the mid-1990s I was the founder editor of *Prospect*, the monthly current affairs magazine, that was loosely affiliated to the liberal centre-left and endorsed New Labour's arrival in 1997. But while editing *Prospect* I also began to detach myself, intellectually, from orthodox liberalism—in particular after writing a rather speculative essay for the magazine headlined 'Too Diverse?'[14] It raised questions about the conflict between rapidly increasing ethnic diversity and the feelings of trust and solidarity required to sustain a generous welfare state. The essay was reprinted in the *Guardian* and caused an almighty row, at least on the centre-left. I was accused of 'nice racism' and 'liberal Powellism'.

That brief notoriety triggered a lasting interest in immigration, race, multiculturalism, national identity and so on (which in 2013 resulted in a book, *The British Dream*).[15] And the more I studied these things and tried to defend my initial, rather accidental, scepticism the more I became convinced that the left had got on the wrong side of the argument on mass immigration (too enthusiastic), and integration of minorities and national identity (too indifferent).

On matters of culture and community the sometimes socially conservative intuitions of mainstream public opinion came to seem to me at least as rational and decent as the individualistic egalitarianism of the middle class, university educated left which now dominates the Labour party. Liberalism, as the late Jamaican-born cultural theorist Stuart Hall once said, is stupid about culture. It can be stupid about parts of human nature too. It understands the yearning for freedom and autonomy much less so for recognition and belonging. As I heard Labour politicians, some of them friends, talking about the fiscal benefits of mass immigration as the party's old working class base drifted away I understood what Hall meant.

Dogmatism and group-think are not the preserve of poorly educated Somewheres. Indeed, progressive Anywheres tend to be more socially tolerant than Somewheres but less politically tolerant.[16]

So I am a kind of Anywhere apostate but I like to think that I can see the point of both worldviews. My social networks are still largely comprised of Anywheres but when the conversation turns to politics I often find myself looking on as an outsider.

That does mean that I sometimes hear Anywhere views in their most unvarnished form—my email inbox was full of angry contempt for the ignorant masses from left-wing professors in the days after the Brexit vote. And here are two examples of conversations I have been part of in the last few years that illustrate one of the book's central theses and lend some support to Theresa May's reprimand to the world citizens 'from nowhere'.

The first conversation took place at an Oxford college dinner in Spring 2011. When I said to my neighbour—Gus O'Donnell, then in his last few months as Cabinet Secretary, the most senior civil servant in the land—that I was writing a book about immigration, he replied, 'When I was at the Treasury I argued for the most open door possible to immigration ... I think it's my job to maximise global welfare not national welfare.'

I was surprised to hear this from the head of such a national institution and asked the man sitting next to the civil servant, Mark Thompson—then Director-General of the BBC—whether he believed global welfare should be put before national welfare, if the two should conflict. He defended O'Donnell and said he too believed global welfare was paramount.

This exchange underlined, rather starkly, what this book is about. Both men's universalist views are perfectly legitimate and may reflect their moderately devout Catholic upbringings. They are views that are quite normal in some circles and may now encompass up to 10 per cent of public opinion. O'Donnell, when I met him again a few months later, confirmed that my recollection of the conversation was accurate and he has subsequently expressed his views in milder form in newspaper articles. Moreover, he thinks that his views about immigration are, notwithstanding some short-term losers, in the interests of the average British person.

But is it healthy for democracy when such powerful people hold views that are evidently at odds with the core political intuitions of the majority of the public? If these were just private views that had no bearing on the job that both men did it would not matter. But O'Donnell was the permanent secretary of the Treasury when important decisions were being made about immigration—not least the decision to open the British labour market in 2004 to the new former communist EU states seven years before required by EU law and seven years before any other large EU state did so. By all accounts he was a powerful advocate for openness.

The second conversation happened a few years before in 2007. I was at a sixtieth birthday party for a well-known Labour MP. Many of the leading intellectual figures of the British centre-left were also there and at one point in the evening the conversation turned to the infamous Gordon Brown slogan 'British jobs for British workers,' from a speech he had given a few days before at the Labour conference.

The people around me entered a bidding war to express their outrage at Brown's slogan which was finally triumphantly closed by Chris Huhne—who went on to become a Liberal Democrat cabinet minister in the Coalition government. He declared, to general approval, that it was 'racism, pure and simple.'

I remember nodding along but then thinking afterwards how weird the conversation would have sounded to most other people in this country. Gordon Brown's phrase may have been clumsy and cynical but he didn't actually say British jobs for white British workers. (In a YouGov poll soon after the speech, 63 per cent of people agreed that employers should have special incentives to hire British born workers and, rather shockingly, 22 per cent said there should be incentives to hire the white British born.)

In most other places in the world today, and indeed probably in Britain itself until about twenty-five years ago, such a statement about a job preference for national citizens would have seemed so banal as to be hardly worth uttering. But in 2007 the idea of a borderless Europe and the language of universal rights had ruled it beyond the pale, at least for this elite centre-left group.

By chance as I was writing this in October 2016 a similar row blew up over a suggestion, indirectly from Amber Rudd the home secretary, that companies should inform the Home Office of the proportion of their non-British employees when applying to sponsor a foreign worker for a work permit. The intention was to signal to employers that they might be over-dependent on foreign workers and not doing enough to train British ones. There was an indignant outcry from business and liberal Britain—in some cases absurdly citing the treatment of Jews in Nazi Germany—and the measure was quickly dropped. Another YouGov poll again found widespread support for the proposal—with 59 per cent supporting (including a narrow majority of Labour supporters) and 26 per cent opposing—proportions that almost map on to my estimate of the Anywhere and Somewhere populations of Britain.

But both Gordon Brown and Amber Rudd were addressing a real issue. As part of the greater freedom and efficiency of British business since the 1980s has come a weakening of the idea of the national corporate citizen, the implicit obligation to train and employ British citizens. As larger businesses have become more global and footloose, employers have come to expect complete freedom to import skilled workers and in some cases unskilled workers—in Britain's biggest manufacturing sector, food and drink, more than one third of production workers now come from eastern Europe, from almost nothing ten years ago. It did not even occur to the Labour party to complain about this.

Business self-interest and the progressive worldview—with its stress on openness, rights and equality—have both become uncoupled from common sense notions of economic justice, still seen through a national lens. It is this uncoupling that has been eating away at European social democracy.

More broadly, it illustrates how the gap between the secular liberal baby boomer Anywhere worldview that dominates our political party, governmental and social institutions and the intuitions of the ordinary citizen has become the great divide in British life.

* * *

In the next eight chapters I will first, in chapter two, introduce in more detail that great divide—as revealed in countless surveys—between Anywheres and Somewheres and then, in chapter three, set this British story in a wider European and American context. In the subsequent five chapters I will take different areas of life and show how Anywhere and Somewhere perspectives and interests differ. Chapter four considers globalisation, European integration and the nation state; chapter five looks at immigration, integration and the London story; chapter six looks at the knowledge economy and the declining status of non-graduate employment; chapter seven looks at the achievement society and its discontents; chapter eight looks at the remaking of family life. These are all huge fields about which libraries full of books have been written. I cannot claim to be an expert in any of them but by looking at them through the Anywhere/Somewhere prism I hope to shed some fresh light.

The final chapter will look at the likely future trends in the Anywhere/ Somewhere tussle and make the case for a new political settlement that can provide Somewheres with more of a stake in our Anywhere-designed open societies.

2

ANYWHERES AND SOMEWHERES

In the immediate aftermath of the Brexit vote there was a long wail of dismay at how Britain had broken into two nations. Those who voted Leave were said to be Britain's losers: the left behind, the white working class of the Midlands and the North, but supplemented by older people from everywhere and Tory southerners. Their experiences and worldviews diverged radically from the core Remain voters, who were winners: optimistic, young, educated and middle class, living in the big metropolitan centres and university towns.

As the dust settled, this polarisation story came to be challenged by a more nuanced view of the multiple tribes of Britain and their internal divisions—a complex patchwork of social, economic and cultural differences, as the think tank British Future put it.[1] It was noted that only 37 per cent of Labour voters had voted Leave, that while most people in public housing voted Leave so too did those who had paid off their mortgages, and that there were large dissenting minorities of around 40 per cent in the main strongholds of both sides—London and Scotland for Leave, and the North East and the West Midlands for Remain.

Yet fundamental truths are often to be found in first reactions, and the Brexit vote did reveal a central divide in British society. This rift is not just about social class, though the Brexit vote was probably the most directly class-correlated political choice of my lifetime, with support for Remain highest at 57 per cent in the top social classes (A,Bs) dropping to 36 per cent in the lowest (C2,D,Es), with 49 per cent in the middle (C1s).[2]

The divide is about education and mobility and, in fact, the combination of the two. More decisive in predicting a Remain vote than affluence and membership of the highest managerial and professional class was whether or not someone was a graduate: more than two thirds of graduates voted Remain.[3]

There are many things that still unite us as a country. Most people accept the continuing reality and importance of the nation state even if the more liberal-minded think of it primarily as a community of interest—revolving around taxes, public services and rules for getting along together—rather than as a community of identity. And many of the so-called left-behinders accept much of the 'great liberalisation' that I mentioned in chapter one—in attitudes towards race, sexuality and gender—even if they are by no means liberals. Indeed, the broad outlines of our politics, encompassing a relatively free-market economy with a big state and a big society—with a culturally permissive and egalitarian ethos—are accepted by the vast majority.

But I also believe that the Brexit vote happened because over the past generation we have allowed ourselves to drift too far off into separate and barely comprehending cultural blocs—the two tribes that I have labeled Anywheres and Somewheres.

The divisions can be seen in what we get angry about. When Nigel Farage complained about feeling uncomfortable in a train carriage with no English speakers in it, the outrage in Anywhere media reverberated for several days, but anecdotal evidence suggested that 60 or 70 per cent of the country thought what he said was just common sense. Or when Jeremy Corbyn did not sing the national anthem on one of his first outings as Labour leader, it was the Somewheres' turn to be infuriated. Anywheres were more likely to think it was an amusing media confection.

A free society has many conflicting values and strands of opinion, but if the value gulf becomes too deep—especially between the dominant class and the rest—we become vulnerable to shocks and backlashes like Brexit.

I am often taken aback at the lack of awareness on the part of Anywheres at just how peculiar their views are to middle-ground

Somewhere opinion. Let me describe a scene that has become all too familiar to me over the past few years.

At the end of 2015 I was at a conference about the refugee crisis. It was a grand gathering in a country house with many experts providing alarming glimpses of Europe's southern and eastern borders—then looking increasingly like Europe's version of the Mexico–US border.

At several points during the two-day discussion the academics, NGOers and government officials talked about migration flows as if they were generals moving troops around the battlefield. There is, for example, a big youth bulge in the Western Balkans and in many of the forty African cities with more than a million residents. At the same time, several Western European countries have rapidly ageing populations. So, hey presto, argued several delegates, we should make it easier for the former to move to the latter and we would have a 'win-win situation' if only European politicians would show political leadership: code for ignoring public opinion.

This idea appeared to have the support of many people in the room. Yet it blithely ignores the fact there is such a thing as society. Societies are not just an aggregation of individuals who happen to live in physical proximity and into which millions of people from elsewhere can be easily transplanted.

Successful societies are actually existing things based on habits of cooperation, familiarity and trust and on bonds of language, history and culture. In modern times successful societies have also been relatively open to movement of ideas and people. But if our European societies—a magnet to millions of refugees—are to continue flourishing they need to retain some sense of mutual regard between anonymous citizens, which means keeping inflows to levels that allow people to be absorbed into that hard-to-define thing we call a 'national culture' or 'way of life'.

Most people in Britain, and in the rest of Europe, when faced with images of desperate people in the summer of 2015 felt compassion—many acted on it as individuals by donating to charities, and most of us wanted our governments to do something to alleviate the suffering. But there are also clear limits—both financial and emotional—to this compassion. Most of us would like to be generous without encouraging further flows and without risking damage to our own country's social and cultural infrastructure. High levels of normal immigration in recent years means Britain is already struggling to properly integrate some incomers, especially those from traditional, often Muslim, societies.[4]

This ought to be common sense, especially to the sort of idealistic people at my conference who were mainly on the political left. Yet when it comes to immigration the left abandons its normally social and communitarian instincts and becomes libertarian in its individualism. Why not another 100,000 desperate people? After all what is there to integrate into? We are all just individual human beings, are we not? The universalism of the left—based on its historic commitment to race equality—meets the 'there is no such thing as society' individualism of the liberal right.

Yet not only do we know that there is such a thing as society we also know that good societies are characterised by high levels of trust and what academics call social capital—the existence of networks and insitutions that make it easier to cooperate for the common good. As the American political scientist Robert Putnam has, reluctantly, conceded, the effect of high levels of immigration and ethnic diversity is to reduce trust and familiarity, at least in the short-term, especially when the people arriving come from places that are culturally distant; absorbing 100,000 Australians is very different to 100,000 Afghans.

Rapidly increasing diversity can also reduce the readiness to share. This is based on the notion that people are readier to share with others they have a fair amount in common with. This does not have to be based on shared ethnicity or religion but it has to be based on something—shared interests and experience most obviously.

We do not all have to be the same, or have the same values, to successfully share a public space. After all, national social contracts and welfare states evolved in European societies that were sharply divided by class and region, but a sense of national solidarity, of sharing a common fate, transcended those differences.

Ethnic differences too can be, and are, absorbed into the national 'we' but it is not always a swift or easy process and liberal societies are reluctant to force the pace. The evidence suggests that ethnically heterogeneous societies show lower levels of support for redistribution and thus in the longer run have weaker welfare states.[5] This is now emerging in Europe having long been evident in the US. (Trump's furious opposition to Obamacare, perceived as obliging the mainly white suburbs and small towns to subsidise the mainly non-white inner cities through their insurance premiums, is said to be another reason for his victory.)[6]

And what if the Anywhere vs Somewhere divide is itself contributing to the feeling that we are no longer a single society? That as social class divisions become more blurred, we are replacing them with this new divide based on education and mobility, and large social groupings which do not comprehend the intuitions of the other side on some of the most important issues of our times.

The binary distinction between Anywhere and Somewhere worldviews will feel too forced to many people, especially if they feel themselves to contain a mix of Anywhere and Somewhere values. Everyone is, of course, an individual political being with their own idiosyncratic mix of views and values. But we are also creatures of our circumstances and experiences, members of families, social groups, educational and ability categories, all of which leave their traces upon us in ways we are often unaware of and incline us towards wider value groups.

The value clusters I am describing are not static and older distinctions based on economics and left/right beliefs cut across them in unpredictable ways—it is possible to be a statist or a free-market Anywhere or Somewhere. Both value clusters lie on a spectrum— Anywheres and Somewheres come in many shapes and sizes—and, yes, there is quite a large Inbetween group (on my estimate about a quarter of the population).

Notwithstanding all those caveats, my two tribes capture the reality of Britain's central worldview divide and help illuminate important aspects of modern politics, including the unexpected Brexit vote. I sketched out the outlines of the Anywhere/Somewhere divide in chapter one, here is some more detail.

The most typical Anywhere is a liberally-inclined graduate. Anywheres vote for all the main parties but particularly the 'progressive' ones: Labour, the Liberal Democrats and the Greens (and the civic nationalist SNP in Scotland). They generally belong to the mobile minority who went to a residential university and then into a professional job, usually without returning to the place they were brought up. They are mainly in the upper quartile of the income and social class spectrum and include a disproportionate number of people who feel a special responsibility for society as a whole. They predominate among decision makers and opinion formers. There is a left-of-centre wing—in caring professions like health and education, and the media and creative industries—and a right-of-centre wing in finance, business and traditional professions like law and accountancy. Anywheres are highly concentrated in London and the other main metropolitan centres, as well as university towns.

This in a nutshell is their worldview: they broadly welcome change and are not nostalgic for a lost Britain; they fully embrace egalitarian and meritocratic attitudes on race, sexuality and gender (and sometimes class) and think that we need to push on further; they do not in the main embrace a borderless world but they are individualists and internationalists who are not strongly attached to larger group identities, including national ones; they value autonomy and self-realisation before stability, community and tradition.

The average Somewhere is on a middling income, having left school before doing A-levels. In voting preference, they lean towards the Conservatives and UKIP (many are ex-Labour). They are most likely to be in the bottom three quartiles of the income and social class spectrum and have not, in the main, experienced higher education. People from Somewhere are numerically a much larger and more widely distributed group than Anywheres but their political voice is weaker. They tend to be older and come from the more rooted middle and lower sections of society, from small towns and suburbia—where nearly 40 per cent of the population lives—and the former industrial and maritime areas.

Their worldview can be characterised thus: they do not generally welcome change and older Somewheres are nostalgic for a lost Britain; they place a high value on security and familiarity and have strong group attachments, local and national; Somewheres (especially younger ones) accept the equality revolution but still value traditional family forms and are suspicious of 'anything goes' attitudes; they are not Hard Authoritarians (outside a small core) but regret the passing of a more structured and tradition bound world.

A worldview is a fuzzy and fluctuating thing, but I estimate (and will show in more detail later) that around 20 to 25 per cent of the British population loosely share the Anywhere worldview as I have outlined it, with perhaps 5 per cent belonging to the more extreme sub-group that I call Global Villagers. Somewheres claim about half the population, with a sub-group that I call Hard Authoritarians of real bigots representing between 5 and 7 per cent of the population. The Inbetweeners account for the rest. Similar patterns exist in many other developed countries, as I will indicate in the next chapter, but my Anywhere/Somewhere distinction is based on British experience.

Attitudes to immigration have probably become the single biggest litmus test of Anywhere/Somewhere difference and over time have come to stand for more general attitudes towards social change and whether people feel comfortable with and feel they benefit from it, or not.

That more than 75 per cent of the population in 2013 wanted to reduce immigration a little or a lot suggests that even some Anywheres and a lot of Inbetweeners may, on this issue, have moved into the 'reduce immigration' camp.[7]

But in broad outline the numbers map neatly onto my estimated proportions for the different categories: 56 per cent want immigration reduced a lot—the Somewheres; 22 per cent want it reduced a little—the Inbetweeners; and 22 per cent want it to stay the same or increase—the Anywheres.[8]

Looking at class and education the expected effects can be found. Those with degrees are now such a large section of the younger age groups that they by no means all sign up to the Anywhere worldview, indeed a full 30 per cent of degree holders want immigration reduced a lot, but that compares with nearly 70 per cent of those with no or low qualifications. And while almost 40 per cent of degree-holders want immigration to remain the same or increase, that applies to just 15 per cent or under for those who were schooled only to GCSE level or below.

A similar breakdown emerges from polling about the European Union, with minority enthusiasm tempered by majority scepticism. In 2013 people were asked whether they thought Britain benefitted from EU membership with replies on a five-point scale. Only 21 per cent ticked the top two most positive boxes with 67 per cent saying Britain benefitted only a little or somewhat. (Though just 12 per cent said the country does not benefit at all.)[9]

Answers to the 2013 question 'would Britain begin to lose its identity if more people from Eastern Europe (for example Poland and

Latvia) came to live in Britain?' produced the same broad outcome, with 60 per cent agreeing or agreeing strongly and 24.2 per cent disagreeing or disagreeing strongly. More straightforwardly, in the same year 24.2 per cent of people said they felt close or fairly close to Europe and 76.2 per cent said they felt not very or not at all close.[10]

The Leave/Remain 52 per cent/48 per cent divide does not map so straightforwardly on to my Anywhere/Somewhere groupings. Almost all Anywheres voted Remain but most Inbetweeners and a few Somewheres voted Remain too; perhaps they accepted the centrality of the economic argument, feared the leap into the dark, or were still prepared to accept the expert consensus. But the values, attitudes, preferences and intuitions of most Leave voters match up with a large part of the Somewhere worldview.

And it is clear from a glance at the policy headlines of the past decade or so how under-represented that worldview has been. The list of policies that go with the grain of Anywhere thinking and interests is long: the 2003 decision to open the British labour market to people from eastern Europe (seven years before the EU required it); the 2007 decision to allow Romania and Bulgaria to join the EU (pushed hard by Tony Blair initially against the wishes of the European Commission); support for more economic integration as represented by the TTIP trade negotiations; support for gay marriage (though many Somewheres would also back it); the big increase in foreign aid; the continuing expansion of and investment in higher education; the big infrastructure and cultural investments in London; the large subsidies (now declining) for renewable energy and the relentless increases in petrol duty (now slowing).

By contrast the list of policies inspired by Somewhere thinking and interests is very short: Britain's semi-detached status within the EU and now exit from the organisation; restrictions on non-EU immigration after 2010; harsher sentencing and a growing prison population; household welfare caps; the living wage (though this is also supported by many Anywheres); and the belated drive to revive apprenticeships.

Later in this chapter I will show how the two groups (and their subgroups) leap out of the vast number of British value and attitude surveys. But first a brief overview about what we know about value changes in developed societies.

The Decline (but Survival) of Traditional Values

Most academic work on the evolution of values over time sees the onward march of Anywhere liberalism, at least in Europe and North America. The most detailed research by the World Values Survey, which has published data in six 'waves' since the early 1980s, continues to confirm the trend.[11] It is not yet clear whether the Trump victory and Brexit are signs of a slow-down or even reversal of that long liberalising trend.

Ronald Inglehart, who has pioneered work on value change, argues that when countries industrialise the traditional values of religion and deference to authority tend to give way to more secular and rational priorities, initially among the educated. And as societies grow richer they cling less to 'survival values'—based on the security to be found in one's family, tribe or other in-group—in favour of self-expression and 'emancipative values'. The new values stress rights and well-being not just for oneself but for everyone. As existential pressures fade, people become more open-minded and they 'prioritise freedom over security, autonomy over authority, diversity over uniformity and creativity over discipline,' as Christian Welzel puts it in his book *Freedom Rising*.[12] (Though this seems to be less true of Africa, South Asia and the Middle East.)

These are classic Anywhere sentiments, but they are held only by a minority even in rich societies. Indeed, the people who hold these views are, in the formulation of a group of American cultural psychologists, WEIRD—they are from a sub-culture that is Western, Educated, Industrialised, Rich and Democratic. They tend towards moral universalism and are suspicious of strong national loyalties. As the World Values Survey stresses, they also tend to prioritise autonomy and self-realisation. They are usually strongly concerned with social justice and unfairness, and also suspicious of appeals to religion, tradition or human nature to justify any departure from equal treatment—differences between men and women, for example, are regarded as almost entirely cultural rather than biological.

This is also what some people call the secular liberal baby boomer worldview in particularly pure form—and it is in many ways an attractive and coherent worldview. It is also, for historical reasons to do with empire and post-imperial guilt, unusually ingrained in the British cultural and political elite—the default position in much of higher education and significant parts of the media.

But it is very unlikely ever to become a majority worldview. Most traditional societies are 'sociocentric', meaning they place the needs of groups and institutions first. Today most rich societies are 'individualistic', meaning that society is a servant of the individual. Yet even in countries that have broken through to individualistic modernity, significant traces of our more sociocentric and 'groupist' past are to be found in people's instincts and moral intuitions.

This has been the message of countless works of popular science, especially since the renewed interest in Darwin and evolutionary psychology. Humans are not 'blank sheets' and only partly respond to a WEIRD worldview; we are still also group-based primates and our moral psychology remains shaped by historic evolutionary forces.

The problem for Anywhere liberals is that Somewhere conservatives understand this better than they do. As one conservative friend put it, 'it has taken modern science to remind us what our grandparents knew.' A seminal book by Jonathan Haidt—out of that remarkable US popular-science-meets-political-speculation stable—called *The Righteous Mind*, explains why.[13]

Haidt was a liberal who began to study political psychology in order to help his political tribe become more effective in its competition with conservatives. Along the way, he became a centrist who believes that each side sees some truths and ignores others.

Haidt's basic insight is simple but powerful: morality is built on many foundations, many psychological systems, and conservatives understand more of these foundations than do liberals. Liberals are very sensitive to issues of harm and suffering (appealing to our capacities for sympathy and nurturing) and also fairness and injustice (related to our innate instinct for reciprocity). All human cultures are sensitive to these two sets of issues, but most of them also respond emotionally to three other things: loyalty to the in-group, authority, and the sacred.

As Haidt puts it: 'It's as though conservatives can hear five octaves of music, but liberals respond to just two, within which they have become particularly discerning.' This does not mean that liberals are necessarily wrong but it does mean that they over-focus on material gains and losses and often have more trouble understanding conservatives than vice versa.

The idea of the sacred is especially difficult for liberals to understand. This isn't necessarily about religion, but about the idea that some things should be untouchable or off-limits regardless of their consequences. If your only meaningful moral concepts are suffering and injustice then it is hard to understand conservative reservations about such things as swearing in public, defending the flag from desecration or most of today's biomedical controversies.

Haidt and his colleagues have not just plucked these moral senses from the air. He explains the evolutionary roots of the different senses from a close reading of the literature, but has also then tested them in internet surveys and face-to-face interviews in many different places around the world.

Morality, he says, 'binds and blinds' which is why it has made it possible for human beings, alone in the animal kingdom, to produce large cooperative groups, tribes and nations without the glue of kinship.

Haidt's book was written partly as an antidote to the more polarised US politics that began in the 1990s, marked by the reaction to the arrival of Bill Clinton and the liberal baby boomers onto the political stage.

The American culture wars began earlier, back in the 1960s, with young liberals angry at the suffering in Vietnam and the injustice still suffered by African-Americans. But when some of them adopted a style that was anti-American, anti-authority and anti-puritanical, conservatives saw their most sacred values desecrated and attacked.

Some conflicts are unavoidable, and Haidt is not suggesting that liberals should stop being liberals. Rather, they wll be politically more successful if instead of telling conservatives that their moral intuitions are wrong, they seek to shift them in a liberal direction by understanding and accommodating their anxieties as far as possible.

For example, if you want to improve integration and racial justice in a mixed area you do not just preach the importance of tolerance but you promote a common in-group identity.

Here are two variations on the Haidt thesis. One comes from American conservative Thomas Sowell. In his book *A Conflict of Visions* he described the liberal and conservative views of human nature, what he calls the 'unconstrained vision' and the 'constrained vision.'[14] Conservatives assume that people need constraints to behave well, liberals assume that constraints cause people to behave badly. And looking at the world from inside these visions people constantly find their assumptions reflected back at them as fact—what is called 'confirmation bias'.

Haidt himself (in a piece of journalism for the Center for Humans and Nature) puts a useful gloss on Sowell's two visions. The unconstrained vision reads like this: 'Human nature is malleable and can be improved ... if social conditions are improved. A better society is possible if the artificial constraints placed on human beings can be removed. We must therefore free people from the petty tribal loyalties that cause mistrust and war.'

The constrained vision reads like this: 'Human beings need external constraints in order to behave well, cooperate and thrive. These constraints include laws, institutions, customs, traditions, nations and religions. These constraints are built up slowly and organically but they can be destroyed quickly by radical reformers who don't understand their value.'[15]

Another variation of the Haidt argument is found in Karen Stenner's work on authoritarianism. She looks at how liberal Anywheres can unwittingly activate more extreme authoritarian views among normally moderate Somewheres.

Stenner's book *The Authoritarian Dynamic* finds that authoritarianism is not normally a stable character trait; rather, it is a predisposition to become intolerant when one's values or security or in-group feel under threat.[16] Rapid change in a neighbourhood can trigger this feeling of threat to the moral order.

She notes that her theory 'explains the kind of intolerance that seems to "come out of nowhere", that can spring up in tolerant and intolerant cultures alike, producing sudden changes in behaviour that cannot be accounted for by slowly changing cultural traditions.'

She might be describing the election of Donald Trump, something unimaginable ten years ago; or the sudden questioning of multiculturalism and mass immigration in the Netherlands in 2002 (see chapter three); or the vote for Brexit, when only 35 per cent of people seemed to support leaving the EU six months before the vote.

Stenner acknowledges the trend towards greater tolerance and openness but thinks it has the potential to generate a powerful backlash. Moreover, she warns: 'All the available evidence indicates that exposure to difference, talking about difference and applauding difference—the hallmarks of liberal democracy—are the surest ways to aggravate those who are innately intolerant … Paradoxically, then, it would seem that we can best limit intolerance of difference by parading, talking about, and applauding our sameness … Ultimately nothing inspires greater toler-ance from the intolerant than an abundance of common and unifying beliefs, practices, rituals, institutions and processes.'

My Oxford college companions mentioned earlier—O'Donnell and Thompson—are unlikely to take Stenner's advice. They form part of that elite group of Anywheres, that I have labeled Global Villagers, making up no more than 3 to 5 per cent of the population—people who would support open borders if it was politically feasible, and are as likely to identify as European or as a citizen of the world as they are British (let alone English).

Global Villagers are the people Theresa May described as the 'Citizens of Nowhere'. They are often secular and mobile and often (though not always) highly successful and are likely to belong to inter-nationalised networks, maybe living in more than one country. They are to be found at the top end of business and the professions and academia (in fact at all levels of academia). Their views are never going to become government policy but they have a disproportionate influence on the climate of opinion and help to tug more mainstream Anywheres towards even greater openness.[17]

Most of them are on the left but there are also liberal Conservatives who think like this. On a BBC Radio 4 Moral Maze programme in 2011 about development aid, the former Tory cabinet minister and born-again liberal Michael Portillo had this to say (though it is possible he was being a devil's advocate): 'It is quite old fashioned to think about national borders, and rather nationalistic to say we must help people who are only moderately poor because they happen to be in the UK rather than helping people who are desperately poor because they hap-pen to be a long way away.'

Some leading business figures like Martin Sorrell and Peter Sutherland are also Global Villagers. Sutherland, the former chairman of Goldman Sachs and a former EU trade commissioner, told a House of Lords committee in 2012 that the EU should do its best to 'under-mine the homogeneity' of its member states and that immigration was crucial for economic growth 'however difficult it may be to explain to the citizens of those states.'[18]

The largest single group of committed Global Villagers is to be found in higher education and among creative people. As a visiting fellow of Nuffield College, Oxford for the past seven years I have lost count of the number of Global Villagers I have encountered, both among the international, post-graduate student body and among the other outside guests.

And collectively the Global Villagers enrage the latent Somewhere authoritarians. In fact they doubly enrage them. First, by actively pursuing a policy agenda—freedom of movement in Europe for example—that is felt to weaken the national social and moral contracts upon which Somewheres rely. Second, by accusing those who object of 'racism, pure and simple.'

Racism is a highly politicised and much abused term that has come to refer to any kind of racial stereotyping or mild partiality towards an in-group—in the Chris Huhne anecdote above, the in-group being all British citizens of whatever colour or creed. Race activists and some people on the left want the widest and loosest possible definition in the mistaken belief that this somehow contributes to the elimination of racism. In fact the attempt to close discussion by appealing to one of the greatest remaining taboos in western society too often serves only to alienate people and devalue the term.

By describing as racist everything from ethnic cleansing to national citizen preference and the greater comfort people (of all backgrounds) often feel in settled communities among people they are familiar with, the term loses precision and force and ends up calling into question what most people regard as normal human feelings.

We need to use far more careful terminology to describe the spectrum from fear of the unfamiliar and clannishness to stereotyping and genuine hatred. And even when racism is racism, when it does involve dislike of or contempt for a particular group, it is not just about skin colour or even religion as such, it is about what skin colour or distinctive dress represent in terms of different values or behaviours or traditions and the challenge they present to mainstream norms. 'These moral concerns may be out of touch with reality, and they are routinely amplified by demagogues. But if we want to understand the recent rise of right-wing populist movements, then "racism" can't be the stopping point; it must be the beginning of the inquiry,' as Jonathan Haidt has written.[19]

Higher Education and Mobility

The value divergence this chapter is describing did not exist, or not to anything like the same extent, in the first half of the twentieth century and into the first couple of decades of post-war Britain. Across classes, regions and educational levels people lived in very different physical and economic universes but strong common norms continued to prevail—a loose belief in Christian teachings; a strong, even chauvinistic belief in Britain; and a set of beliefs on gender, race and sexuality that would now be regarded as extremely conservative.

Even in the 1960s life did not change much for most people. A New Society/Opinion Research Centre poll in 1969 asked people to look back on the decade and select from various options the changes they were most and least pleased about. The change that got the greatest support (51 per cent) was 'better old age pensions', and the changes that attracted most hostility were 'easier laws for homosexuality, divorce, abortion' (26 per cent) and 'immigration of coloured people' (23 per cent). The New Society magazine concluded: 'Shouldn't one talk of the Cautious Sixties, rather than the Swinging Sixties…If the 1960s meant anything special to most people in Britain it was because they got, during them, a better chance to lead a not-too-poor, not-too-insecure life.'

Nevertheless new value divides were opening up, in the metropolitan centres, in the universities and in pop culture, most visibly between the young, liberal and secular and the old, authoritarian and Christian.

While value and interest differences based around property ownership and class did not disappear, they came to be supplemented by differences based on lived experience—above all the degree of physical and social mobility and level of education. One of the features of the last few decades of the last century and the first decade of this century has been the convergence between social classes on economic and left/right issues—represented perhaps by the support for New Labour at its peak of popularity—and a divergence on social/moral/cultural issues, albeit within a broader liberal drift.[20]

In almost all societies since the industrial revolution there has been a connection between affluence and education, and between both of them and mobility. But thanks to the post-war expansion of higher education what had once been the life-style of a small elite came to be characteristic of a much larger group, as the 70s and 80s turned into the 90s and 2000s.

And while in the past many small groups of the intelligentsia, such as the Bloomsbury Group in 1920s London, have rejected traditional, socio-centric views in favour of individual freedom and autonomy, this kind of liberalism has remained on the fringes of society. Yet in the latter part of the twentieth century a kind of 60s 'trickle down' effect began to emerge, especially visible from the early 1980s. As educational qualifications became the main condition of career success, meritocratic liberalism became the dominant worldview of this educated group.

Educated people tend to have liberal views on race, sexuality and gender not because of the books they have read at college, though the books may reinforce the message. It is to do with self-interest. As the political writer Daniel Finkelstein has put it: 'If you have high human capital (you are educated and intelligent), what can prevent you from succeeding? A system in which prejudice erects barriers to the success of clever people.'[21]

Those most in favour of challenging racism, sexism and elite privilege tend to come from rising social groups with high human capital as well as already-dominant groups who can re-legitimise their superior status via educational attainment. The rising groups—successful minorities such as British Jews or Indians or upwardly mobile individuals from lower social classes—will often have faced direct discrimination in living memory and are not nostalgic for all aspects of Britain's past.

At the same time the descendants of the already-elite groups, whose parents or grandparents may have been responsible for discrimination in the past, can atone for past misdeeds of class or colonial oppression by ostentatiously shifting in a more liberal direction.

Anywheres generally regard themselves as tolerant, socially aware and progressive but the key ingredients of the Anywhere worldview—openness, meritocracy, autonomy and embrace of change—tend to benefit the affluent, the able and the fleet of foot and are much less likely to benefit those in the bottom parts of the income and ability spectrum, at least in the short-term. Partly to deal with this contradiction, bourgeois Anywheres are often attracted to identity politics—the politics of gender, race or sexuality is more likely to provide them with a cause than socialist economics. So, on the left too, socio-cultural politics increasingly trumps socio-economic politics. Moreover, as Mark Lilla has pointed out, this is an identity politics that is 'expressive not persuasive', so not very good at changing minds or winning elections.[22]

Robert Ford and Philip Cowley have shown how progressives tend to be socially tolerant but politically intolerant. Nearly one third of Labour voters said they would be upset if one of their children intended to marry a Conservative supporter compared to just 10 per cent vice versa. And 57 per cent of Labour supporters would be upset by a child bringing home a UKIP fiancée.[23]

Nevertheless the top-down liberalism in social norms of the cognitive elites marches on and has been significantly amplified by the expansion of higher education—the single most important institutional driver of contemporary Anywhere liberalism. As recently as fifty years ago just 6 per cent of school-leavers in England and Wales went to university, and though about 90 per cent came from private or grammar schools it was still a relatively unusual path even for the privileged. But then came successive waves of expansion, culminating in the 1992 conversion of the thirty-five polytechnics into universities and the drive towards a truly mass higher education in the late 1990s (see also chapter six). In 2016 nearly 50 per cent of school leavers were heading to university, and only 13 per cent came from private or grammar schools.[24]

Unusually by international standards British universities are overwhelmingly residential or boarding universities. Young men and women leave home and move to a different town, sometimes hundreds of miles away, to mix with their generational peers from other places, social classes and, increasingly, ethnic groups. This will often be the first time young people will have mixed with people different from themselves and have had the opportunity to experiment with new ideas and life-styles.

The boarding tradition became established in Britain in part because of the domination of the Oxbridge model and the boarding school tradition of the upper classes (itself related to the requirements of colonialism). Many of the big city 'red brick' universities founded in the latter part of the nineteenth century, often with a science and engi-

neering focus, recruited students locally. But the victory of the boarding principle came with the next big expansion of higher education in
the early 1960s when the Robbins report of 1963 backed a new wave
of residential universities—York, Kent, Sussex, Warwick and others.
Eric Robinson, an adviser to Labour Education Secretary Tony Crosland,
complained that the new universities were established by people seeking 'to reaffirm the boarding school principle.'

Mass higher education in Britain is elite higher education written a
little larger, according to educationalist Guy Neave. The proportion of
boarders is now actually declining as the university intake broadens and
students have to cover most of their own living costs. It was 92 per cent
in 1984 and is now about 73 per cent.[25] That is still far more than in
continental Europe or the US. About half of European countries offer
students no support for living costs, discouraging all but the richest
from leaving their local area. And in the US more than half of students
live at home—the main exception being the prestigious, residential Ivy
League colleges—and public universities usually charge lower fees to
students from their home state.

The boarding university can be a creative and stimulating transition
to adulthood. As we will see, mobility and experience of higher education tends to change people's worldview—making them more open to
change, less connected to particular places, shifting in essence from a
Somewhere to an Anywhere worldview. This is a welcome evolution
towards a society that is more egalitarian, more feminised, less likely
to consider force as a legitimate way of resolving disputes. But it may
also help to shape an elite that is more tightly bonded and more separate from the rest of society in networks and attitudes—if you are a
boarding graduate you are much less likely to stay in touch with the
non-graduate friends from your childhood—and this may legitimate a
liberal snobbery, a contempt for more rooted Somewhere intuitions
that was clear to see in the hostility and incomprehension towards
Brexit voters after 23 June.

The idea of the university is based on the pursuit of reason and sci-
entific inquiry and is thus institutionally inclined to challenge authority
and tradition. The pursuit of truth recognises no national boundaries.

British universities are for that reason exempt from the requirement
to prove that no national citizen could do a particular job before

recruiting from abroad. If a university needs a new professor of mathematics it will recruit the best it can find from anywhere in the world, for the salary it can afford. The internationalist ethos has been reinforced in recent years by the rapid internationalisation of the student body, about 20 per cent of students (13 per cent of undergraduates, 38 per cent of post-graduates) at British universities are from abroad and about 28 per cent of the academics.[26]

It is easy to see why British universities, and especially the elite twenty-four Russell Group universities, are such a vocal lobby for Anywhere openness and against any immigration restrictions that might deter foreign students. Universities have a big financial incentive to take international students from outside the EU so long as they can charge them anywhere between 50 per cent and three times more in fees than British or European students. One senior Cambridge academic said to me recently: 'We are so desperate for the fees of overseas Masters students that I can say that the only condition for a place is filling the application form.'

Whether universities are more generally a disinterested lobby for rational inquiry, at least in the humanities, might be called into doubt by the extent of political uniformity—according to a *Times Education Supplement* survey only 11 per cent of academics voted Conservative at the 2015 election and 90 per cent voted to remain in the European Union.

Many students, especially in humanities subjects, will be heavily influenced by this liberal and internationalist ethos of higher education, though research in the US and Switzerland suggests that many students are already self-selected for Anywhere type attitudes before they go to college.[27] University confirms a kind of social status in which liberal attitudes are part of the ethos differentiating Anywhere students from the mass of Somewheres.

Mobility is especially strongly correlated with Anywhere liberal values in Britain because of our residential university system, which is then reinforced by the dominance of London in building professional careers. Getting on in Britain means getting out, shaking the Somewhere dust off one's boots and forming new bonds with one's fellow Anywheres in London or another metropolitan centre.

But according to data from the Understanding Society surveys most other British born people are not particularly mobile. Amongst white

British people, 42 per cent live within 5 miles of where they lived when they were fourteen and 60 per cent live within twenty miles.[28] (Mobility is, if anything, rather lower for ethnic minorities, especially South Asians.) But of the 19 per cent who live more than 100 miles from where they lived when they were fourteen, the vast majority are graduates.

A separate Understanding Society survey finds that only 22 per cent of graduates live within fifteen minutes of their mother, compared with 47 per cent of those who only have GCSEs. And 26 per cent of graduates live more than two hours from their mother, compared with 10 per cent of those with only GCSEs.[29]

Looking at political affiliation, nationalist party voters had the highest levels of rootedness: more than 50 per cent of BNP voters live within fifteen minutes of their mother, compared to 42 per cent of UKIP voters, 60 per cent of Plaid Cymru voters, 37 per cent of SNP voters (and all the Northern Ireland parties are over 50 per cent). Those least likely to live close to their mothers are Green voters, on 25 per cent, and Liberal Democrats, on 30 per cent.[30]

Those who feel they most belong to their neighbourhood (according to the 2010 Citizenship Survey) are also most like to have higher levels of attachment to their national identity and their ethnicity. And that is unlikely to be Anywhere graduates.[31]

The Great Liberalisation

I have referred several times already to the 'great liberalisation', it's now time to take a closer look. Many readers of this book will have lived through it, and maybe experienced some of the upheavals associated with it as a young man or woman—alternatively if you are under forty you will never have known anything else. As recently as 1983 a clear majority of people thought that homosexual relationships were wrong and would mind a lot or a little if a close relative married a black person.

The change in public attitudes between the early 1980s and today has been painstakingly tracked by the British Social Attitudes surveys. The BSA is an annual face-to-face sample of up to 3,000 people who get asked the same, often quite detailed, questions over many years and decades so one can compare the responses over time.[32]

The surveys only began in 1983 so it may be that the liberalisation had really begun in the 1960s or 1970s but was only properly recorded from the early 1980s. In any case, the story since 1983 is by now a relatively familiar one. There has been a sharp decline in racist, homophobic and male chauvinist attitudes, with the sharpest declines among the young and the highly educated. There has been an equally sharp decline in religious observance and a sharp rise in acceptance of sex before marriage.

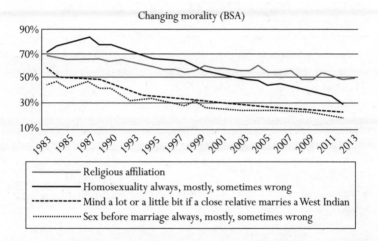

Changing morality (BSA)

_____ Religious affiliation
_____ Homosexuality always, mostly, sometimes wrong
----------- Mind a lot or a little bit if a close relative marries a West Indian
.... Sex before marriage always, mostly, sometimes wrong

There have been gentler declines in support for the death penalty—75 per cent supported it in 1986 and it is now down to just below half—and draconian punishment for criminals.

And in a few other areas opinion has stayed the same or has actually become *less* liberal: on welfare payments to the unemployed and welfare spending more generally; on the authoritarian-libertarian axis (which has stayed broadly constant); on European integration, on immigration (admittedly in the light of a large increase); and on Muslims and attitudes to multiculturalism. (Actually, the story on multiculturalism and integration is a complex one, with less racial views on who can be part of the British national club coinciding with more overtly integrationist views once people are here, see chapter five).

Students of public opinion look at changes to attitudes in three different ways: Is it a cohort effect mainly affecting one group, such as young people? Is it a temporary life-cycle effect that will change as people age? Or is it a period effect that impacts almost the whole society?

The liberalisation, especially on race, gender/family roles and sexuality, seems to be both a period effect and a cohort effect, with the young leading the liberal charge.

So, here is a snapshot of some of the data. First, race. In 1983, 57.3 per cent said they would mind a little or a lot if a relative married a black person. By 2013 22.1 per cent of respondents said they would mind a little, and 9.1 per cent 'a lot'. For the youngest age cohort, those minding a little were 9.2 per cent in 2013, and only 2.8 per cent minded a lot. Older age cohorts continue to be much more hostile.

Among graduates, 44.1 per cent said they would mind in 1986, falling to 8.8 per cent in 2013. For those with little education the share fell from 49.2 per cent to 16.5 per cent. In 1983 there was little to distinguish the highest and lowest income quartiles. In 2013, while both income groups were more accepting, a gap had opened up: just 12.9 per cent of the highest income quartile said they would object compared with 29 per cent of the lowest income quartile.

What about gender roles? In 1984, 42.8 per cent of people agreed that a husband should earn money and a wife look after home and family. In 2012, the share had fallen to 12.4 per cent. For the youngest cohort the shares fell from 16.5 per cent to 4.9 per cent over the same period. Even for 65 to 74 year olds, it fell from 70.9 per cent to 18.5 per cent—a good example of a period effect.

For graduates the share agreeing was 35.1 per cent in 1987, falling to just 4.1 per cent in 2012. For the least well educated it dropped from 45.2 per cent to 12.9 per cent. Interestingly, there is a significant difference between income groups, suggesting full gender equality is much more entrenched among the affluent and educated (see chapter eight).

There are also striking changes in our willingness to accept gay relationships. In 1983, 62.6 per cent of people said they thought such relationships were always or mostly wrong, falling to 22.2 per cent in 2013. Among 15 to 24 year olds the share dropped from 60.1 per cent to 7 per cent, while for 65 to 74 year olds the drop was less pronounced, from 80.9 per cent to 30.1 per cent. For graduates, the share rejecting homosexual relationships fell from 41.4 per cent in 1985 to 10.5 per cent in 2013; for the least well educated it fell from 72.1 per cent in 1985 to 27.4 per cent in 2013.

So alongside the general liberalisation we can also detect a significant divergence emerging between the better educated and the less well educated. I now want to look at a wider set of attitudes—connected to what are called the 'security and identity' issues, things like immigration (which I considered earlier in the chapter), national identity, ethnicity, law and order—to further tease out the Anywhere/Somewhere divide.

Polling on national identity finds indifference to national feeling only among a small minority, though growing slowly among the highly educated and affluent. Those who are very proud to be British is dropping slightly thanks to the higher number of graduates in the population (see chapter four for more details) though those who are very or somewhat proud to be British remain around the 80 per cent mark.

Attachment to ethnicity is harder to measure because the category is not in everyday use and, for the ethnic majority, is associated with racism. But it is pretty evident from the data that white British people, especially those from lower income and educational backgrounds, do still wish to retain a non-supremacist ethnic identity.

For example, when asked whether it is impossible for people who do not share Britain's customs and traditions to become fully British just over half agree or agree strongly, with one quarter disagreeing or disagreeing strongly (strong disagreement rising to over 40 per cent among graduates). And when white British people are asked directly about whether the proportion of ethnic minority people in their neighbourhood matters to them or not, about one third express indifference but over half admit that they might feel uncomfortable if the proportion rises too high. When asked about particular proportions, nearly 60 per cent say that a neighbourhood that is one quarter ethnic minority or more would make them feel uncomfortable.

Caution about openness, preference for the familiar, and a belief that charity begins at home attract majorities or large majorities in a host of further surveys relating to economic openness, global obligations, foreign aid, attitudes to whether Britain feels like a foreign country, and Muslim immigration.

On the latter point, well over half the population thinks that Britain would begin to lose its identity if more Muslims came to live here, with as many as 35.6 per cent agreeing strongly. Strong agreement is less prominent, as one would expect, among graduates (12.6 per cent), people aged 15–24 (21.7 per cent) and the richest quartile (24 per cent). Those who disagree with the proposition, or disagree strongly, are only 22.2 per cent.

And on the issue of Britain as a foreign country—mentioned at the start of the book—a YouGov poll in 2011 asked people to agree or disagree with the statement 'Britain has changed in recent times beyond recognition, it sometimes feels like a foreign country and this makes me feel uncomfortable.' As many as 62 per cent of people agreed, with just 30 per cent disagreeing. Only 16 per cent of graduates agreed strongly, compared with 41 per cent of non-graduates.[33] (Support for such sentiments is, if anything, slightly higher among the supposedly optimistic Americans.)

A similar result can be found in another poll about discomfort with the modern world, this time by Ipsos MORI in 2014, which asked people to respond to the statement 'People led happier lives in the old days when they had fewer problems to cope with.' Just over 60 per cent agreed and 30 per cent disagreed, with 15 per cent of graduates agreeing strongly compared with 50 per cent of non-graduates.[34]

These 'change is loss' sentiments are generally mocked by Anywhere commentators as the 'bring-backery' of provincial, small town Britain. Jeremy Paxman described it thus: 'We should recognise that this atavistic desire to resurrect defunct institutions is a symptom of social necrophilia. The success of the Vote Leave campaign ... has set off a positive epidemic of the disease ... What this amounts to is an obvious attempt to turn the clock back.'[35]

It is customary when making such comments to point out, as Paxman does, that for most people life has never been better. And that is certainly true in terms of income (leaving aside the last few years), health, longevity and most material comforts. But maybe in other respects life really isn't better for many people in terms of belonging, social recognition, having a valued role, feeling wanted and respected and so on. Wanting to turn the clock back is not a foolish instinct for those who feel the non-material aspects of life really were better in the past.

So we can see clearly the outlines of my two value groups in the attitude data. The graduate/non-graduate divide is one very broad proxy for Anywhere/Somewhere group membership. As we have seen there are some Somewhere minded graduates (30 per cent want immigration reduced a lot) and Anywhere minded non-graduates but the vast majority of graduates are at the liberal end of the attitude spectrum, some at the extreme liberal end, and vice versa for non-graduates. Age plays a part too, as many graduates are under forty-five and may shift towards Somewhere values as they age.

Further support for my 'great divide' thesis can be found in the influential British Values Survey, started in 1973 by Les Higgins and Pat Dade, which arrives at a broadly similar conclusion about the value tribes of Britain, though with three main groups. The values 'map' is constructed from responses to various propositions—such as: 'I feel that people who meet with misfortune have brought it on themselves. I see no reason why rich people should feel obliged to help poor people.' (About 30 per cent of the British population agrees with this statement and the differences between class and age cohorts are small.)[36]

The three British Values Survey groups are called Settlers, Prospectors and Pioneers. Settlers are socially conservative, pessimistic about the future and care strongly about social order and group belonging. They overlap significantly with my Somewheres (and Hard Authoritarians) and come mainly from lower social classes, though nearly 20 per cent of affluent ABs are Settlers. The proportion of the population who are Settlers has fallen from about 50 per cent in 1973 to about 30 per cent now.

Prospectors are more optimistic than Settlers but can be either socially conservative or liberal. They care about status and respect but are pragmatic and not particularly egalitarian, in political terms they are the aspirant swing voter that all parties target. They are about 32 per cent of the population and tend to be younger and more affluent than Settlers.

Pioneers have a strong sense of agency and care about creating a better society. They are socially tolerant or liberal and positive about change and diversity. They tend to be more highly educated and relatively affluent. They overlap with my Anywhere group, though are somewhat bigger, and now encompass 38 per cent of the population.

Pat Dade says that all the evidence shows a liberal shift in the centre of gravity over the past forty years, as one would expect from all the attitude evidence we have seen, with the number of Pioneers growing and Settlers shrinking. Though he also points out that the last few years has seen a slight increase in the number of Settlers and believes that the events of 2016 suggest that Pioneer liberalism has, for now, been 'stopped in its tracks'.

The Outriders

Having established my two broad value tribes, I now want to pin-point the two sub-tribes—the Global Villagers (already identified) and the Hard Authoritarians—and take an educated guess at their size too.

The following small groups I classify as Global Villagers. In the 2013 British Social Attitudes immigration survey 4.2 per cent of the public said that the number of immigrants should increase a little or a lot. In the same year just 3.1 per cent disagreed strongly with a statement designed to tease out how nationally or internationally minded people are: 'Britain should follow its own interests even if this leads to conflicts with other nations.' In 2014 just 2.6 per cent of the public identified as European before any of the nations of the United Kingdom.[37]

On social and cultural matters, 5.9 per cent supported the idea of the gender neutral family, disagreeing strongly with the view that men and women are different and therefore cannot be expected to play the same family roles, and 7 per cent said that it is not important for Muslims to integrate into British society.[38]

What about the Hard Authoritarians and the reactionaries? One of the key questions here is how old they are, and therefore whether they are dying out or renewing themselves, as Karen Stenner argues, in reaction to Anywhere dominance.

The answer appears to be that authoritarian views are not dying out with the older cohorts; new authoritarians are emerging to take their place. The BSA's authoritarian-libertarian axis (mentioned in chapter one) is constructed from responses to these six statements: 'young people today don't have enough respect for traditional British values'; 'people who break the law should be given stiffer sentences'; 'for some crimes the death penalty is the most appropriate sentence'; 'schools should teach children to obey authority'; 'the law should always be obeyed, even if a particular law is wrong'; 'censorship of films and magazines is necessary to uphold moral standards'.

On the BSA scale there has been remarkably little movement over the past twenty years between the five categories of libertarian (virtually zero), liberal (4 per cent), centrist (25 per cent), illiberal (57 per cent) and authoritarian (13 per cent). Even if one might want to dispute the BSA categorisation system, the interesting point is the consistency over time and the persistence of Hard Authoritarian views—on mainly law and order related issues—at a little over 10 per cent.

And on race there is a stubborn core of those who admit to being very prejudiced against people of other races that has fallen from 4.4 per cent in 1983 to 2.8 per cent in 2013—which is probably an underestimate given how socially unacceptable such views have become. As recently as 2000 as many as 9.3 per cent of the sample said that equal opportunities have gone 'much too far' for black and Asian people. That number was quite evenly spread across age groups, with the over 65s only a bit higher at 12 per cent.

A few years ago in 2003 (the question has not been asked more recently), 14.4 per cent of people agreed that you had to be white to be truly British, with 4.7 per cent agreeing strongly. Similarly a larger proportion of respondents, 23.4 per cent, said they would mind 'a lot' if a close relative married a Muslim. And although that number is just over 40 per cent for the over 65s, it is still over 15 per cent for people in their 30s.

By way of an extended footnote to this section I want to approach my four main categories (Global Villager, Anywhere, Somewhere, Hard Authoritarian) from another angle to persuade you of their reality in roughly the current proportions of the population that I have indicated. But instead of looking at the data and putting labels on it I want to do it the other way around: by establishing some rough definitions for my four groups and then interrogating the data to see who signs up, and in what numbers.

For mainstream Anywheres, three defining characteristics would be feeling comfortable about the modern world, having a loose and open idea of national identity, and putting liberty before security in the civil liberties debate.

For mainstream Somewheres, three mirror-image defining characteristics would be feeling uncomfortable about the modern world, having a more 'fellow citizens first' view of national identity, and being prepared to sacrifice liberty for security.

For my two mainstream groups the numbers broadly turn out as I would expect. In relation to Anywhere comfort about the modern world, I have chosen to look at those who disagree or disagree strongly with the claim that Britain sometimes feel like a foreign country, and that number is 30 per cent—somewhat higher than my estimate of Anywhere size (so including a fair number of Inbetweeners). For Anywhere openness about Britishness, I looked at those who disagreed strongly with the idea that you have to be white to be British, and it comes out at 26.4 per cent, around my Anywhere estimate. And, finally, for my civil liberty question I looked at answers to the question 'should religious extremists be allowed to hold public meetings?', and in 2014 24.2 per cent of people agreed. (That was down from 35 per cent in 2004, no doubt reflecting the 7/7 bombing of 2005.)[39]

For Somewhere discomfort about the modern world, we have 53 per cent saying they would like Britain to be the way it used to be (and 62 per cent saying it sometimes feels like a foreign country), which is close to my 50 per cent Somewhere estimate. On fellow citizens first, the number of people who support the idea that employers should be given special incentives to hire British workers is 63 per cent. And 76 per cent of people do not think religious extremists should be allowed to hold public meetings (which includes a lot of Inbetweeners).[40]

For Global Villagers, three defining characteristics are putting global before national welfare, being indifferent to national identity, and not caring whether Muslims integrate or not. For Hard Authoritarians, my three characteristics are being a completely uncritical nationalist, having a highly restricted view of who can join the national club, and strongly opposing gay marriage.

The number of people who strongly support putting global before national welfare, or do to some extent, is 10 per cent, slightly above my estimate of the Global Villager proportion of the population. For a measure of national indifference I chose those who disagree with the statement 'I would rather be a citizen of Britain than any other country in the world', which turns out to be 7.5 per cent of respondents. And those (non-Muslims) who say it is not important for Muslims to integrate into British society are 7 per cent of the population.

For the Hard Authoritarians, as a measure of uncritical nationalism I took those who strongly agree that people should always support their country even if their country is wrong, which turns out to be just 5.1 per cent—rather at the low end of my hard authoritarian estimate. As a measure of a restrictive, racial, view of national membership I took those who think that to be truly British you have to be white, which is 14.4 per cent (4.7 per cent agreeing strongly). And, finally, 10.1 per cent strongly disagree with gay marriage.

So, to conclude, three things have emerged from our investigation of the 'great liberalisation'. First, the liberalisation surveys broadly confirm the reality of my two main value groups (and two sub-groups). Second, there is a core of resistance to liberalisation that appears not to be dying out with older generations. Third, and more significant, there is a range of subjects where liberalisation is simply not happening, or not to any marked extent, despite the increased number of graduates in the population—immigration, European integration (obviously), welfare, and national (and to a lesser extent ethnic) identity.

A final piece of evidence for the persistence of more traditional and socially conservative views can be found in the extraordinary consistency with which people have answered the clichéd question as to whether 'young people do not have enough respect for traditional British values.' In 2014, 66.6 per cent of respondents agreed or agreed strongly and just 12.8 per cent disagreed or disagreed strongly, and these are almost exactly the same numbers as in 1986.[41] Yet how many people among the students and staff of Britain's elite universities would agree?

3

EUROPEAN POPULISM AND THE CRISIS OF THE LEFT

A couple of years ago I was sitting in a bar in Amsterdam with two Dutch friends when one of them, the political writer René Cuperus, came up with a phrase (adapted from Tony Blair's famous couplet on crime)—'tough on populism, tough on the causes of populism.' I have had occasion to borrow it on many occasions since.

We were talking about the rise of European populism over the past fifteen years and how 2002 was the year that changed everything. Political systems dominated by competition between a main party of the centre-left and the centre-right had been slowly fraying in much of continental Europe in the last decades of the twentieth century, with proportional representation making it easier for small parties to eat into the voter base of the big ones.

But then came 2002. It was the year in which Jean-Marie Le Pen unexpectedly beat the Socialist Lionel Jospin into the final round of the French presidential election before going down to a heavy defeat to Jacques Chirac. It was also the year in which the myth of a benign, happily multicultural Netherlands was unmasked.

My other Dutch friend in the bar, the academic Paul Scheffer, had played a small role in that unmasking. Scheffer, a charming man in his early 60s, wrote an essay in 2000 called 'The Multicultural Tragedy', taking a critical look at the hands-off way that the Netherlands had managed immigration, Islam and national cohesion.[1] He was, and remains, an influential member of the Dutch Labour party but his challenge to liberal squeamishness about minority segregation and illiberalism led to a heated national 'integration debate'.[2]

That Scheffer debate in the Netherlands helped to clear intellectual space for the anti-multiculturalism candidate Pim Fortuyn to gather a growing wave of support in the 2002 Dutch election. When Fortuyn was assassinated two days before the election by an unhinged vegan activist his death swept away any remaining taboos about opposing immigration and multiculturalism in the Netherlands.

A series of governments, of both centre-left and centre-right, have subsequently implemented more overtly integrationist policies—pushed hard from the outside (and briefly from the inside) by Geert Wilders and his anti-immigration, anti-Islam Party of Freedom (PVV). The Wilders party, which emerged in the 2006 election, has consistently claimed between 10 and 20 per cent of the popular vote ever since, which in the Netherlands' fragmented political system usually makes it the second or third largest party in popular support. In the run up to the 2017 general election Wilder was scoring 24 per cent in the polls, his support swelled by a trial in which he called for fewer Dutch Moroccans. In the end he came second in vote share, with 13.1 per cent after the centre-right VVD on 21.3 per cent. The Dutch Labour party, a recent ruling party, scored just 5.7 per cent.[3]

Being 'tough on populism' requires challenging the sometimes bizarre and contradictory policy programmes of populist parties like the PVV (which wants to ban the Qur'an and close mosques), their caricature of elite self-interest and the very real xenophobia that is sometimes found beneath the surface. Being 'tough on the causes of populism' requires challenging the mainstream politicians, especially of the centre-left, who too easily convinced themselves that the virtues of openness—of more intrusive globalisation and EU integration and increased immigration over the past twenty-five years—were self-evident. The solutions that populists come up with are often unworkable—see President Trump—but the problems they address are real enough.

When a small, rather homogeneous country like the Netherlands, with a population of 17 million, in the course of a few decades acquires an immigrant and minority population of over 20 per cent, when about half of the Moroccan minority in Amsterdam schools do not identify as Dutch, when only one third of asylum seekers who have arrived in the last twenty years are in work, a political reaction is inevitable.

This chapter is a general reflection on populist politics—in continental Europe and the US as well as in Britain—and what happens when Somewhere priorities are disregarded by the political mainstream. Somewheres are a large and varied group and by no means all of them vote for populist parties, but almost all populist voters are Somewheres or the more extreme Hard Authoritarians.

We may not like strident populists like Wilders but they are a predictable reaction to the excesses and blind spots of Anywhere liberalism. Mainstream populist sentiment is a restatement of certain basic political intuitions that the dominant Anywhere classes have paid insufficient attention to: the importance of stability and secure borders, the priority of national citizen rights before universal rights, the need for narrative and recognition for those who do not easily thrive in more education-driven economies.

Right wing populism is, of course, an imprecise, irresponsible, reactive, rejection of a faster-moving, more open society. And as we have seen across Europe, and in the US, it can in skillful hands bring large sections of the population together at the ballot box—the old, part of the former working class, the soft and hard authoritarians unsettled by modern liberalism, people from the places that have had the life and purpose sucked out of them, and all those 'forgotten people'—in Donald Trump's phrase—who feel adrift or in some way unrecognised in our post-modern societies.

Liberals customarily think of populism as representing something old and atavistic—a xenophobic rejection of the 'other', a gut rejection of liberal reason and a yearning for a lost unity and simplicity. But it is also very modern: since the demise of socialism it is the political instrument used by the less successful to restrain, to bring down to earth, the more successful—the cognitive elites—in what are still, by historical standards, extraordinarily rich and flourishing societies.

It is often seen as mainly an economic phenomenon: a reaction against globalisation-related job loss or competition on the part of people who feel they are losing out from it. It is sometimes that, but as I argued in chapter one, populism is a socio-cultural and identity phenomenon more than a socio-economic one, which is why so many conventional politicians, especially on the left, do not know how to respond to it. And it is in cultural matters, not economic ones, that the consensus in liberal democracies is most broken. In Britain, at least, the cross-class consensus on economic matters has actually grown in recent decades as working class opinion has become less statist and middle class opinion more egalitarian.

Populism might even be seen as idealistic, as another wing of the 'postmaterialist' politics more normally associated with the environmental movement; a quest for meaning and collective identity in a secular, individualistic, economistic modern world. When people in Sunderland voted for Brexit apparently against their material interests it was considered stupid; when affluent people vote for higher taxes it is considered admirable.

Modern European and American populisms have emerged in rich and relatively secure societies. Very few populist voters are hungry or cold and most have access to a cornucopia of cultural, educational, sporting and musical stimulation. But political discontent in modern times has always been more about relative access to the good things in life, about feelings of loss and sometimes humiliation, about disappointed expectations and about the conflicting worldviews of elites and masses, rather than the absolute condition of the world.

One of the best explanations for inchoate anti-establishment sentiments can be found in the famous social psychology experiment, the 'ultimatum game'. In a one-off deal someone is given £100 to share with someone else in whatever proportion they choose, but if the other person rejects the share they are offered as unfair neither person receives anything. The experiment usually finds that if the second person is offered much below £30 the deal is rejected and neither party gets any money, showing that people place recognition, reputation and a sense of fairness before simple gain.

This explains why the Remain camp's complaint that working class people who voted Brexit or who oppose a more globalised economy are only harming themselves is missing something important. People are prepared to trade economic gain for political agency and the prospect of a society that takes them more seriously. (They may also be acting out of sheer vindictiveness, 'if I cannot have the good life, why should the other lot'.)

It is well put by management writer Charles Leadbeater: 'The Remain campaign was all about money and how much people would lose if Britain exited the EU. The Leave campaign was all about restoring a semblance of meaning to people's lives, despite not having much money. As a vote for something more than money—for pride, belonging, community, identity, a sense of "home"—it was a rejection of the market ... The result was a reminder that people need something in their lives that feels more important than money—especially perhaps when they have little prospect of having much.'[4]

There are a great many varieties of modern European populism, from extreme left (Syriza in Greece, Podemos in Spain and, arguably, the Corbyn Labour Party and Momentum in Britain) to more mainstream right (UKIP and Alternative für Deutschland) and extreme right (Jobbik of Hungary), while others like the French Front National are in a process of transition represented by the different leadership style, rhetoric and indeed policies of Marine Le Pen, who when elected leader in 2011 distanced the party from the explicit racism of her father Jean-Marie. Others, like the Five Star Movement, are not really classifiable on the old spectrum.

There are also special cases like the Scottish National Party which as its name suggests is a nationalist party with a majority ethnic appeal at the grass-roots but a civic nationalist, centre-left leadership and a rhetoric that can straddle the two: 'Decisions about Scotland taken by the people who care most about Scotland.' As Andrew Marr has pointed out, the 'yes' movement in the Scottish referendum campaign of 2014 drew on some of the same anti-system impulses as UKIP and the anti-EU uprising in England: 'a sense that the system no longer works for "people like us" ... and that power needs to be returned much more locally.'[5]

Brexit was a movement to reclaim control/sovereignty from a supranational EU and the SNP is a movement to reclaim control/sovereignty from a multinational United Kingdom (though happy to cede sovereignty to an even more remote Brussels).

There are some parallels between the SNP and the Liberal Democrats in their recent ascendancy. Both are parties with strongly Anywhere leaderships that claim to represent Somewhere interests (as all parties have to do at a basic level because there are so many Somewheres). This worked for the Liberal Democrats until it joined the mainstream in sharing power in London during the Coalition government.

Power in Edinburgh has not yet destroyed the SNP, though its wings were clipped in the 2017 general election. That is partly because it has governed competently, or at least has stayed disciplined, but also because it has something stronger than Liberal Democrat localist resentment to draw upon—Scottish national feeling. And it can wield that feeling in a civic nationalist manner by attacking Westminster—rather than the English—for granting insufficient power, funding and general welfare to the Scottish people.

Populism Goes Mainstream

There is no agreed definition of populism. It means slightly different things at different times and places, and parties or movements seldom self-describe as populist. Academics disagree about whether it is a style, a set of core beliefs or a psychological disposition. The American historian Richard Hofstadter delivered a famous paper at an LSE conference in 1967 entitled 'Everyone is Talking About Populism, But No One Can Define It', which could just as easily have been written today.[6] The word covers so many different political phenomena that it has little explanatory power. If there is a single idea that unites almost all variants it is this: that the interests of the virtuous, decent people and the corrupt, liberal elites are fundamentally opposed.

It was first used to describe Russia's nineteenth century agrarian radicals the *narodniki*. A People's Party of small farmers and workers known as the Populists was briefly a force in the US in the 1890s and Theodore Roosevelt's Progressive Party founded in 1912 was also labeled populist. In the US and Latin America the term has generally been associated with the left and in Europe with the right. Actually there has been a left-wing anti-corporate elite strand to US populism and a right-wing strand that is also nativist and anti-immigrant. The latter strand of populism influenced the 1882 Chinese Exclusion Act and the immigration pause starting in the early 1920s. Donald Trump combines aspects of both left and right populism.

Two things that populists are said to have in common is a hostility to elites of many kinds—bankers, governments, cosmopolitans, intellectuals—and the belief in a virtuous 'general will', the idea that the

people form a largely homogeneous body with shared ideas and interests. This usually pits populists against liberals, with their stress on
individual and minority rights and antipathy to majoritarianism.

Populism has exposed the inherent tension between the two terms
in the phrase liberal democracy—between the will of the people on
the one hand and constitutional rights and law on the other as the
source of legitimate decisions.[7] To put it another (anti-populist) way:
the right to be governed wisely versus the right to vote. When pushed,
populists place democracy before liberalism and liberals when pushed
place rights and reason before democracy—witness some of the progressive outrage after the Brexit vote, which sounded like those nine-
teenth-century liberals who wanted the suffrage restricted to those
with the respectable views acquired through property ownership (now
it would be a good degree from a Russell Group university).

The liberalism-democracy conflict is a very real issue in some parts
of Europe, especially with so many issues now removed from national
democratic choice thanks to independent central banks, judicial creep
in areas like human rights, and the growth of EU law. In central
Europe, as the Bulgarian political scientist Ivan Krastev has pointed
out, it was hostility to the post-communist elites that partly drove
popular enthusiasm for EU membership, but less than ten years later
Brussels was seen as the enemy, usually in cahoots with local elites.
'The outcome is a sort of politics in which populists are becoming
openly anti-liberal, and elites are becoming secretly anti-democratic,'
says Krastev.[8]

But this classical populist paradigm of a conflict between liberalism
and democracy does not work in other parts of the developed world.
The phenomenon that I have labeled 'decent populism' does not fit the
old categories. Most, though not all, of the British Somewheres who
voted Brexit or for UKIP, would support minority and gay rights while
also rejecting European integration and mass immigration.

Populism has a mainstream face in parties like UKIP or the Five Star
movement in Italy or the Danish Peoples' Party. And people who vote
for such parties have a perfectly good reason to do so. Most of them are
former centrist voters expressing normal political disaffection—they
do not necessarily want the populist party they vote for to form the
government. Rather they want their vote to act as a brake on Anywhere

preferences. (Many Brexit and Trump voters almost certainly cast their votes as a protest without expecting their choice to win.)

They also want to register a complaint about elite performance. Compared with the political achievements of the immediate post-war period it is quite reasonable to be critical of western elites and the elite consensus over the past generation: the creation of a flawed Euro; foreign policy blunders like the Iraq war; the British Parliamentary expenses scandal of 2009; the failure to think through the consequences of large scale immigration (and in Britain the particular failure to predict the flow of eastern Europeans after 2004); the failure to deliver the protections from globalisation promised for the bottom half of society; the failure to tame the financial sector or the global imbalances that led to the financial crisis of 2007–2008. Moreover, as the writer John Lloyd has put it, political elites have neither vigorously enough renewed their offerings to the electors nor shared their disillusionment.[9]

Populism's reaction against the established order obviously has multiple causes and the balance of motivations behind the movement differs from country to country. Ed Conway, the Sky Economics Editor, has neatly punctured the claim that economic failure—falling wages or growing inequality—is the prime mover by pointing out that both Austria and Sweden have seen healthy wage growth in recent years. Inequality has been static in several countries with growing populist movements and has fallen sharply in Poland which actually has a populist government.[10]

Nevertheless, a delayed reaction to the 2008 crisis and disillusionment with the broader economic and social order—including inequality, falling living standards after the crisis, and fewer good jobs for school leavers not destined for university—is clearly one of the recruiting sergeants for populist disaffection (see more detail in chapter six).

The more important factor can be encapsulated in the notion that 'Britain increasingly feels like a foreign country'—immigration, speed of demographic change and so on. It is worth noting that the populist right, including Donald Trump, can mobilise around both of those disillusionments—the modern left has only been able to mobilise around, indeed can only really comprehend, one of them. Only where the Euro has made disaffection overwhelmingly economic—as in Greece and Spain—has left populism made significant headway.

Another key point about populism, made by the Dutch political scientist Cas Mudde, is that it is normal. Many liberal commentators and academics, like Pippa Norris of Harvard University, see populism as an irrational, xenophobic, backlash against a more fluid and open world. Or even as a kind of political illness created by charismatic individuals at moments of crisis, appealing to extreme and paranoid voters. There is, of course, a fringe that does fit this description—that is racist, violent, anti-semitic, neo-Nazi, conspiracy theory driven and so on. And there are some parties of the populist right that emerged from that fringe and still cling to some parts of the belief system.

Mudde argues that the three things that define the populist radical right—nativism, authoritarianism and mistrust of elites—are also in milder form at the centre of orthodox politics, while the trinity of populist policy concerns—immigration, security and corruption—are shared by significant sections of the electorate in the US and Europe.[11]

Populism thus becomes a difference not of *kind* from mainstream parties but of *degree*, almost a matter of temperament—mainstream beliefs held with extra passion or bitterness or certainty.

Nativism, for example, is based on the idea of the primacy of the interests of native people. But in practice, even for most right wing populists, that has come to mean the primacy of fellow citizens, which is a concept right at the heart of mainstream politics—which still talks of the 'people' and the national interest as if they were self-evident political facts. Nativism, stripped of ethnic exclusivity, is no more than placing national citizen rights before universal rights.

Similarly authoritarianism, meaning a strictly ordered society in which infringements of authority are punished, sometimes severely, is also a completely mainstream conservative view, as we saw in the last chapter. Most citizens want harsher sentences for most crimes and more discipline in schools.

Finally, populist mistrust of elites is the most mainstream idea of all. It is an idea deeply embedded in western society—thanks perhaps to the Christian idea of original sin—that people will abuse their power if they are allowed to do so. The US constitution itself and its complex separation of powers is based on this supposedly populist idea.

Indeed, many of today's mainstream parties—including both of America's main parties and, arguably, the Labour party in Britain—

started life as populist movements. And when as a young reporter in Leipzig in 1989 I accompanied the East German marchers chanting 'We are the people' it was a legitimate popular claim for democratic voice in the face of a communist elite that locked them out. Popular and populist are not, of course, always the same thing.

Moreover, there is a kind of soft populist rhetoric common to all the mainstream Westminster parties. What could be more populist than Theresa May's refrain at the start of her premiership that she will govern for the 'many not the privileged few.' The establishment itself has become anti-establishment, perhaps starting with the Thatcher/Reagan right in the 1980s which encouraged working class voters to replace the plodding communitarianism of the labour elites with a vigorous individualism and cultural conservatism.[12]

So populism, at least in its measured versions, is a normal reaction to Anywhere liberal over-reach, a change of political tone as much as a backlash. But there are other explanations as to why it has emerged with such force in the past generation which are connected with the practice of modern politics and the new technologies of communication.

A more confident populism has emerged out of the convergence of two political trends. On the one hand, conventional party politics has become narrower, less ideologically distinct, more insider dominated, both in personnel and also in the interests represented. On the other hand, technology has lowered the barriers to political voice and removed the old elite 'filter' that controlled who could play the political game.

Rates of social mobility in Britain do not tend to change very much over time but whereas there used to be a variety of routes up there is now just the path of taking A levels, going to university and starting a professional career.

Similarly in politics. There used to be many routes to becoming an MP, from the unions, from business, from the law, now almost all MPs elected since 1992 have gone to university and into a profession—many of them professions directly related to politics. (In fact 25 per cent of today's MPs had worked in politics before becoming an MP and a further 18 per cent had worked in the media or public affairs. About 90 per cent of MPs are graduates.)[13]

The passing of the old, more rigid class system is rarely to be regretted but thanks to the more class-based politics of the immediate post-war period in Britain more people probably felt represented in the nation's deliberations. As a sociologically flatter graduate class has emerged some people have become nostalgic for the distinctive accents and manners of the old class system.

Identification as working class remains quite high—anything from one quarter to 60 per cent of adults in Britain, depending on how the question is posed—yet there is also a strong sense that class identities are much fuzzier. As Julian Baggini puts it: 'When it is no longer even clear what it means to be working or middle class, there is no clear sense of belonging to a group that can be represented. "The likes of us" are no longer members of a well-defined group, spread all over the country, but more fragmented groupings, such as the people "born and bred around here" or "from the estates"'.[14]

The professionalisation of politics is not necessarily a bad thing in itself but it has coincided with a slump in party political member-ship—from 750,000 in 1970 to 190,000 in 2013 for Labour (prior to the Corbyn surge) and from 1.2 million to 150,000 for the Tories over the same period. This shrinkage means that most members and activists will be from similar backgrounds to the MPs and are likely to form an echo chamber around them.

The Labour Party has, at least for now, reversed this long decline in party membership with a surge of mainly young leftists joining the party to support the leadership of Jeremy Corbyn, which has taken membership back up to 515,000 (plus affiliated supporters). The Corbyn movement could be described as populist in economics but extreme Anywhere in most other respects. What it has not done is change the social composition of the party—about three quarters of Labour party members are middle class, about 60 per cent are gradu-ates, and almost 40 per cent live in London and the South East.[15]

The decline of corporatism has also had a narrowing effect on poli-tics. Corporatism, for all its faults, provided many millions of people with a second way to influence public policy through their union branches or business or professional associations. Moreover, in Britain, thanks to the first past the post system, most constituencies never change hands. This means a limited sense of political agency in national politics for the people stuck in the rotten boroughs, while local gov-ernment politics, at least outside big cities, is often barely visible to most people (thanks in part to the sad decline of good local newspapers). Surveys regularly reveal that 70 to 80 per cent of the population do not feel they can have any impact on politics. The number is usually a bit more positive for ethnic minorities perhaps because they still feel they have a quasi corporatist or pressure group relationship to the state through their minority organisations.

The claim that low voter turnout is a sign of relative contentment with the status quo is not a ridiculous one and probably had some validity in the middle and later decades of the twentieth century when incomes were rising and the future looked relatively bright for most people in the middle and lower ends of the income spectrum. (Percentage turnout in general elections hovers around the mid-sixties in the UK and mid-fifties in the US.)

Even looking around the world now you might argue that successful countries have apathy and anger, unsuccessful ones have high voter turnout and mass rallies for politicians. The idea that western electorates en masse are 'angry' is plainly not the case. There are pockets, sometimes quite big ones, of disaffection and the US in particular has a high level of negative partisanship, but Obama's approval ratings on leaving office were about the same level as Ronald Reagan's in the 1980s.

Nevertheless, by the time the populist surge took off in Europe at the turn of the century the non-voters were no longer seen as lending their consent and had come to be regarded as sullen and alienated—'active' non-voters because they thought that all the main parties represented variations on Anywhere progressive individualism, the politics of Tweedle Dum and Tweedle Dee, and they no longer saw people like themselves represented in politics. It is estimated that 3 million people who didn't vote in the 2015 General Election did vote in the EU Referendum (which had a higher 72 per cent turnout), the vast majority for Leave.[16]

Does this amount to the emergence of a 'two nation' politics, not so much rich and poor but insiders and outsiders? Insiders being the connected graduate class who understand the technocratic language of politics, listen to the *Today* programme and watch *Newsnight*. Outsiders being the rest: people who are now far less likely to be connected, even indirectly, to a political party—in 2013 membership of the three main Westminster parties hit an all time low of 0.8 per cent of the population.

In fact, outsiders are far less likely to be a member of anything—church group, community group, charity, club—they are often people whose social universe has shrunk to work, the family and the virtual reality of television, radio and the internet. An outsider nation makes a decreasing effort to be politically informed, as books like *Democracy for Realists* by Christopher Achen and Larry Bartels have shown in chilling detail.[17] Most voters are not only extraordinarily ignorant of current affairs but also reveal only the most tenuous connection between what they believe and how they vote. They end up voting, if they do so at all, for people who they think will stick up for people like them.

Here is American political writer Michael Lind: 'Insider Nation on both sides of the Atlantic is extraordinarily homogeneous, in spite of its professed dedication to diversity ... Although meritocracy is the official creed of Insider Nation, its allegedly self-made men and women are almost always born into the wealthy or professional classes, seldom into working class or poor families. The new oligarchy is linked by education at a few institutions, like the Ivy League universities in the US, and increasingly by intermarriage. ... The ideal of Insider Nation is nonpartisan technocracy, staffed by the best and brightest graduates of a few elite schools. It is assumed that domestic and foreign policy consist of a set of discrete problems, each of which has an optimal solution upon which rational, disinterested, nonpartisan individuals can agree. The style of Insider Nation is that of corporations, think tanks, consulting firms—soft-spoken, analytical, emotionless.'[18]

Insider Nation exists in Britain too. As one rising Labour politician, himself from a working class background, said to me: 'My generation of Labour staff and activists in London—pre-Corbyn—were drawn from quite a narrow social background, often second generation political professionals or otherwise from the intellectual/professional elite. The four principle staff of the Stronger In campaign all grew up within two square miles. Two went to the same north London state school. One's father was Labour Home Secretary, another's godfather was Peter Mandelson.'

And, as it happens, the populist claim that all the main parties over-represent the interests of the affluent and liberal turns out to be broadly true, as Martin Gilens has shown in his study of public policy and public preferences in the US as revealed in responses to thousands of questions from national surveys conducted between 1964 and 2006.[19]

Americans actually agree on many aspects of public policy across the class and income spectrum (as do Britons) with about half of policy proposals attracting broadly similar support—foreign military action, education spending, the War on Drugs, childcare and job training for welfare recipients.

When preferences diverge the views of the affluent make a big difference. Low and middle income Americans have been united since the 1970s in opposing free trade agreements such as NAFTA but the affluent favoured freer trade and got their way.

On moral and religious issues the affluent tend to be more liberal than poorer Americans and still generally get their way. Lower income people want the consent of the biological father to an abortion, tighter limits on stem cell research and more support for school prayer.

According to Gilens if a policy is favoured by 80 per cent of the affluent it has a 50 per cent chance of being adopted. In contrast, except close to election time or when partisan competition is particularly acute, support or opposition from poor and middling Americans makes no difference at all. The most simple explanation for representational inequality is that high-income Americans are more likely than less well off Americans to vote, volunteer in campaigns, and make political donations (large and small). They are the political class.

Democrats used to be the party of the working class but now remain so only on social welfare issues. What Thomas Frank has called the 'liberalism of the rich'—with its focus on gender equality, environmentalism and so on—is of little interest to lower income Americans who are far closer to Republicans than Democrats on cultural and religious issues. On economic issues neither main party, at least until Donald Trump, has represented the anti-free trade, anti-big business preferences of the poorer, especially since the Democrats shifted in a more free-market, free trade, direction twenty years ago.

The policy preferences of the affluent Anywhere classes have been similarly dominant in Britain in the past generation. Poorer Britons are generally less socially conservative and religious than poorer Americans but in other areas their priorities have been ignored: tighter control of immigration; less European integration; more public housing; more decently paid ordinary jobs; better vocational education; the opportunity to lead a respected and successful life without having to move away from one's family and home town. Many of these things are hard to achieve, but public policy and rhetoric can at least be tilted in their direction, as the post-Brexit May government was aiming to do. (See my overview of how Anywhere priorities have dominated public policy over the past twenty years in chapter nine.)

This pattern, with national variations, has broadly been the story of politics in Europe and America in the past generation or more. There has been a growing convergence between Anywhere centre-left and centre-right on the 'double liberalism'—more market friendly, pro-globalisation economics combined with more individualistic social and cultural policies and state enforcement of greater race and gender equality. This reflected the political settlement of the Thatcher-Reagan era in which the right won the economic argument and the liberal-left won the cultural argument. There are exceptions to this rule: the left did not win the cultural argument so clearly in the US, hence the long 'culture wars'. And the right may now be partly losing the economic argument as markets are more constrained, the world experiences a limited deglobalisation and austerity fatigue sets in.

This 'double liberalism' is the reason for that familiar refrain 'they are all the same, what's the point in voting?' And almost everywhere that convergence left a 'missing majority', or at least a substantial minority, of lower income, less well-educated people who remain significantly less liberal than the graduate Anywhere class but still prefer moderately social democratic economic and tax-spend policies and better protection from globalisation.

In Britain, Red Toryism and Blue Labour were belated attempts to point the two major parties away from Anywhere liberalism in the direction of this ideological coalition, but it was UKIP, Britain's first mainstream populist party (with the most working class voter base), that first gave it voice, especially after it shifted sharply to the left in the run up to the 2015 election.

Yet alongside this *narrowing* of official politics, as Anywhere people and preferences have held sway in both Britain and the US, the opportunity to make one's voice heard, albeit in a disorganised way, has multiplied.

People in most advanced democracies are less deferential and trusting of authority, more conscious of their rights, readier to engage in one-off activism to stop a hospital closing or a motorway being built and, armed with the internet, better equipped to challenge professional expertise. Indeed, the end of deference seems to have spilled over beyond the rejection of authority based on unmerited class power to include a rejection of authority based on cognitive ability too— hence Michael Gove's notorious comment about experts. And through social media and other networking technologies it is easier for people to make their voices heard and to cluster together for temporary political, or social, purposes.

The elite political filter once provided by the conventional party system and traditional media has been broken; the voice of the people, angry or otherwise, spills out everywhere. And not just through new digital media, the old media of newspapers and mainstream broadcasters constantly beg for our participation and feed-back. Moreover, the opinion sampling industry has never been more sophisticated or ubiquitous, we know more about what our fellow citizens think they think than ever before (though, of course, the polls were wrong about the 2015 and 2017 elections, Brexit and Trump).

So as the emotion and conviction has drained out of conventional politics it has reappeared in the chaotic and often shrill digital world. This is not always pleasant. A mass media that rewards the shocking and belligerent can act as a de-civilising influence; it is hard to imagine the triumph of Donald Trump in a pre-social media age. As Michael Lind pithily expresses it: 'If Insider Nation is a nation of technocrats, Outsider Nation is a nation of trolls.'

Yet many people have found voice and agency, perhaps for the first time, in cyberspace. Not all of them are populists, but many are. As Jamie Bartlett, author of *Radicals*, puts it: 'Digital politics has been an enormously important mechanism for the new populists. It has allowed them to circumnavigate elite interests and connect to the "general will" online.'[20] Populists as varied as UKIP, the Wilders party, Jobbik in Hungary, Podemos in Spain, Corbyn's Momentum movement and the Five Star Movement in Italy have all eagerly adopted the new political currency of posts, shares, likes and re-tweets.

America and Europe: The Populist Convergence

The election of Donald Trump was seen by most Europeans as another example of the weird exceptionalism of US politics. But although

Trump's brand of vulgarity is peculiarly American the social forces he represented in his successful bid for the presidency actually signify a convergence between populism in the US and Europe. (As Ivan Krastev has pointed out, the American demagogue in his crude directness and news media manipulation is surely a pupil of the former Italian prime minister Silvio Berlusconi.)[21]

Race and ethnicity has always been more central to US politics than to European, thanks to America's history as an immigrant nation and its history of mass African slavery. By contrast, social class—so important to European experience over the past 200 years—has been a weaker force in the US. Yet thanks to the rapid increase in immigration to Europe in the past generation, race and ethnicity has now also moved to the centre of European politics, while at the same time the economic discomfort of lower income America and the stagnant living standards and sharp increase in inequality since the 1970s has put social class closer to the centre of US politics.

The sharper line between the successful college-educated professional with a degree of security and career progression in the knowledge economy, and the bottom half of the US workforce has cast a long shadow over the American Dream. The median household income of $53,600 is down nearly 7.5 per cent from the peak twenty years ago—but while the incomes of college graduates have risen 22 per cent in that time those of white men who didn't progress beyond high school have fallen by 9 per cent.[22] (And although headline unemployment remains low in America there has been a sharp decline in the employment rate of prime age men.)

One of the survey results most often cited to explain the unexpected success of the Trump insurgency is that, according to Gallup, 33 per cent of Americans described themselves as 'working class' in 2000; by 2015 that figure had risen to 48 per cent.[23] Despite his own privileged background and business tycoon career, Trump—the 'blue-collar billionaire'—crafted an economically protectionist, pro-social security platform that was way to the left of his Republican challengers, and even parts of the Democratic party, as he set out to appeal to the new working class Republican base—the 'country and western' Republicans who have replaced the 'country club' Republicans. These new Republicans are as opposed as Democrats to social security benefit cuts.

Fewer than 20 per cent of Americans say they have no religious affiliation compared with almost half of Britons. And it is often said that poorer Americans sacrifice their economic interests for their cultural or religious preferences—such as the right to carry arms or hostility to abortion.

But the Trump ascendancy suggests that the decades-long culture wars between religious conservatives and secular liberals is winding down. It is being replaced by a 'border war' between nationalists, mainly on the right, and multicultural globalists, mostly on the left. Trump was not engaged by the old culture wars. In spring 2016 the Supreme Court moved to block new Texan laws restricting abortion. Normally this kind of intervention would provoke angry rhetoric from leading Republicans—Trump said nothing.

Borders, though, did interest him a great deal. His shocking comments about Mexican 'rapists' and bans on Muslims attracted the most media attention but his speeches were far more about trade and jobs.[24] His main message was about reassuring American losers that a revived American nationalism can protect them better than in the recent past. 'I love uneducated people,' he liked to say in the campaign. And uneducated people loved him back: almost 70 per cent of whites without college degrees voted for Trump.[25]

It is true that a majority of the poorest voters—those earning less than $50,000 a year—divided 52 per cent/42 per cent in favour of the Democrats. But those who switched from Democrat to Republican were almost entirely from middle and lower income groups. Indeed, according to Torsten Bell of the Resolution Foundation, a full 16 per cent of voters earning less than $30,000 switched to Trump. This explains his unexpected success in the de-industrialised Midwestern states like Michigan and Wisconsin, hit hard by the China shock.[26]

Even more than in Britain, white Americans tell pollsters that they think 'Things were better in the past'. A YouGov poll in 2016 found nearly 60 per cent agreeing and only 21 per cent disagreeing.[27] Those who perceive loss—whether due to age, lack of opportunities, personalities that favour stability, sense of declining status—are much more anti-immigrant and populist.

And the Democrats, like the centre-left in Europe, have not found a way of talking to these voters. The presidential election was not just an anti-incumbent vote, it was strongly anti- the Democratic party of Obama and Clinton, seen as the party of liberal metropolitan whites and minorities. The Republicans now hold the presidency, Senate, the House of Representatives and two thirds of state legislatures and most state governors.

Donald Trump's populism is, of course, about race as well as class. And majority ethnic anxiety is clearly a factor behind both American and European populism, as much research evidence confirms.[28] Trump's popularity among poorly educated older white males was attributed in part to ethnic anxiety, as whites become a minority in many parts of the country and stand at just 62 per cent in the country as a whole—with minority status beckoning in 2044 (unless, as is possible, a significant proportion of Hispanics assimilate into the white population).

Most white Americans already think they are in the minority, as they are in large states like Texas and California.[29] And 45 per cent of Trump supporters in 2016 said that whites in America face a lot of discrimimation.[30] Poorer whites have, indeed, fallen in status relative to other racial groups and to their own group in the recent past—and for the first time in US history the life-span of white, middle aged Americans is actually falling thanks to addiction and suicide (see the 2015 study by Anne Case and Angus Deaton).[31]

Many Europeans are puzzled that an immigrant country like America could have been seduced by Trump's flirtation with white identity politics. But it is often forgotten that the US had a long immigration pause between the early 1920s and the late 1960s. In 1970, not only was America about 84 per cent white it was also only 4 per cent foreign born. Race plays a larger role in US life and politics because of the legacy of African slavery but middle-aged and older white Americans grew up in a country where the white European ethnic majority was almost as dominant as it was in European countries.

Since then there has been another immigration surge in the US and, as noted, the non-Hispanic white population has fallen to just 62 per cent. Moreover, because of an overwhelming consensus in favour of legal immigration on the establishment centre-left and centre-right there has been almost no debate about this big demographic shift. The immigration debate, prior to Trump, was *only* about what to do about the estimated 12 million illegal immigrants in the US and even in that debate opponents of 'paths to citizenship' measures were rountinely accused of racism.

Will Trump's extraordinary campaign and early immigration curbs leave an even starker racial divide in US politics with a core of disaffected whites, now stirred into political consciousness? It is certainly the case that while in 2012 Barack Obama took 39 per cent of the white vote, Hillary Clinton could not even match that with just 37 per cent. And the shift from a Republican politics with a predominantly religious accent to one that was more explicitly ethnic in the Trump campaign was supposed to alienate many minorities, especially Hispanics. Yet when the votes were counted it turned out that Trump had won a higher proportion of black (8 per cent), Hispanic (29 per cent) and Asian (29 per cent) voters than the two previous Republican candidates Romney and McCain. In fact, his vote increased proportionately more among those minority groups than it did among whites.

Trump is not a white supremacist—he would not have been elected if he was—but he did in some of his campaign speeches nod towards white America's anti-integrationist, anti-black traditions and joined in the absurd questioning of President Obama's birthplace and religion. And, more legitimately, he did start to address lower income whites as a group with their own interests and concerns overlooked by the country's elites. This was not entirely novel—Pat Buchanan had done something similar in the 1990s. But it does beg the question of whether it is possible to create a politics—within either main party or outside them both—that can respond to the grievances embodied by Trump but in a way that reaches across class and race divides.

In parts of Europe too, majority ethnic anxiety appears to be one element in the rise of populism as whites are forced to think about their ethnic identity, often for the first time, when their symbols and priorities no longer automatically dominate in a neighbourhood—as the pub closes and the Polish shop or Halal butcher opens.[32]

Even more than in America, opposition to a growing Muslim minority is close to the heart of European populism (though less so in Britain). And ethnic anxiety is expressed in a range of ways: more intense opposition to immigration, worries about lack of integration, the feeling of abandonment by political and economic elites who seem to be more concerned with minorities than the white working class.

In the next section I will give a brief overview of the varieties of European populism, from the moderate and legitimate to the extreme and menacing.

Populist Parties: The Necessary, the Weird and the Ugly

Since European populist parties announced their arrival in the political mainstream in 2002—with Jean-Marie Le Pen reaching the final round of the French presidential election and Pim Fortuyn emerging in the Netherlands—they have experienced mixed fortunes but have remained on an upward trajectory.

The average share of the popular vote taken by west European populists in the 2014 European elections was 17 per cent, more than double the share in 2001 and one third higher than 2009.

Several populist parties have been in government in that period, though they have only been the main governing party in eastern Europe in Hungary (Fidesz), Poland (Law and Justice party) and Slovakia (Smer), as well as Greece (Syriza).

I have included the east European countries in this overview but they are *sui generis*. There is no widespread Anywhere influence in these societies and very little immigration. The publics are considerably less tolerant than in western Europe and the elites more nationalist, so there is much less of an elite/mass divergence. Indeed, the whole region grew more Eurosceptic in the wake of the refugee crisis and German attempts to impose refugee quotas on the former communist countries. Victor Orbán, the Hungarian leader, who is often the main spokesman for the Visegrad Four (Hungary, Poland, Slovakia and the Czech Republic) talks explicitly about 'illiberal democracy,' a new kind of conservative 'EU of capitals' and contrasts federalism with an EU based on the family, the nation state and Christianity.

In western Europe populist parties of the right that have either been in coalition government or have overtly supported a government coalition from the outside include: the Freedom Party in Austria; Lega Nord in Italy; the Peoples' Party in Denmark; the PVV in the Netherlands; the Finns in Finland; and the Progress Party in Norway.

Other significant populist parties with at least 10 to 15 per cent of the popular vote include UKIP in Britain, the Front National in France, the Five Star Movement in Italy, the Sweden Democrats in Sweden and, most recently, Alternative für Deutschland in Germany.

Two things are needed to give a useful overview of this populist trend. First, some estimate of the influence these parties are having on the politics of their respective countries, in or out of government. Second, a classification of the different populist parties on a mainstream to extremist spectrum.

As we have seen, populists have had a taste of power in a number of countries. In some cases joining the system has led to a moderation of their views and a fall off in support—support for the Finns has almost halved since they joined the government in 2015. The Danish People's Party has also been compromised by power and seen its support fall. The Freedom Party of Austria has seen its support fall after joining coalitions but only narrowly failed to win the Austrian Presidency in December 2016. The lesson seems to be that populism cannot be eliminated but it can be moderated and co-opted.

In a few countries, for example Sweden and to a lesser extent France in its presidential elections, there has been an intense effort to ostracise the main populist party and close ranks against it, even at the cost of diminished political competition between the main non-populist parties.

In Sweden this has not worked. In the 2014 general election, the Sweden Democrats polled 12.9 per cent and became Sweden's third largest party. It is a working class party combining left-wing economic policies with conservative social policies. It still supports voluntary repatriation of immigrants though on its journey to the centre is likely to jettison the policy or, at least, play it down. And, despite having been shunned by the mainstream media and parties, in February 2016 the Sweden Democrats emerged briefly as the most popular party in polls thanks to their tough response to the refugee crisis—160,000 asylum seekers arrived in Sweden during 2015, more per capita than any other country in Europe. The party's leader, Jimmie Akesson, is a relatively mainstream figure who defected to the Sweden Democrats from the Moderate Party (though some of those who founded the party in the 1980s had neo-Nazi pasts). At the end of last year he told *Bloomberg News* that populist success was not mainly about economics. 'It's mainly about values ... about how we manage to keep society together.'[33]

The main influence of populists comes not so much through participating in government and more through sharpening the populist strand in existing public opinion and influencing the main competitor party, normally the main party of the centre-right, in a more populist direction. UKIP, for example, since its breakthrough in the 2009 European elections was never far from the thinking of leading Conservatives and its presence was a big factor behind their 2013 decision to hold a referendum on EU membership.

Yet, surveying European politics since 2002 it is hard to find elsewhere as clear-cut a case of significant populist influence as UKIP and Brexit. In fact in many ways it is remarkable how little *direct* influence the populist surge has yet had either on the politics of the whole EU or on individual countries. It has probably helped to keep immigration at the centre of national politics. And more extreme, fringe populists have made life on the streets a bit less pleasant for minorities, especially Muslims, but the open society consensus has largely held.

The populist voice has not led to a change of policy on the Euro or any significant change to freedom of movement within the EU—and did not prompt the leading EU countries to offer David Cameron an attractive reform package that he could have sold to British voters. Neither the EU nor any leading country within it has clamped down hard on immigration, with the possible exception of Denmark, nor implemented any significant anti-globalisation economic measures. The initial reaction to the 2015 refugee crisis was hardly draconian (even if Angela Merkel's initial welcome message was unrepresentative), though it did become tougher after a few months, especially in eastern Europe. Nor, despite a wave of jihadi terrorism, has there been any weakening of the rule of law or minority rights. (Again, the Law and Justice government in Poland and the Fidesz government in Hungary are, arguably, partial exceptions.)

Populist leaders and activists—especially those from far right backgrounds—are often ugly messengers, at odds with the general moderation and liberalisation of European societies, especially on race, over the past two generations. The bulk of the Somewhere classes are not xenophobic. Decent populism shares many harder populist concerns with pace of change, erosion of national favouritism and good jobs for non-graduates, but most Somewheres find race politics weird and alien.

Populism is the new socialism. Almost all European populist parties now have an overwhelmingly working class voter base and most have policies towards economics and globalisation that have more in common with the left than the right, or might better be described as statist/protectionist. Indeed, several of the big parties—including both UKIP and the Front National—have been dragged sharply to the left in recent years.

UKIP started life as a libertarian anti-EU party but after it achieved that unexpected breakthrough it shifted increasingly to the left—£350 million extra a week for the NHS may have been an exaggeration but it is hardly a right wing slogan. It won 22 per cent of the popular vote at the 2013 local council elections and came top of the poll in the 2014 European Parliament elections with 27.5 per cent of the vote. UKIP had the most working class voter base in Britain and nearly 4 million voted for the party in the 2015 general election (12.6 per cent of the vote) contributing to Labour's poor performance but winning only one seat. UKIP came second in 114 English constituencies in 2015 and hoped to make inroads into Labour seats in 2020. Instead the party experienced a nervous breakdown after the Brexit vote and was then wiped out at the surprise 2017 election, its vote share slumping from 12.6 per cent to 1.8 per cent. Nearly 60 per cent switched to the Tories and just 18 per cent to Labour.

The Front National in France has also been on a journey, though from extreme right roots. When founded in 1973 its appeal was mainly to rural and lower middle class voters in parts of the south, and especially to the 'Pieds Noirs' former French colonists in North Africa. In the 1980s and 1990s it began to pick up former Communist party voters in the industrial north, combining economic and anti-immigrant grievances. In 2014, the FN won the European Parliament elections in France with 24.9 per cent of the vote—a similar breakthrough to UKIP's in Britain—and went on to win 28 per cent of the vote in the 2015 regional elections, making it the official opposition in four regions. 'It has now become the party of the working class,' according to political analyst Bruno Cautres.[34] Opinion polls in October 2016 found that 45 per cent of blue collar workers supported the FN and 38 per cent of the unemployed. Older voters are less drawn to the party's anti-EU positions, though younger voters are more supportive. Marine Le Pen focuses heavily on unemployment but also on security issues—the country has been in an official state of emergency for more than a year—and the threat of the banlieue as a breeding ground for jihadi terrorism. The FN was never expecting to win the 2017 presidential election and gained only a few seats in the National Assembly. But a vote of almost 34 per cent for Le Pen, including defectors from mainstream parties, is another step towards respectability.

So how should one categorise the different populist parties of the right across Europe? Here is one attempt.

First, the Mainstream: parties that can mount a challenge to Anywhere liberalism but are most appealing to decent populist Somewheres, and more mainstream voters generally, and do not have roots in the far right. These include UKIP in Britain; the Five Star Movement in Italy; the Danish Peoples' Party; Alternative für Deutschland in Germany; the Finns; and three of the four governing parties (as of late 2016) in the Visegrad Group (the alliance of four Central European states)—the Law and Justice party in Poland, Fidesz in Hungary, and Smer in Slovakia (the Czech Republic has a populist, and popular, president in Milos Zeman but does not have a populist government).

Second, the Anti-Islamists. Hostility to Islam is important to most European populists but some are overwhelmingly driven by it, and it has caused some groups to drop any traces of anti-semitism (if they had them) and often stress their support for homosexuality, female equality and free speech. Party of Freedom in the Netherlands is one of these, the Danish People's Party also has a strong anti-Islam focus as does Pegida the German-centred movement (though it is largely a street movement and attracts violent off-shoots).

Next are the Reformed Far Right: parties which have roots in more extreme organisations, in some cases even neo-Nazi ones, but have reformed substantially and are keen to become 'clean' (or at least some of their factions are). Amongst these are the Front National in France, the Sweden Democrats, the Austrian Freedom Party and Vlaams Belang in Belgium.

Finally, the Unreformed or Barely Reformed Far Right. Many of these parties or street movements, the unconstitutional populists, are overtly racist and white supremacist and generally support repatriation of non-natives: Jobbik in Hungary, Golden Dawn in Greece, Phalange in Spain, Kotleba in Slovakia.

The populist parties, at least the mainstream ones, are generally no longer insurgents and most have been rendered more moderate by office or the attempt to reach it. They have filled a gap left by Anywhere domination of the main parties of centre-left and centre-right. If populists are an unappealing but necessary counter-balance, they have also been a coarsening influence on politics; even mainstream populists who repudiate racism tend to reinforce ideas of insiders and outsiders that allow real racists to grow more confident, at least for a time (as they seemed to do after the Brexit vote).

Populists also tend not to be interested in the complexities of policy and, as their opponents never tire of pointing out, usually offer merely simple solutions to complex problems. And the problem with simple solutions is that they raise expectations that are almost always disappointed, which then encourages even simpler or more radical solutions in a downward spiral of anger and denunciation. This could be one of the consequences of the Trump presidency.

Leaders of populist parties are frequently opportunists, narcissists and sociopaths—one reason why the parties are so often torn apart in enormous ego clashes. Nevertheless a full-scale political disaster cannot be completely ruled out: in the wake of huge new waves of immigration and/or jihadi terrorism a modern European state could fall into the hands of an unreformed or only semi-reformed populist party with a plausible sounding leader who then proceeds to partly suspend the rule of law, persecute minorities, take control of the media and perhaps even provoke border disputes with neighbouring countries. (Something similar is also possible in the US—imagine if President Trump is assassinated by a jihadi or black power extremist.)

Such dystopian visions are usually conjured up to promote all out opposition to populism. But 'tough on populism' will only be politically effective so long as it is also acknowledged that populists channel discontents that are legitimate and salient. It is, indeed, the failure of the established parties, especially of the centre-left, to respond to Somewhere grievances that has allowed modern European populism to become so solidly established since 2002.

EUROPEAN POPULISM AND THE CRISIS OF THE LEFT

Why Populists Damage the Left Most

When I intermittently attended my local ward meetings of the Islington South Labour party in the couple of years prior to the 1997 election it was still possible to hear a few cockney accents in the room. There were still a few regulars from blue-collar backgrounds—a postman, a hospital porter, a retired print worker. Fifteen years later they had all gone, or so I am told (I had gone too).

Early New Labour turned out to be the last hurrah of the old alliance between the progressive, often public sector, middle class and the trade union base of the Labour party—what one might have called, fifty years ago, the Hampstead/Hartlepool alliance. The party is now overwhelmingly middle class in MPs and activists and, narrowly, in voters too—in the 2010 election its middle class vote (ABC1) of 4.4 million just outstripped its working class vote (C2DE) of 4.2 million for the first time and the balance remained roughly the same in 2015. As recently as 1997 the working class Labour vote of 8 million comfortably outstripped the middle class vote of 5.5 million. And back in 1970 it was 10 million to 2 million.[35] (The working class in the occupational sense also declined sharply during that period, from outnumbering middle class voters two to one in the 1960s the workers are now in turn outnumbered four to three.)

UKIP and the SNP siphoned away working class support from Labour in the 2015 election. The peculiar Brexit election of 2017 saw a return to two-party politics and Corbyn's Labour sharply increased its working class vote share (from 34 to 42 per cent) but was still outstripped by the Tory working class share (32 to 44 per cent). In the 1980s, the Labour party's problem was conveying its support for working class affluence and aspiration—a problem that New Labour emerged to answer. Now culture is its problem and it has no long-term answer.

The value divide between the Anywhere and Somewhere classes that this book is partly about runs right down the centre of the voter base of the Labour party and other parties of the centre-left in Europe, and this has been slowly strangling them for a generation.

Indeed, the break-up of the progressive class alliance and the decline in working class support for the main centre-left party was already well established by the end of the last century in France, Belgium, the Netherlands and elsewhere; Labour in Britain and the Social

Democratic Party in Germany held on to working class support for longer than most.

Some continental European centre-left parties have experienced the squeeze from both ends, losing working class support to populists and middle class support to greens and leftists. The French Socialist party, until recently one of the main parties of government, scored only 6.4 per cent in the 2017 presidential election. Similarly, support for the Dutch Labour party has fallen from nearly 30 per cent to less than 6 per cent in recent years as educated people in big cities and university towns have peeled off to the Greens and a liberal party called D66, while working class strongholds in places like Rotterdam have switched to the Geert Wilders party.

The Anywhere/Somewhere value divide has been only one part of the story of social democratic decline. Others include the achievement of many historic social democratic goals; de-industrialisation and the shrinking of the unionised working class; and the more mainstream legitimacy of populist parties. From a high point at the end of the 1970s electoral support for the centre-left across Europe has fallen by around one third and looks likely to fall further—it is hard to see where the sociological or ideological impetus for another Clinton/Blair style revival might come from. And as recent Conservative governments have shown, it is possible for others to borrow the policies—living wage, apprenticeship levy—and even the language of social democracy.

Parties of the centre-right have seen their vote share fall in many countries too, and have also lost votes to right-wing populists, but have generally found it easier to straddle the Anywhere/Somewhere divide. At least in the British Conservative Party opposition to liberal openness on immigration and European integration has co-existed, if not always happily, with support for free markets and business de-regulation.

Cross-class and cross-value appeal has been achieved by the centre-right through a liberal 'modernisation' drive tempered by a more traditional Conservative belief in a strong nation state. To the extent that there has been an Anywhere/Somewhere divide in the party it has probably been over the EU itself (one reason for the deep persistence of the argument) and less dramatically over gay marriage. Apart from the EU, the noisiest internal debates have continued to be largely socio-economic—over market orthodoxy, the size of the state, tax and so on.

The Tories have the lowest proportion of graduates among party members out of all the main parties (38 per cent to Labour's 60 per cent), which might be one of the secrets of their recent success—they do not struggle to understand Somewheres because they often are Somewheres, albeit more affluent than most.

In the longer run it is possible that Labour will benefit from the growth of the graduate population, a more politicised younger generation and other liberalising trends and will become, or some successor party will become, the liberal wing of the expanded middle class while the Conservatives will remain the conservative wing and various populist parties will compete for the rump working class voters. But years of turmoil on the centre-left looks inevitable not withstanding Labour's temporary 2017 revival.

Why has the Anywhere/Somewhere division wrought such damage on Labour? After all, the gulf between the liberalism of the centre-left's leaders and activists and the more conservative communitarianism of its working class voters is an old story.

One reason is the simple expansion of liberal Anywhere numbers and influence on the left. From a minority voice sitting astride a largely Somewhere Labour party for much of the early post-war period, the Anywhere voice is now loudest. As recently as the end of the 1970s nearly 100 MPs came from manual working class backgrounds and less than one third of Labour MPs were graduates. The number of graduates is now close to 90 per cent and even Labour voters are now about one quarter graduates. The activists are now overwhelmingly Anywheres but the voters are probably less than a third Anywheres.[36]

The Labour party, like other parties of the centre-left, has become institutionally dominated by minority and progressive causes and has been the natural home for ethnic minority voters since the 1960s. This is changing as the minority middle class slowly shifts to the right in voting allegiance—successful groups like British Indians and Chinese are losing a sentimental attachment to Labour and voting in their economic interest. But the minority intelligentsia is solidly on the left and would place some limits on Labour's ability to follow the Danish Labour party in a radically restrictive immigration or hard integrationist policy.

This has set up a possibly fatal dynamic for the centre-left throughout Europe. As white working class Somewheres are alienated by the louder Anywhere voice on the centre-left, or are lured away by popu-list parties, the liberal Anywhere/ethnic minority influence and voter base gets even bigger on the centre-left, further alienating the white working class Somewheres, and so on.

The attempt to evade this spiral is one reason for the strangulated language and lack of passion or coherence on the Labour side in recent years, prior to the Corbyn takeover. Figures like Ed Miliband could not speak clearly and openly for fear of alienating what remains of a substan-tial Somewhere voter base.[37] Labour leaders have had to speak warily—outside of a few issues like reducing poverty or increasing public spending—because they know that so many of their intended audience do not feel as they do on socio – cultural issues. (Corbyn's support for Brexit in 2017 helped to shield him from this problem.) When they have addressed immigration it has been mainly as a public spending and employer exploitation issue, not in terms of cultural change. Labour leaders could often understand Somewhere complaints and even sym-pathise with them but they seldom spoke from the heart about them. And voters could hear the inauthenticity—it was like public school boys talking in socially rootless mockney accents (also a common sound on the Labour benches!).

The other reason why the left has found it harder to paper over its internal divisions is the much greater salience in recent decades of the 'security and identity' issues—immigration, national identity, extrem-ism and so on.

The value divide within the centre-left's class coalition was borne out by some polling I commissioned in 2011 a few months after the 2010 election. Peter Kellner of YouGov and I designed some questions to tease out the value divide among 'progressive' voters (Labour or Liberal Democrat voters)—between the middle class graduate pro-gressives and the non-graduate working class progressives.[38]

Asked whether employers should be given special incentives to hire British workers—working class progressives agreed by 65 to 25 per cent, but middle class graduate progressives disagreed by 52 to 35 per cent. Asked whether Britain now feels like a foreign country—working class progressives agreed by 64 to 26 per cent, but middle class graduate progressives disagreed by 67 to 28 per cent.

Asked to choose between two statements about immigrants, one saying they should integrate, the other suggesting it would be fine for them to keep their own culture and traditions, 72 per cent of working class progressives backed integration compared with just 53 per cent of middle class graduate progressives. And on foreign aid one third of working class progressives said it should be axed completely in favour of spending more on public services at home, compared with just 12 per cent of middle class graduate progressives.

Looking at the public as a whole, middle class people are more likely to say they are left of centre than working class people. And in another YouGov poll from 2012 the middle class was way to the left of the working class on immigration and foreign aid. It is little surprise that the centre-left has been so vulnerable to the populist surge.[39]

Hampstead and Hartlepool never had identical concerns, even fifty years ago. They had (and have) a shared preference for high public spending but the middle-class left was generally more interested in foreign policy issues and liberal reform (divorce law, gay rights and so on) than, say, rights at work. In the 1970s these differing priorities could happily co-exist. Fifty years later the two groups have not only different priorities but conflicting *interests*: over the economics of immigration, national citizen favouritism, spending on higher education and more.

Fifty years ago there was no such thing as identity politics; now, it is what mainly motivates the young, London left—increasingly the centre of gravity of the party. The Twitter accounts of Labour activists are more about rape culture or bullying than economic inequality. With middle class radicals in search of non-economic justifications for their radicalism—in gender politics or refugee support or environmentalism—the Somewhere voters have become an embarrassing historical legacy: the annoying, unsophisticated relatives one wishes one did not have to invite to family occasions.

4

GLOBALISATION, EUROPE AND THE PERSISTENCE OF THE NATIONAL

In the first two chapters I set out the great divide in modern Britain and other developed societies, and in the last chapter we saw how that divide has driven the rise of populist politics. Not all of politics is about these Anywhere/Somewhere divides. As I have stressed, people from the two groups might well be on the same side when it comes to some of the big questions of political economy: the size of the state or structure of the tax system, or if they are on different sides it is not necessarily because of their Anywhere/Somewhere instincts.

But when the gulf in attitudes between Anywheres and Somewheres does translate into conflicting material interests and political priorities, especially on the security and identity issues, the Anywhere worldview has invariably prevailed in the past twenty-five years—hence Brexit, Trump, the populist reaction and the urgent political task of finding a new settlement between the two worldviews.

In the next two sections I want to return to one of the themes of the first chapter and challenge the contention that globalisation in its current form is a force of nature that we must adjust to on its terms.

A World on the Move?

There are two commonplace Anywhere assumptions that inform the debate about mass immigration and globalisation. The first is that humanity is on the move on an unprecedented scale and the second is that the nation state is inexorably losing out to global markets and institutions. Neither is true.

Human beings have not given up the largely settled life they have lived since hunter-gathering gave way to the first agricultural revolution 10,000 years ago. There is, it is true, a vast movement within poor countries from the rural to the urban, but the world's people have not suddenly become country-hoppers. Rootedness is a strong human impulse.

In 2015 the number of people living in countries other than the one they were born in was 244 million, or 3.3 per cent of the global population of 7.3 billion. That is a significant increase on 2000 when the total was 173 million, or 2.8 per cent. But the global migration rate actually reached its recent peak between 1990 and 1995 when the Iron Curtain had fallen, Afghanistan had descended into civil war and there was genocide in Rwanda.[1]

International agencies like the UN and international refugee NGOs have a vested interested in talking up the numbers, as do politicians of left and right for different reasons. Indeed, the UNHCR often refers to 60 million people fleeing conflict but actually most of those are internally displaced in their own countries, in places like Syria or Iraq or Afghanistan. Only about 15 million are international refugees in the terms laid down by the 1951 Geneva Convention regulating how refugees should be treated.[2]

It is true that the bulk of non-refugee migration flows are now to the rich world of Europe and North America—and the reason that many parts of Europe seem so preoccupied by immigration and related issues is that the number of immigrants to Europe has more than doubled in the past thirty years.

Numbers could get far higher. There is the apparent paradox that as poorer countries get richer they develop a larger middle class, many of whom are desperate to leave and often have the means to do so. The gulf in income and stability between rich and poor places will remain for many decades or even centuries. Professor Dani Rodrik points out that poor people in rich countries (meaning the bottom 10 per cent) are three times richer than rich people in poor countries (meaning the top 10 per cent).[3]

Moreover, as Ivan Krastev observes: 'The spread of the internet has made it possible for young Africans and Afghans to see with one click of a mouse how Europeans live. People no longer compare their lives with those of their neighbours but with the planet's most prosperous inhabitants. They dream not of the future but of other places'.[4]

There are also unknowable factors relating to future conflicts or the effects of global warming on poor countries. Africa's population is currently a little over 1 billion and it is expected to stabilise at anywhere between 3 billion and 4.5 billion—if it stabilises at the higher number, or even higher, it may produce unstoppable pressures to move.

Thanks to its geographical position Britain was partly insulated from the European refugee crisis of 2015/2016 (though asylum claims rose to over 40,000 in the year to September 2016 making it the sixth highest recipient in the EU). But British governments have been arguing, rightly, that seeking to protect someone who may be in danger or in a war zone does not necessarily require offering them a place to live in Britain or a similar rich county. Instead Britain has put money, more than £1 billion in the last two years, into improving refugee camps in the Middle East and elsewhere, from where small numbers of the most vulnerable can be selected and brought to Britain.

Rich, liberal, Christian countries like Britain feel a moral obligation to suffering humanity—both politicians and the general public. But there are many ways in which those obligations can be fulfilled—through foreign aid to poor and fragile states, through helping countries to trade their way out of poverty, through military intervention to restore order, and through providing either temporary or permanent refuge to people in trouble.

Too much emphasis has been placed on this last method for helping the desperate: we have the resources and technology to help at a distance. We can fulfill our moral obligations without disrupting our own societies and tempting the most able and dynamic people from the poor societies that desperately need them. And every dollar spent helping someone in a poor country goes a lot further than it does in London.

For decades the grounds for claiming refuge or asylum have been steadily widened. The 1951 Geneva Convention, established during the Cold War as a signal to Soviet dissidents that they would not be returned to their countries, has been subject to constant legal evolution and it has been supplemented by the EU's 2004 Humanitarian Protection directive, and underpinned by the European Convention on

Human Rights. According to former Labour home secretary, Charles Clarke, there are now 'hundreds of millions' who could legitimately claim permanent protection in Europe. Such open criteria for seeking asylum could only be feasible in an era when people were too poor or ignorant or too locked up in prison states like Iraq or Libya to take advantage of this theoretical generosity.

In 2015 Europe's bluff was called and about 1.3 million people walked through Europe's half-open back door (with some encouragement from Angela Merkel). In doing so they exposed the promise to give shelter to refugees not as a foundation stone of European civilisation, as the refugee lobby claims, but as an embarrassing example of European hypocrisy and wishful thinking.

We need different rules to reflect our somewhat more mobile times and to keep numbers to a level that is broadly acceptable to European publics—that means keeping the offer of permanent refuge to individuals facing state persecution (as described in the 1951 Convention)—people such as African opposition leaders, many Ahmadiyya Muslims in Pakistan or NATO interpreters in Afghanistan—but not extending it to everyone who lives in an authoritarian state or whose country is experiencing some kind of conflict.

Britain, and countries like it, should also continue to offer at least time limited refuge to those caught up in particularly all-consuming natural disasters or conflicts like Syria. Though even in the Syrian case we should select the most needy—not allow the most mobile and affluent to select us, as we do now—and for the rest turn refugee camps into decent, temporary small towns with schools, clinics and jobs, where people can remain as close as possible to their homes and prepare to rebuild once peace returns.

Root and branch reform of the main UN refugee organisation, the UNHCR, is also necessary according to the development economist Paul Collier. Collier points out that the UNHCR is only allowed to provide food and shelter and cannot adapt to the needs of those condemned to refugee status lasting many years. As a result most refugees just by-pass the UNHCR camps and work in the black economy in countries neighbouring the disaster zone. Collier himself has been working on plans with the World Bank and Jordanian government to create business parks in refugee camps to give people security, income and dignity.

It is up to us in the rich world to make sure both that the conditions in temporary towns are good enough and that the neighbouring countries where they are mainly situated are adequately compensated for the disruption.

Moreover, the relentless focus on refugees, often the best educated and affluent—between a third and a half of all Syrians with tertiary education are now in Europe—means that more deserving causes, producing less dramatic pictures and stories, can get overlooked.[5] Almost 1 million children, mainly in Africa, still die of malaria each year.

Protection at a distance my be morally convenient for those of us in rich countries but an apparently more generous offer risks making the best the enemy of the good. The claim that you often hear from people in the refugee lobby that 1.5 million refugees a year is trivial for a European continent of 500 million ignores the cumulative effect of such small changes and the fact that they are not spread evenly but are mainly coming to thirty or forty urban areas in north western Europe. Illegal Mexican immigration into the US started as a trickle in the late 1970s and in another twenty years the US will be one third Hispanic—one of the factors behind the rise of Donald Trump.

As Paul Scheffer has put it—we in Europe tend to underestimate our ability to control our borders and vastly overestimate our ability to integrate people into our complex, liberal, modern societies.

The Globalisation Overshoot

So what about globalisation and the nation state? It is increasingly recognised that the globalisation hype which took off in the 1980s and 1990s—partly prompted by a significant increase in cross-border activity—never matched the more prosaic reality.

It is right to say that the world is significantly more economically interdependent than fifty years ago, and nation states have voluntarily vested more of their sovereignty in international regulations and institutions such as NATO, the World Trade Organisation and the Basel financial regulators club. Moreover, global tourism and the internet reinforce the metaphor of a 'borderless world'. But it is mainly a metaphor.

Thomas Friedman's paean to globalisation, *The World is Flat*, is now widely regarded as 'globaloney'.[6] Professor Pankaj Ghemawat, one of the leading critics of globaloney has shown convincingly that distance most certainly does still matter. Less than 25 per cent of global economic activity is international, and most of that is regional, and foreign direct investment accounts for less than 10 per cent of all fixed investment worldwide.

Ghemawat also has an entertaining list of activities which remain stubbornly domestic even in areas that one might associate with global connectivity. International mail is just 1 per cent of the total; international telephone calling minutes, 2 per cent; international internet traffic, 17 to 18 per cent; Facebook friends not in their home country, 10 to 15 per cent; foreign owned patents, 15 per cent; stock market equity owned by foreign investors, 20 per cent; first generation immigrants, 3 per cent.[7]

He points out that for the past couple of decades globalisation has been driven by trade, investment and other interactions between developed countries and developing ones—rich country trade with China in the vanguard. Now more of the activity is found among the developing countries themselves, which is re-regionalising many economic flows. According to Ghemawat: 'South to south trade is now growing faster than south to north or north to south, while north to north trade has basically stagnated.'

Even the rise of Chinese manufacturing has disguised the continuing dominance of companies based in the three most populous developed nation states—the US, Japan and Germany. The iPhone, for example, is assembled in China using components from those three countries, together with Korea and Taiwan. Imported components account for the lion's share of the total cost of an iPhone, whereas assembly in China accounts for just 4 per cent of the total cost. The most successful transnational corporations tend to be those with the largest home market.

Global trade used to increase at about twice the rate of global economic growth but since the financial crisis trade has been growing more slowly than global GDP. The overall level of global connectedness has not yet returned to 2007 levels, in some areas of finance it probably never will (as former Bank of England governor Mervyn King put it, banks turned out to be global in life and national in death). Cross-border bank lending is sharply down. Indeed, global capital mobility is now out of intellectual fashion: an IMF paper published in early 2016 identified 152 capital 'surge' episodes between 1980 and 2014 in fifty-three countries, with 20 per cent leading to a banking or currency crisis.[8]

But even if the reach and rigidity of globalisation has been exaggerated and may, in any case, now be in retreat, greater economic openness has had a big impact on many British lives in recent decades. The rapid de-industrialisation from the 1970s onwards was partly a policy choice of successive governments but it was hastened by the unusual openness of the economy (and the sharp rise in the pound in the 1980s, partly the result of North Sea oil). And thanks to that openness if you work for a non-public body that employs more than 1,000 people there is a more than 50 per cent chance you will have a foreign owner. And of course the large immigration flows of recent years from Europe and further afield are part of the same story.

The changes overall have brought many benefits to many people in rich and poor countries. The globalisers' case for more economic openness enabled by more transnational rules—governing everything from public subsidies to health and safety standards—is a coherent one and the increases in trade and global wealth and the decline in global inequality makes for powerful supporting evidence. The number of people living in extreme poverty—less than $1.90 a day—is now down to 10 per cent of the global population.[9] But it does not follow that China should be allowed to dump cheap steel on the British market, jeopardising what remains of the steel industry.

Today's globalisation represents two historic inversions—poor countries now send manufactured goods and flows of people to rich countries, the reverse of what was happening in colonial times. This is sometimes seen as a kind of revenge for colonialism. But if so it seems unfair that it is discomforting the European descendants of the 'poor bloody infantry' rather than those who sat in the governor's mansions.

The one major group that has lost out from the most recent wave of globalisation are poorer people in rich countries. One of the most influential charts in modern economics looks at global income from 1988 to 2008—the so-called elephant curve (created by Christoph Lakner and Branko Milanovic)—and it shows that all groups have benefitted apart from those on middling and lower incomes in rich countries, who have seen zero income growth.

Others, such as the Resolution Foundation, argue that the income stagnation for those groups was a result of domestic policy more than globalisation.[10] It was, no doubt, some combination of the two but just consider the decline in decently paid manufacturing jobs in Britain in four sectors between 1995 and 2015: clothing fell from 200,000 to 70,000; leather goods from nearly 200,000 to 40,000; machinery from 400,000 to 250,000; and medical equipment from 150,000 to 30,000.[11]

In the longer run everyone may benefit from such shifts in economic activity, especially as consumers, but in the shorter term the adjustment costs are mainly borne by people in the bottom half of the income spectrum. There is some evidence that in rich economies trade increases the proportion of high paid to low paid jobs,[12] but an LSE paper by Joao Paulo Pessoa also finds that British and American workers in sectors most impacted by Chinese imports had worse job and income outcomes after China joined the WTO in 2001. (By 2013 China had captured 20 per cent of all global manufacturing exports, compared with just 2 per cent in 1991.)[13]

This second phase of post-war globalisation starting in the 1980s, and put on pause by the financial crisis, has been very different to the first Bretton Woods/GATT regime which governed the world economy from the 1950s to the 1970s.

In the first phase trade liberalisation remained limited to manufactured goods, mainly between industrialised nations. Tariffs fell sharply and trade and investment flows grew rapidly. But capital controls remained in place and it was assumed that national preferences and national social contracts would remain undisturbed. Indeed, when imports of textiles and clothing from low-cost countries threatened jobs in rich countries special controls were introduced.

This regime came to be seen as inadequate in the 1980s and a big push was made for what Dani Rodrik has called 'hyperglobalisation'— the attempt to eliminate all transaction costs that hinder trade and capital flows. Tariff barriers were only a small part of this, it was also about all the domestic market rules and regulations, from product standards to national currencies, that required elimination or harmonisation. 'The World Trade Organisation was the crowning achievement of this effort in the trade arena. Common rules were now extended to services, agriculture, subsidies, intellectual property rights, sanitary standards, and many other areas of what had previously been considered domestic policy. In finance, freedom of capital mobility became the norm … with regulators focusing on the global harmonisation of financial regulations and standards. A majority of European Union members went the furthest by … adopting a single currency.'[14]

The result was a weakening of national accountability without a legitimate global, or European, authority to take its place. In so many policy areas—from finance to GM food—there is a trade-off between risk/innovation and stability and different societies will draw the line in different places. When such national choices become impossible thanks to intrusive global rules it creates a political backlash against the WTO and Brussels and a crisis of legitimacy.

After the financial crisis and the rise of populism, the rich world is clearly in retreat from hyperglobalisation, symbolised by the apparent failure of the TTIP trade negotiations between the US and the EU, the election of a protectionist US president and by Brexit. A recent WTO survey found that countries in the G20 rich country club had themselves applied 145 new trade restrictive measures in the first part of 2016. The slow-down in Chinese growth in the past couple of years is a big factor too.

Global villagers, who generally regard the nation state as a hindrance to desirable economic and social outcomes, have had too loud a voice in the globalisation story in the past generation. It was their choices that led to hyperglobalisation, including at the regional level with the attempt to create a single fiscal and economic space within the European Union. Under the banner of free global trade and European integration they battled against the market 'frictions' which many people regard as vital national interests.

As Rodrik points out, the US, Japan and Europe have all grown rich with very different histories and institutional arrangements governing labour markets, corporate governance, welfare systems and approaches to regulation. 'That these nations have managed to generate comparable amounts of wealth under different rules is an important reminder that there is not a single blueprint for economic success.'

A new settlement is needed between the nation state and the international economic order that allows for a greater variety of institutional forms reflecting different national preferences and traditions. Some people, especially on the left, fear that without rigorous harmonisation of institutional regimes there will be a race to the bottom on labour, environmental or financial regulation (the same argument is made within the EU). This fear is not groundless but is exaggerated, and the only area where there seems to be some evidence for it is in corporate taxation. Most institutional money is risk averse and sees low regulation countries as risky. In any case if there can be global agreement through the WTO to bring down barriers to trade why not also tougher agreements to establish clear minimum standards in these areas?

The globalisers are right that free trade is a great benefit to humanity—and that free trade requires some intrusions into national sovereignty—but there are many different kinds of free trade and the globalist version is evidently losing ground in the democratic marketplace. In its place Rodrik has proposed a 'sane globalisation' based around the right of countries to safeguard their national institutional choices. (This might also be a useful blueprint for the future of a looser EU.)

He writes: 'Advocates of globalisation lecture the rest of the world about how countries must change their policies and institutions to expand their international trade and to become more attractive to foreign investors. This way of thinking confuses means for ends. Globalisation should be an instrument for achieving the goals that societies seek: prosperity, stability, freedom, and quality of life. Whether globalisation sets off a "race to the bottom" or not, we can break the deadlock between the proponents and opponents of globalisation by accepting a simple principle: countries can uphold national standards in labor markets, finance, taxation, and other areas and can do so by raising barriers at the border, if necessary, when international trade and finance demonstrably threaten domestic practices that enjoy democratic support.'[15]

Rodrik argues that this principle rules out extremism on both sides. It prevents globalisers from winning where international trade and finance erodes widely accepted standards at home. Similarly, it prevents protectionists from obtaining benefits at the expense of the rest of society when no clear public purpose is at stake. 'In less clear-cut cases, in which different values have to be traded off against each other, the principle forces internal deliberation and debate—the best way to handle difficult political questions.'

So, a moderated globalisation would, for example, be able to prevent US health care companies taking over functions currently performed by the NHS. It would also allow governments to impose local content conditions (insisting, for example, that a significant proportion of a product was made, and not just assembled, in Britain) on companies wanting to invest in Britain and permit governments themselves to use state procurement rules to encourage domestic production.

This moderated globalisation may be exactly what is emerging now, according to Barry Eichengreen writing in *Prospect*.[16] He sees a 'recalibration' rather than a retreat. 'If by globalisation we mean an era when flows of merchandise, capital and labour across borders grew several times faster than GDP, then we can say this phase in global affairs is already over. But if we mean a state where national economies are linked together by those flows—subject to adjustments as different countries see fit—then globalisation remains firmly in place.'

Support for 'sane globalisation' has also come from the American economist Larry Summers, who was closely involved with securing big trade deals such as NAFTA and now admits they may have been oversold. Writing in the *Financial Times* he, perhaps unintentionally, echoed the comment from Michael Gove during the Brexit campaign about people being fed up with experts, when he said: 'The willingness of people to be intimidated by experts into supporting cosmopolitan outcomes appears for the moment to have been exhausted.'[17]

He continued: 'What is needed is a responsible nationalism—an approach where it is understood that countries are expected to pursue citizens' economic welfare as a primary objective but where their ability to harm the interests of citizens elsewhere is circumscribed. International agreements would be judged not by how much is harmonised or by how many barriers are torn down but whether citizens are empowered.'

The European Tragedy

The European Union has been our local version of the globalisation story. European integration has been an Anywhere project par excellence, and in its technocratic elitism and drive to transcend the national it has become another story of Anywhere over-reach.

What seemed at its foundation in 1957 like a utopian experiment in trans-national cooperation had, by the early 1990s, achieved far more than might have been supposed. It had apparently made war in western Europe impossible, won the Cold War by uniting half the continent against the Soviet threat, solved the German problem by locking the country into European political and economic institutions, and inspired healthy levels of economic growth.

In fact, most of those achievements were only partly the result of the actual policies or institutional structures of the European Economic Community—or European Union as it became known in 1991—which was essentially a customs union and a farmer subsidy machine (until the end of the 1980s more than three quarters of EU revenues were spent on the Common Agricultural Policy). NATO and the US nuclear guarantee were just as important in the first two and economic growth of 3.5 per cent a year in the 1950s, rising to 4.5 per cent in the 1960s, was largely the impetus of reconstruction after war and depression, with some help from the Marshall Plan.

But institutional Europe did provide a framework of cooperation and stability and helped Europe, and its nations, restore a sense of morale and self-belief. For the War generation, including in Britain, it was an obvious success. And economic integration did boost growth in the 1970s and 1980s. It was a club that people wanted to join, swelling from six to fifteen states by the early 1990s. That moment represented a high-water mark of success and prestige with the single market—a deeper form of economic cooperation than a simple customs union—established and the Cold War over. The EU was a peculiar hybrid that worked: a non-federal integrated economic space with a high degree of political cooperation. No wonder the former communist states of central and eastern Europe were so keen to join, and their incorporation as EU market democracies was another enormous geo-political achievement.

How, then, did the EU plunge from those heights to its current mess: a Euro crisis with low growth and high unemployment (Eurozone growth picked up in 2017 but since 2008 has been almost flat compared with 27 per cent growth in the US), the inability to secure Europe's external border in the refugee crisis, and now Brexit? (Not to mention lower level crises such as the inability to respond properly to the renewed threats from Russia and even the corrupt nature of EU decision-making revealed by the Volkswagen emissions scandal.)

Neither the introduction of the over-extended Euro between 1999 and 2002 nor the sudden surge in the numbers taking advantage of freedom of movement (especially to Britain) after the arrival of the much poorer former communist states after 2004, were necessary answers to pressing problems and they have both been achieved at a very high political price for the EU, including now Brexit.

Both a single currency and free movement have some economic benefits when functioning properly but neither have been able to do so, or at least with democratic legitimacy, because of the continuing attachment to national ways of doing things among political elites and even more so among voters across the EU. The idea that a country's tax and public spending levels should be decided by a committee in Brussels and that all EU citizens must be treated as if they are national citizens of all EU countries clashes with common sense ideas of national sovereignty.

It is one thing to pool sovereignty for demonstrable economic gains or increases in political clout—in global trade negotiations for example—it is quite another to relinquish most national control over economic life, which is the likely fate of Eurozone members. Most of the nineteen Eurozone countries (minus the nine who remain outside the Euro) now find themselves in a barely functional half-way house from which the only rational path appears to be to edge towards fuller integration of economic decision making over the next decade or two. This is no coincidence, as we shall see. But first we need some historical background.

If there was still some doubt when Britain belatedly joined the EEC in 1973 as to whether it was joining a free trade association or signing up to ever closer political and economic union, that doubt had largely gone by the end of the 1980s—even prior to the great leap forward of the single currency. (Hugo Young called the claim that Britain was merely joining a customs union 'the mendacious reassurance').[18] The question by then was what sort of balance would be struck between the national and the supranational. Some countries, above all Britain itself, continued to see the EU as a form of intense economic cooperation between nation states, with the sharing and sometimes pooling of sovereignty, where it made sense to do so, but functioning under a broadly 'inter-governmental' assumption. Others wanted to go further than this and chart a path towards much greater integration with a view to creating a quasi-state called Europe.

These 'true believers'—the disciples of Jean Monnet and Robert Schumann, the French founding fathers of the EU—have always been a powerful influence both within the Commission and in some national capitals. Their belief is that Europe can and must dissolve into some sort of single political entity—a European version of the United States of America albeit with stronger linguistic and cultural differences between individual states.

Monnet was quite explicit about this goal and also quite explicit that this would only be achieved behind the backs of European publics. He wanted to build a union 'among people' not just between states and argued that 'the fusion of economic functions will compel nations to fuse their sovereignty into that of a single European state.'

Having seen in the 1930s how democracy could be captured by demagogues—Hitler, after all, was elected—technocratic elitism was a more respectable view in the 1950s than it is today. And the so-called Monnet method was about taking a succession of small steps towards economic integration, each of them making sense in their own terms but also nudging towards the bigger endgame of political union.

The Eurozone, as I have argued, is now on the verge of a classic Monnet small economic step with enormous political implications: the half-way house created by a single currency without a single finance ministry or fiscal policy is clearly not working well and probably now requires the pooling of national debts, the creation of Eurozone bonds, a single form of bank regulation and centrally-determined annual spending and debt limits. That would be a big further step to removing all national control over economic matters and creating a 'transfer union' in which richer countries would transfer more resources to poorer ones, much as regions now do within nation states.

The prior story of how Europe got to this point is bound up with Jacques Delors, Commission president from 1985 to 1995, who—with the backing of Germany's Helmut Kohl and France's François Mitterrand—oversaw a big expansion of EU influence in the domestic affairs of member states.

In a long procession of conferences and treaty signings in the 1980s, 1990s and 2000s—the Single European Act 1986, Maastricht 1992, Amsterdam 1997, Nice 2000, Lisbon 2009—the EU extended its hand into defence, security cooperation and foreign affairs, policing and criminal justice, regional aid, social and labour market regulation and so on.

There were other memorable landmarks. In 1985 the Schengen agreement was signed by a core group of countries abolishing internal border controls but a properly policed external border was never really established—as the refugee crisis of 2015 revealed.

The single market was also first announced in 1986, and was seen as a liberalising free market measure against the more protectionist instincts of countries like France, and, not coincidentally, it was championed by Margaret Thatcher's Britain. (Britain's dramatic liberalisation in the 1980s had more to do with the EU than is generally acknowledged, symbolised by the so-called 'big bang' deregulation of the City of London partly inspired by EU competition rules.)

Moving from a tariff-free customs union to what is sometimes called the 'common economic space' of a single market is a bigger step than it sounds. The idea was to make a reality of the so-called four freedoms of goods, services, capital and people by harmonising and coordinating a huge range of factors, from state subsidies to product specifications. It was also supposed to open up the services sector, particularly important to Britain, which is often subject to a thicket of non-tariff barriers. (Thirty years later about 60 per cent of the EU's services market remains closed to cross-border trade.)

These changes involved significant intrusions into national life, and many measures were even subject to majority voting, meaning countries could no longer apply national vetos if they felt their fundamental interests were threatened. But in general the trade-off made good sense. There were clear and visible benefits from sharing or relinquishing sovereignty. The Schengen agreement, for example, was a godsend to the many millions of people who live close to an EU border.

The EU also provided strength in numbers, especially for smaller countries too weak to flourish as independent actors. As the Cold War ended and China began to emerge as an economic power, the idea of a world dominated by powerful 'blocs'—North America, Europe and the Far East—able through their collective muscle to manage the anarchic force of global markets, became popular in Brussels. (Some of the true believers, though not Monnet himself, had always wanted a more integrated EU bloc as a challenge to US hegemony.)

This sort of thinking was not common in the UK, it had not needed the EU to restore its national prestige. Moreover, as a late-joiner Britain had never benefitted economically from the first phase of European cooperation as much as the other bigger states like France, for whose small farmers—22 per cent of the population in 1958, compared to Britain's 4 per cent—the Common Agricultural Policy was partly designed. (Small farmers had been a key constituency of the extremist political forces of the 1930s and post-war Europe was determined to keep them protected.)

Although weakened and exhausted after 1945, Britain had experienced several hundred years of more or less unbroken success: the gradual evolution of liberal constitutionalism, no serious internal conflict since the seventeenth century, the industrial revolution, empire, victory in two world wars in the twentieth century and the creation of a democratic welfare state—all of which inspired strong attachment to venerated political institutions that it did not want superseded. This contrasted sharply with France, Germany and Italy all of which had experienced dictatorship, defeat, or both in the twentieth century.

For that reason, among others, there has never been much emotional commitment to the European project in Britain or enthusiasm for political integration—apart from brief flirtations with the idea under Edward Heath in the early 1970s and Tony Blair in the late 1990s.

Britain, albeit as a somewhat semi-detached member, was reasonably comfortable with the EU of the late 1980s and early 1990s. The liberal nation state had been restored to health across Europe and the high degree of economic cooperation, with some political cooperation, was largely undertaken within an inter-governmental framework that gave countries many veto options. Moreover, Britain increasingly established a special leadership role in financial services just as the Germans did in the motor industry or the French in agriculture.

But instead of the pause that Britain would have preferred, the early 1990s—partly as a result of German unification—saw a dramatic new integrationist surge, orchestrated by Delors, embodied in the Maastricht Treaty of 1992 with its flight path to the single currency (and its creation of the category of European citizen).

There had been a long-standing interest in a single currency at the federalist margins, but German unification gave it a chance. A single currency linking economies at a similar level of development provides the obvious advantages of reduced transaction costs and greater predictability, especially in cross-border trade. Delors also believed Europe faced a particular problem that he thought a single currency would solve: he feared that the liberalisation of capital controls introduced by the single market would destabilise the ERM mechanism, which had since 1979 loosely linked EU currencies, which would in turn unravel the single market. (The ERM did, indeed, nearly fall apart in 1993.)

Another worry was that Germany had become too dominant in the ERM system—whenever the Bundesbank shifted interest rates other countries had to follow suit whether it suited their economic conditions or not.

But what should have been a common currency for a small number of core economies was extended by political ambition to a far larger group, including the weaker southern Europeans. As with freedom of movement there was no powerful economic case for this.

Historians will argue about the exact mix of factors that drove the EU towards the over-large and badly designed single currency that was finally established on 1 January 2002. François Mitterrand is said to have made it a condition of German unification, but it seems unlikely that he could have carried through with his threat if Germany had said no to the single currency. Some in the German establishment wanted to reject it, but not a majority.

The fact that Yugoslavia was violently tearing itself apart only a few hundred miles away from the capitals of western Europe may have helped the argument that Europe must peddle faster forward to prevent slipping back into such barbarism—the so-called bicycle theory of political union.

I recently spoke to Pascal Lamy—Delors' chief of staff at the time the Euro was being planned who went on to run the WTO. He was sceptical about both those explanations and took me back to Monnet: 'It was about those steps that you could take. And monetary policy was easier for national governments to give up because most countries already had independent central banks, the politicians were not losing control of anything. It became a technocratic matter between central bankers and people at the Commission.'

Andrew Cahn, the British chef de cabinet to Neil Kinnock 1997–2000, agrees with Lamy. 'It was the classic tactics of advance. You establish the ERM, that runs into trouble, so you have to go forward to a single currency. And when the half-way house single currency without fiscal convergence runs into trouble you have to go forward to the full-blooded single currency.' He also thinks there was at times a triumphant atmosphere in Brussels at the end of the Cold War, a feeling that Europe could step up as an equal of the US.

The strict rules that required countries to have budget deficits of no more than 3 per cent of GDP and debt to GDP ratios of no more than 60 per cent were allowed to slip soon after the Euro's launch and then blown apart when the sovereign debt crisis struck in 2009.

Unlike the 2007/8 credit crunch, the Eurozone crisis was one of the most widely predicted economic disasters of modern times. The apparently reduced risk of lending in hard Euros to weaker economies and governments like Greece and Spain created unsustainable government deficits in the case of Greece and an unsustainable property bubble in Spain (and Ireland).

The no bail out rule was quickly abandoned after the economic crisis made several states insolvent, and the Eurozone economy has been living in a twilight zone ever since. Germany and other northern European states have forced austerity on several of the southern European states, as a condition of their new loans, which has held back growth and created strident anti-German feeling, especially in Greece. But states and companies, argue the thrifty north Europeans, cannot be rewarded for living beyond their means.

The Euro in its current half-way house has been kept alive without any drop-outs but this intermediate stage is unlikely to be sustainable and the richer countries are probably going to have to accept some kind of shared fiscal space and transfer union. In the meantime the European economy has been badly damaged, the over-mighty Germany problem is back with a vengeance and the tarnished reputation of the whole EU project was probably a factor behind Brexit.

But it is worth noting one remarkable thing: none of the countries most affected by the austerity measures want to go back to their old currencies or national political systems. (Indeed two small countries, Slovenia and Latvia, have actually joined the single currency since the crisis.) Rebellions against austerity have been half-hearted, as were the various rejections in referenda of integrationist EU treaties over the past couple of decades by a range of countries including France, the Netherlands, Ireland and Denmark. A few cosmetic changes were usually made and the referenda were held again and won.

The one rebellion that is most unlikely to be revoked is Brexit. That is because, in the words of historian Brendan Simms: 'Europe was designed to fix something [national democratic sovereignty] that was never broken in Britain.' He argues that with its economic strength (the sixth largest economy in the world), its permanent seat in the UN Security Council, its independent nuclear deterrent and general military prowess, Britain remains one of the top three or four powers in the world.[19]

A divergence of some kind between Britain and the rest, or most of the rest, was perhaps inevitable but in retrospect it is a shame that London did not put more strategic effort into creating and leading an 'outer ring' of countries with no interest in a single currency or a shared fiscal space but a continuing attachment to the single market (without full freedom of movement) and to cooperation on foreign and security policy. (The only politician of note who has consistently argued along these lines is David Owen.)[20]

Such a role would have suited Britain's history and political temperament and might also have saved the EU from forcing countries into economic or cultural straitjackets that might suit Germany or France but do not suit Greece or Hungary. A two, or even three, tier EU could have sidestepped the clash between its inter-governmental soul and its supranational one, and thus avoided the nervous breakdown of the Eurozone crisis—the product of a compromise between these two incompatible approaches to integration.

There was some movement in this direction with 'opt-outs' for Britain and others over the single currency, Schengen and so on. And it is possible that some multi-tier approach might yet emerge from the Brexit negotiation. The Scandinavian countries share some of Britain's reservations about further integration, as do the Visegrad Four countries in the east with their conservative-populist politics. Could Britain retain access to the single market in return for defence of Europe's eastern flank or help securing the EU's external border? Could countries outside the

Euro be allowed more control over freedom of movement, making it easy for skilled workers to move but harder for unskilled?

The governments of central and eastern Europe, whose citizens are the most mobile, will battle to retain the rights of those already working in northern Europe but they would most likely be open to a compromise on future flows partly because they need the workforce back home just as much as they need their remittances. A bigger obstacle is the European Commission which will hold on to the acquis communautaire, the powers acquired by the Union, as tenaciously as possible and would far prefer to see a clean British exit than to sub-divide the EU into different tiers or speeds.

One of the main stumbling blocks over any future British involvement with the EU will be over freedom of movement. The shock of 2004 in Britain when a few thousand people were expected from the new member states in the east and then more than 1 million came over the next few years—with British politicians impotent to do anything about it—was probably the biggest single factor behind the Brexit vote.

Freedom of movement is the most controversial of the 'four freedoms' of goods, services, capital and people, and is the one that is least compatible with a normal nation state. A single market in goods and services and, with some reservations, capital, is compatible with multiple nations trading with each other. Freedom of movement of people takes the relationship to a different level.

British reservations are, to a somewhat lesser degree, shared by many of the richer northern European countries like Germany, the Netherlands, Denmark and Sweden—yet freedom of movement in these countries also underpins a vision of a borderless Europe, with citizens mixing freely as Europeans, that has a favourable echo especially among young people. This is, in part, based on a misunderstanding: freedom of movement is conflated with all movement around Europe, yet visa free travel and various forms of special intra-European movements, of students for example, are perfectly compatible with the normal national immigration controls that freedom of movement prohibits.

The number of EU citizens who actually identify first as European is small—in single figure percentages in most EU countries—but the creation of European citizens is regarded as a noble goal even by more pragmatic EU politicians. More than the Euro, freedom of movement has been an intensely political priority with only marginal economic benefits.

Trade theory from Ricardo onwards assumes the immobility of labour. The whole point of trade is that you can buy goods and services from people in other countries, they do not have to come to your country to provide them. It is true that service industries may require more exchange and intermingling of people than making cars or fridges. And London after Brexit will certainly need a large continuing flow of EU citizens to thrive. But this service sector anomaly may, increasingly, belong to the past. Communications technology already connects London's magic circle law firms to Singapore in the blink of an eye.

Freedom of movement was included among the 'four freedoms' in the Treaty of Rome in 1957 for largely symbolic reasons, and to offer something to the Italians (who were the eastern Europeans of those times). It was never envisaged that it would become a mass movement from poorer to richer countries as it did after 2004, partly because it was always assumed that member states would be at similar levels of economic development.

During the golden years of post-war economic growth for the European economy there was relatively little movement between countries, a few Italians moved to Belgium and Germany and, later, there was an Iberian exodus to France (but as those poorer sending countries became richer the movement trailed off). Indeed, movement has remained negligible for about half the life span of the single market. Even since 2004 the overall numbers have remained relatively small and significant inflows have been limited to a handful of northern European states, including the UK (which was most exposed because it opened up its labour market seven years before the other big states).

By 2014 around 3.5 per cent of the EU's population was born in another member state compared to just 1 per cent in 2000. In the UK the figure was just over 6 per cent and EU citizens accounted for about 8 per cent of low skill jobs. (There are just over 1 million UK citizens working or resident in other EU countries, compared with 3.3 million EU citizens working or resident here.)[21]

From the point of view of Europe as a whole there is a clear benefit in an unemployment safety valve which makes it easy for people to move temporarily from poorly performing economies with high joblessness to booming ones with tight labour markets—some British workers famously took advantage of that in the early 1980s, their experience immortalised in the TV comedy series 'Auf Wiedersehen Pet'. It happened on a much larger scale after 2012 when large numbers of young unemployed southern Europeans unexpectedly arrived in Britain—sometimes called Europe's employer of last resort.

There might also be some theoretical benefit in having a more Europeanised labour market in some niche areas, like parts of academia and some low skill sectors like agriculture, food processing and social care. Employers certainly benefit in the short-term from having a much larger pool of already trained or willing workers though if this leads to a lower level of investment in training in the national labour market (or lower wages) the result may be negative for society as a whole. There are also brain-drain issues for the poorer, sending countries in central and eastern European societies as highlighted in a recent IMF report which estimates that 20 million people have left eastern Europe over the last twenty-five years with 80 per cent heading for western Europe.[22] Romania is estimated to have lost nearly one third of its doctors to other EU countries between 2011 and 2013.[23]

And for some countries it is not just brain-drain but real demographic meltdown. Thanks to low fertility and high emigration (courtesy of freedom of movement) the Estonian population, 1.5 million in 1993, is predicted by the UN to be below 1 million in fifty years. And Bulgaria, 8.9 million in 1988, and 7.4 million today, is predicted to fall to 3.5 million by the end of the century.[24]

Freedom of movement at moderate levels, like immigration itself, is a benefit both to the movers and the country they move to. But the Anywhere economists and politicians who have dominated the EU debate gave little thought to the scale of the movement nor to the fact that, like much immigration, movement between EU countries tends to be economically regressive: those in the bottom part of society in richer EU countries who are least likely to take advantage of free movement themselves are also the ones who are most likely to be disadvantaged by the extra labour market competition and disturbed by sudden changes to neighbourhoods.

The relatively small, and qualified, benefits of free movement have been bought at a very high price in terms of the popularity of the

European project especially in the heavily receiving countries such as Britain. But there is no reason why some of the benefits could not persist with a better designed and more controlled form of movement. (Visa-free travel and some special terms for labour migration are likely to be on offer to EU citizens as part of the Brexit deal.)

It is often said that the principle of free movement is inviolable but freedom of movement has not always been as free as it is now. It has been substantially widened and extended by the European Court of Justice over recent decades. This culminated in the creation of the legal category 'EU citizen' in the Maastricht Treaty of 1992 which entrenched the principle of non-discrimination, meaning that citizens of other EU countries have to be treated like national citizens in all important respects. The distinction between citizen and worker is crucial here. Prior to 1992 it was workers that moved not citizens and the worker usually had to have a job offer.

Hardly any citizens of EU countries actually believe in the principle of non-discrimination—most people remain attached to the common sense notion that national citizens should be ahead of non-citizens in the queue for public goods—yet the EU appears to be stuck with it.

Too many European Anywheres have a sentimental attachment to it—an attachment that made it impossible to make the concessions that David Cameron needed as part of his renegotiation of Britain's membership prior to the referendum. The European citizenship legislation has, in effect, made it impossible to make the qualifications to free movement that would have made it more acceptable, if not popular, in Britain and elsewhere.

The EU's Monnet–Delors-inspired post-national hubris has led directly to the Euro crisis, and, similarly, the inability to reform freedom of movement has led directly to Brexit. The EU sees itself as a bulwark against nationalism but by making itself the enemy of moderate nationalism it has ended up fostering more extreme versions in the EU-wide populist uprisings.

And the timing has been bad: just as the EU was making its integrationist great leap forward in the 1990s many of the Somewhere people around Europe, and maybe especially in Britain, were becoming more and not less attached to national social contracts as more open, knowledge-based economies increased economic uncertainty for the less well educated. Similarly, just as income growth in Britain was slowing in the mid-2000s, and then stopped altogether after 2008, EU immigration was rising sharply and the two things were probably correlated in many people's minds.

Britain's political traditions and its continuing weight in the world were always going to make it an awkward partner in the EU project. And a more populist media and political culture than is typical in the rest of Europe has made outspoken hostility to the EU mainstream in Britain.

But contrary to the claims that have sometimes been made after the Brexit vote, Britons are not particularly insular or anti-European (as opposed to anti-EU). A comparative study of six EU countries by Ettore Recchi of Sciences Po in Paris found British people to be generally more internationally connected—in terms of travel, friends and contacts and living abroad—both in Europe and beyond. Indeed, unlike most other Europeans, their global connections were as strong as their European ones, if not stronger. They have a bigger sense of abroad than most Europeans.[25]

What they do not have is a sense of being part of a European people or demos. Who in Europe does? Yet it is hard to see how the precipitate leap forward inspired by Monnet and driven forward by Delors can work without properly functioning European political parties and political institutions, which require a much stronger sense of Europeanness than currently exists or is likely to exist in this century.

The Persistence of the National

The destructive force of extreme nationalism in the first half of the twentieth century, and the unprecedented death toll it left behind, continues to reverberate in modern politics, especially in Europe. This is hardly surprising. The desire to weaken and eventually transcend the nation was at the heart of the European project and for some, as we have just seen, remains at its heart today.

What is surprising is how hostility to nationalism became so indiscriminate, at least among the highly educated. Recoiling from the horrors of Nazism and late colonial conflicts in Indo-China, Algeria and Africa, the European intelligentsia generally disdained even mild expressions of national sentiment and identity, giving full support to the EU project, celebrating globalisation (except when it was American-led) and welcoming mass immigration and ethnic diversity.

So even in 1980s/1990s western Europe despite the entrenchment of a gentler form of nationalism—more concerned with the welfare of one's fellow citizens than with conquest—much of the continent's political class and intelligentsia supported what turned out to be a reckless further stage of European integration. And they did this in part for fear that old nationalist demons might return.

Yet it is this refusal to accommodate moderate national feeling that has reinvigorated some of those demons in the more extreme populist parties. The Euro crisis has created Greece's fascistic Golden Dawn.

Post-nationalism has turned out to have some of the same group-think qualities as nationalism itself only wrapped in moral self-regard. Unlike the British patriotic left of the Second World War and New Jerusalem period, the post-1960s new left saw nationalism in the context of European colonialism. It was not only part of the apparatus of class oppression but indistinguishable from racism too. And working class national sentiment was merely false consciousness.

A narrative of progress, shaped by the history of civil rights reforms in the past few generations, saw the abolition of slavery and the emancipation of women and minorities, as a prelude to the transcending of all exclusive communities—including the nation state. Many elite progressives and conservatives could agree that policies designed to protect national producers against foreign competition, or national workforces against immigrant competition, were not only inefficient but also illiberal. If it is wrong to discriminate within a nation on the basis of the accident of race, why is it not equally wrong to discriminate in favour of one's fellow nationals on the basis of the accident of nationality?

But, as Michael Lind points out, if the nation state is an illegitimate expression of bigotry, like racism, then the legitimacy of democracy and the welfare state, which today exist only in national forms, is also thrown into doubt.[26]

Post-nationalism was never a majority view, even among Anywheres, but a looser notion that the national was unfashionable and embarrassing—partly because of the imperial legacy—became part of the common sense of the liberal wing of the educated and affluent in 1970s and 1980s Britain. This discomfort about the national also overlapped with a more establishment view, in part of the business class and the City of London, which favoured maximum openness to financial globalisation, immigration and as much European integration as possible.

Anywheres with wide but loose attachments tend to have little sympathy for the communitarian ambivalence about immigration of the Somewheres. In any case, they say, we are surely a 'mongrel nation'. Britain is, in fact, rather less mongrel than most countries unless you regard successive waves of people arriving between one and two thousand years ago as somehow invalidating its national status. Trying to define a nation, for which there was a Gordon Brown-inspired craze in the mid-2000s, is a tricky exercise. You quickly become essentialist or random. That does not, of course, mean nations or cultures do not exist.

Group attachments of many kinds remain strong. Indeed they are hard-wired into us. Societies are composed of groups of people who come from somewhere, who speak a certain language, have certain traditions and ways of doing things. Anywheres accept this idea for minorities, it is called multiculturalism, but feel uneasy about it for majorities. Somewheres on the other hand have not lost the society instinct, however bluntly it may sometimes be expressed.

The idea of the nation has always been Janus-faced. On the one hand, at least since the French Revolution, it is associated with democracy and the idea of equality between all national citizens. On the other hand it is also associated with the exclusion of non-members and violent chauvinism. The argument rumbles on in many parts of the world often described in rather simplified form as the contest between civic and ethnic ideas of the nation. But the benign side of nationalism's historic Janus-face came to be forgotten, or just taken for granted by too many liberal baby boomer Anywheres: the way it had curbed warlord violence, expanded networks of solidarity beyond local communities, enabled industrialisation and mass markets and representative political institutions.

National identity has become weaker among the highly educated and most globally mobile in rich countries. The globalisation narrative about growing interconnectedness and weakening nation states is their story, partly because it reflects their lives. And as we have seen modern higher education tends to inoculate people against national parochialism.

In Britain as older people with more chauvinistic views die out and more people go through the liberalising experience of higher education, the number of people who say, according to the British Social Attitudes survey, that they are 'very proud' to be British has fallen from 43 per cent in 2003 to 35 per cent in 2013 (though the very proud and somewhat proud together are still 80 per cent, 85 per cent in some polls). Fewer than 20 per cent of graduates say they are very proud and the graduate proportion of the population increased from 26 per cent in 2003 to 38 per cent in 2013.[27] (There might also be perfectly valid reasons for feeling less proud in 2013 than 2003—the latter year was a period of relative optimism with strong economic growth and a still popular New Labour government, in 2013 the country was still recovering from a sharp recession and had also experienced two unsuccessful small wars in the previous decade.)

Almost two thirds of people in 2013 still said they would rather be a citizen of Britain than of any other country in the world (despite the bad weather), down only slightly from 1995. Yet an uncritical, chauvinistic nationalism is clearly fading: just a third of people agreed or agreed strongly that the world would be a better place if people from other countries were more like the British, and only 20 per cent agreed or agreed strongly that people should always support their country, even if the country is wrong. In both cases support was highest among the old and the poorly educated.

Most people in Britain still attach great importance to national symbols and feelings—just consider the renewed popularity of the monarchy after its low point with Princess Diana's death, the pageants, the jubilees, the standing of the military, Help for Heroes, Team GB, the popularity of BBC history programmes and so on. Moreover, almost everything that matters is still rooted in national institutions: law, democracy and accountability; tax and spend and welfare states; cross-class and generational redistribution; labour markets; the national media.

Indeed, throughout the rest of the world this continues to be the age of the liberal democratic nation state and of liberal (or in some cases illiberal) democratic nationalism—European integration is a global exception. The collapse of the Soviet empire in the early 1990s saw another burst of nation creation, just as there had been earlier in the twentieth century with the disappearance of the Ottoman and Habsburg empires and later the French and British empires. More of the world's problems arise because nation states are too weak rather than too strong: why, for example, was rapid economic development possible in the East Asian Tigers but not in Africa? It was partly because national solidarity has been too weak in parts of post-colonial Africa to prevent the state being hijacked by sectional interests.

Why should this be remarkable? Only because the ideology of globalisation has told us that the nation state is an increasingly empty vessel. Open one of the serious newspapers any day of the week and you will read paragraphs like this one from Philip Stephens in the *Financial Times*: 'Governments have ceded power to mobile financial capital, to cross-border supply chains and to rapid shifts in comparative advantage. Control of information now belongs to 24-hour satellite television and the cacophony that is the web ... Citizens expect national politicians to protect them against the insecurities—economic, social and physical—that come with global integration. Yet governments have lost much of the capacity to meet the demands.'[28]

This is not completely wrong. Officials at the UK Borders Agency will say that the internet, for example, has helped to internationalise job hunting, university study and even marriage. But by focusing on those forces—trade, finance, transport/communications technology, immigrant diasporas—that do flow constantly across national borders, it ends up painting a partial picture. In any case, as we saw earlier in this chapter, most of those things are far less globalised than most people think and they are still regulated by national laws or international agreements drawn up by national governments. And this description leaves out of the picture the areas like welfare, tax systems, consumer and environmental protection, employment law, family policy, health and safety rules, where the nation state is more, not less, enmeshed in people's lives than fifty years ago.

Meaningful international agreements are still notoriously difficult to reach, but as global governance grows in importance so too must the nation state. As the power centre closest to where people live and have their attachments, it is only the nation state that can confer legitimacy and accountability on global bodies and thus prevent the emergence of the kinds of global leviathans imagined in Orwell's *Nineteen Eighty-Four*.

A world in which people had unrooted emotional and social attachments would be a bleak one; global government would be an Orwellian nightmare. That does not mean humanity remains imprisoned in national boxes. As countries, and individuals, grow richer and more secure and more mobile their sympathies usually grow wider too. For the first time in recorded history the rich countries of the western world have, in recent decades, actively encouraged poorer countries to catch up with them.

Indeed, all in the West are 'universalists' now in the sense that almost everyone, with the exception of some of the Hard Authoritarians, accepts that all human lives are of equal worth (the political philosopher David Miller calls it 'weak cosmopolitanism').[29] The universalist shift after the Second World War, and partly prompted by the war and the Holocaust, represented a major cultural evolution. The old religious and political idea of human moral and political equality was laid down in the UN Declaration of Human Rights in 1948 and found its way into constitutions and legal systems declaring an end, on paper at least, to the old hierarchies of race and sex and class. Yet as recently as 1919 Japan had asked for a League of Nations protocol in favour of racial equality and the idea had been rejected by the British, French and Americans.[30] And many respected figures continued to defend British rule in India in the 1940s partly on the grounds that Indians were too immature for self government.

The moral equality of all humans is taken by many Global Villagers to mean that national borders and boundaries have become irrelevant and that any partiality to one's fellow nationals is morally flawed. But this is to conflate two separate things. It does not follow from the idea of human equality that we have the same obligations to all humans. Somewheres and Inbetweeners and even many Anywheres believe that this universalist ethos must be tempered by moral particularism: all humans are equal but they are not all equally important to us; our obligations and allegiances ripple out from family and friends to stranger fellow-citizens in our neighbourhoods and towns, then to nations and finally to all humanity.

This does not have to be a narrow or selfish idea. People from Somewhere can be outward-looking and internationalist, generous in their donations to charity (usually more so than Anywheres in proportion to their incomes) and concerned about the progress of the world's poor countries. But they also think it is perfectly reasonable that most European countries put their own citizens first and spend about ten times more every year on domestic health services than on development aid. As Paul Collier has put it, charity may still begin at home but it doesn't end there.

Nor is this kind of particularism morally inferior to the more universalist views of some Anywheres. If everyone is my brother, then nobody is—my emotional and financial resources are spread too thin to make a difference. The novelist Jonathan Franzen puts it like this: 'Trying to love all of humanity may be a worthy endeavour but, in a funny way, it keeps the focus on the self, on the self's own moral or spiritual wellbeing. Whereas to love a specific person, and to identify with his or her struggles and joys as if they were your own, you have to surrender some of yourself.'[31]

Anywheres often see national sentiment as something atavistic and primitive. But the vague feeling of mutual regard that national citizens feel towards fellow-citizen strangers is, in fact, quite a modern phenomenon and is related to Robert Putnam's idea of social capital. Social capital—a sense of trust and cooperation and common interest—is what holds together the political consensus that supports welfare states and the redistribution of resources across classes, generations and regions. It is what permits the so-called 'Cathedral projects'—those cross-generational undertakings, such as the formation of the welfare state, that require some sense of the nation existing through time. Historically, it is usually found where the state is neither too strong nor too weak, allowing the rule of law, civic institutions and a presumption of trust between individuals to emerge. It is the lack of social capital in many poor, low-trust, authoritarian countries that makes it so hard to create the public goods and public cooperation that we take for granted in Europe.

National identities are seldom culturally uniform. Even a small country like Scotland was found by the research organisation Webber Phillips, when analysing the Scottish referendum, to have eight significant national sub-divisions from the Scandinavian heritage Scots in the Orkney Islands to the border Scots who are closer to the English.[32] And national identities across Europe have in recent decades become more fluid and less attached to majority ethnicities partly because of immigration and the growth of the ethnic minority populations.

People now connect to their national story in many different ways. Native citizens may identify most through history and ancestry and have a strong sense of continuity with the past; more recent citizens may stress the political dimension of living in a rich, free society. For most people, their connection is a mixture of these ethnic and civic factors. The blurring of that distinction is perfectly healthy, though it does raise the question of whether some minimal myths of common ancestry—which have always held societies together in the past—may also be necessary.

A strong, confident national identity does not thereby solve a country's social and economic problems but it provides a template, an idiom, through which the discussion can take place and which assumes certain shared norms and common interests. A confident national story also helps to integrate newcomers, providing a symbolic pathway to belonging that new citizens usually welcome. And if we really are all in this together, as a national identity assumes, then it ought to make us want to narrow the gaps between regions, rich and poor, native and minority. Contrary to the old leftist idea that national feeling blinds the masses to class injustice, national identity ought to have an in-built social democratic bias reminding elites of their obligations to those they live amongst.

One reason it often doesn't have that bias in Europe, and Britain in particular, is that the national story for almost 200 years was associated with war, imperialism and domination of others. But too many people from Anywhere have failed to notice the liberalisation of national attachment in the past fifty years. The bigoted, you-have-to-be-white-to-be-British tribe is now a tiny minority.

Danny Boyle's Olympic opening ceremony in 2012 reflected how our national story has become more open, less chauvinistic and grounded in a sense of specialness but not superiority. Decent national sentiment is reinforced by what the American Bonnie Honig calls 'objects of public love'—such as the NHS or Team GB—things that make us feel connected in a joint endeavour.[33]

Despite this normalisation of national sentiment in recent years the Anglo-British story has been complicated by the rise of Scottish nationalism and the belated emergence of an English identity that was more submerged into Britishness than was the case with the smaller nations of the UK. But Englishness too, despite its historic association with dominance, both within the British Isles and around the world, is also on the way to becoming a normal modern nationalism inside a residual British framework of monarchy, the BBC, the armed forces and foreign policy. The generally agreed goal for the UK (minus the SNP) is a looser relationship between the nations of these islands within a continuing British structure, but it may be a bumpy journey there. (And an English-inspired Brexit has temporarily revived old resentments from Ireland and Scotland at England's disproportionate size within the neighbourhood and its carelessness about the interests of its smaller neighbours.)

It used to be the case that the educated and affluent were more nationalistic than the masses because they had a larger stake in the country. The ordinary people had to be literally 'press-ganged' into defending the nation. Now the opposite is true. The richer and better educated you are, the more global your attachments are likely to be. The rich and well educated are also less dependent on national social contracts, while many in the bottom 50 to 60 per cent of the income spectrum have become more dependent on national social contracts in recent years. The national welfare state has been expanding—think of tax credits and the growth of housing benefit—and although state employment has been shrinking, if you live in a rundown area of Britain you are more likely than ever to be a state employee. And as the old working class communities have faded away so, if anything, the imagined community of the nation has loomed larger.

A special attachment to fellow citizens is not a prejudice but an asset in a more individualistic and diverse society. Somewheres have noticed, however, that the Anywheres don't always share that view and that their sympathies (especially those of the Global Villagers) are less likely than in the past to be directed their way—with the global poor or domestic ethnic minorities now ahead of ethnic majority Somewheres in the queue. The elites have lost their fear of the masses and have found other objects for their *de haut en bas* affection.

The more universalist and post-nationalist assumptions of the Anywheres have had political consequences in recent years, particularly in their openness towards immigration and—until Brexit—European integration. And the Anywhere worldview has also embraced the philosophy and legal practice of human rights, almost as a substitute national identity. Somewhere people are also in favour of rights, but do not like the way human rights legislation tends to erode the distinction between citizen and non-citizen.

Rights do not fall from the sky. People who are fortunate enough to be citizens of European countries through birth or choice are richly endowed with legal, religious, political and social rights thanks to a long struggle to establish them. These rights are made real by institutions including parliaments, courts, police forces and the welfare state.

Much of today's human rights rhetoric is utterly ahistorical. It also individualises and de-politicises rights, disguising the degree of interdependence that underpins them. Rights are also inseperable from obligations and duties. Some rights, such as the right to equal treatment if you are gay, simply enforce widely accepted norms. But in many cases the right claimed by one person, especially those that require funding—such as the right to education or decent housing—creates a corresponding obligation on another person to supply the means, usually through the tax system, to make its exercise possible.

A strong sense of one's rights as a citizen does empower and protect but in recent years there has been a 'rights disconnect': a declining willingness of those called upon to fund, through their taxes, the rights of others. Redistribution often lies behind rights, and that requires the willingness of the strong and affluent to recognise their connection to and sympathy for the weak and the struggling. And that, in turn, requires some sense of shared citizenship and national community.

Yet human rights, as the name suggests, is a transnational ideology that asserts that people have rights as a result of their humanity and not, as is usually the case, as a result of their membership of a national community. As the human rights lobby works to reduce the distinction between national citizens and outsiders, by pressing for more powers for European courts for example, it unwittingly undermines the national solidarity on which most rights continue to be based.

There is a case for some international minimum standards on rights, though such standards are usually only enforceable where they are least needed. But once human rights courts move beyond minimum standards they run up against the reality of quite sharp national value differences, even in Europe national legal systems reflect national histories and priorities but human rights courts tend to over-ride them. How, for example, can European human rights law reflect the strongly differing national traditions in Europe on relations between church and state?

And what alternative allegiances are capable of generating solidarity in the way that national allegiances have? There is almost no appetite in

Britain, or throughout the developed world, for a European or a global identity—regular polling by GlobeScan does find support for the idea of global citizenship, especially in developing countries, but not instead of the national.[34] What about local attachments? Young Anywheres will often say they are proud to be Londoners but indifferent to national identity. But they are the exception, most people with strong identification with a local community also have correspondingly strong national identities.

The word community has been rendered almost meaningless by over-use but most people still place a high priority on relatively stable and familiar living conditions, especially when they are young or old or raising a family. Hence they are likely to swap high-churn, diverse, low-trust, inner city areas for the more stable suburbs or small towns when they want to start a family. Hackney to Hertfordshire.

As people have become richer and more mobile, and as families have become looser, the personal diasporas, the chosen networks of friends, interest groups, workplaces and cyberspace have become more significant alongside the given communities of neighbourhood and family. It is often said that our social relations have become shallower but our networks wider. And though people seem to choose this, they do not like the consequence of their choices.

YouGov rather ambitiously posed this question back in 2011: 'In recent times thanks to television, the internet and the growth of the free market people have become less focused on their immediate communities and see themselves more as individuals. It is said that our social relations have become shallower but our networks wider. Have we gained or lost more through this process?' The answer that came back was decisive, only 13 per cent of the 1600 asked thought it was a net gain with 50 per cent saying it was a net loss (and nearly a quarter saying we have lost a lot).[35]

Evidently people still value their face-to-face neighbourhoods and regret their declining sociability. A more recent 2016 poll of 2,000 people for the social network Nextdoor found that one third of people in Britain did not know any of their neighbours well and only 12 per cent feel strongly committed to their neighbourhood.[36]

Community can be felt as oppressive or as an interference with individual choice. Indeed, much of modern culture describes the individual's struggle to free him or herself from tradition and small-town convention. Progressive individualism usually celebrates escape from community and communal obligation. Matthew Parris has written movingly about the great liberation he felt as a young gay man in the 1970s relocating from the censorious, intimate, provinces to liberating, anonymous London. And people from ethnic minority backgrounds may also prefer big cities where their difference from the majority stands out less.

Yet there is clearly a powerful impulse to belong to something bigger. Hence the fascination with programmes like the Great British Bake Off and the X-Factor which catch the national imagination and are often watched by up to 10 million people. This, however, is a fraction of the numbers that once gathered around the nation's campfire—about 22 million used to tune in to the Morecambe and Wise Christmas television special in the 1970s. Indeed, the technology that once brought us together is just as likely to now divide us into different class, generational, political and ethnic echo chambers (see Trevor Phillips on the ethnic divide in television viewing).[37] As *Financial Times* writer Janan Ganesh has put it: 'The modern world has been a disaster for water-cooler moments and a miracle for personal immersion in a chosen interest.'[38]

Nostalgia for the greater social intimacy of the past is often denigrated by Anywhere commentators who will usually point to the gross gender inequalities or racism or homophobia of the 1950s or 1960s. But why is it not possible to have both more stable, human communities and equality?

Anywheres, as I mentioned in the first chapter, tend to have what the American sociologist Talcott Parsons called 'achieved' identities—which is to say that their sense of their worth comes from their educational and career success. This means that it is something they can carry around with them and makes them less sensitive to where or among whom they live. Somewheres, who generally have more 'ascribed' identities—meaning their identity derives from bonds of place or group—are more likely to feel disturbed by rapid change.

For this reason Anywheres and Somewheres tend to have rather different attitudes to immigration, integration and London, as we shall see in the next chapter.

5

A FOREIGN COUNTRY?

'Culture represents not only difference but the elimination of difference,' points out the philosopher Kwame Anthony Appiah.[1] Put another way, all human associations and communities have boundaries. Boundaries can be hard or soft but all have some means of demarcating between insiders and outsiders. The modern democratic nation state has become far more internally inclusive in recent generations—the idea of the equal status of all national citizens is now supported by historically unprecedented social provision, usually free to all insiders. And for that reason it has become, if anything, more exclusionary towards the outside world.

There is nothing perverse or mean-spirited about this exclusion so long as one accepts the idea that countries belong to their citizens—that existing citizens have a right, through their politicians, to broadly control the character of their society and therefore who joins it and in what numbers. And as the value of national citizenship in rich countries has risen, and the cost of physically reaching those countries has fallen, so the bureaucracy of border control has had to grow. The EU has partially bucked this trend internally through the Schengen agreement but cannot resist it at its external border.

If that bureaucracy of border control were to be abolished or even relaxed it would lead to more random and pernicious exclusions at a lower level. The American philosopher Michael Walzer talks about 'a thousand petty fortresses'.[2] It is already possible to see signs of this in the growing levels of both ethnic and social class segregation in some of Britain's major towns and cities.[3]

But that still begs the question of how open to newcomers a country like Britain should be. Is the current roughly 550,000-plus annual gross inflow (250,000-plus net) of people coming for more than a year too high? (About half is work related and the rest, in order of size, is students, family reunion and refugees.)[4] How does it impact different groups and national social contracts: employers and employees, affluent and struggling, big cities v suburbs/small towns, highly educated and those with just basic education.

It is an enormously complex and multi-faceted issue that cannot, it is often argued, be reduced to a binary—more people or fewer? But democracy requires some simplicity on big questions and democracy has delivered a very clear answer on mass immigration: fewer.

The Brexit vote was evidently not just about immigration. But if there is a paramount reason for Britain's shock decision to leave the EU it is the seething discontent of a large slice of public opinion created by twenty years of historically unprecedented immigration and the insouciant response of the Anywhere-dominated political class to this change—a change that never appeared in an election manifesto and was never chosen by anyone.

The consensus of Anywhere and establishment opinion over the past generation—minus several influential tabloid newspapers—has ranged from a happy embrace of the cultural and economic benefits to a belief that it is an uncontrollable force of nature. Yet, as we have seen, around 75 per cent of the population (including more than half of ethnic minority citizens) has consistently told pollsters that immigration is either too high or much too high, with the salience of the issue rising steadily to the top, or near the top, of the list of national concerns in recent years.[5] It is true that people are swayed by sometimes alarmist media reporting and are often ignorant of the facts of current immigration but it is also the case that increasing anxiety about immigration since 2000 has very closely tracked increases in the actual numbers.

Of course, immigration has become a metaphor for the larger disruptions of social and economic change, especially for those who have done least well out of them. In the quiet of their living rooms most people have quite nuanced views on the value to the country of different types of immigrant—people are much more favourable towards highly skilled immigrants and students[6]—and tend to be more positive about the local story. Yet immigration overall still stands for 'change as loss.'[7]

This should be no surprise. Large scale immigration is always and everywhere unpopular. Canada is a partial exception, where mass (albeit highly selective) immigration has become part of the country's national identity.[8] It is a basic human instinct to be wary of strangers and outsiders. In rich, individualistic modern societies, tribal and ethnic instincts may have abated but they have not disappeared completely and have been supplemented by anxiety about sharing economic space and public goods with outsiders.

Immigration, at least on a significant scale, is always hard for both incomer and receiver, especially when people are coming from very different, and more traditional, societies. When social scientists like Norbert Elias and Michael Young in the 1950s and 1960s discovered the significance people in settled working-class communities attached to stability and continuity, and how it was often lost in new housing developments, it was considered something to celebrate and defend against bureaucratic indifference. But when, a few years later, those same communities objected to that continuity being disrupted by mass immigration—in the east end of London for example—their views were often ruled beyond the pale.

Britain has not become a country of angry nativists. Indeed, one of the remarkable things about the growing opposition to immigration in recent years is that it has been accompanied by increasing liberalism on most cultural matters, including race, as we saw in chapter two.

But this requires several caveats. First, as we have seen, there is a core of Hard Authoritarians and racists, maybe 5 to 7 per cent of the population. The BNP won nearly 1 million votes in the 2009 European elections. And a 2013 BSA survey found a small uptick to 28 per cent in the proportion of people admitting to being 'a little prejudiced' about race.

Second, there is a much larger group—most Somewheres—who broadly accept the shallow liberalism that is the dominant ethos of modern Britain and are comfortable with difference at a micro-level at work or in social life, yet still do not like the macro changes to their city or country as a whole and worry that too many newcomers are not integrating into British life. They are not hostile to newcomers or people from different backgrounds but do not want to lose a sense of ownership of their area, a sense that people like them set the tone in the kind of shops and the way of life. They mainly belong to that large group that many Anywheres claim does not exist: pro-immigrant but anti-mass immigration.

Third, although chauvinistic nationalism is much rarer in modern Britain than it was a couple of generations ago, attachment to national social contracts and the common sense belief that national citizens should be first in the queue remains as strong as ever (as we saw in chapter four). This does not necessarily make you a flag-waving nationalist but it might make you more sensitive to competition with people you see as outsiders for school places or hospital beds or social housing.

The 2016 BSA survey finds that 71 per cent of people think immigration increases pressure on schools and 63 per cent say it increases pressure on the NHS. The same survey finds that 42 per cent think that immigration is good for the economy with 35 per cent saying it is bad. But there is a sharp class division: just 15 per cent of graduates think immigration is bad for the economy compared with 51 per cent of those with no educational qualifications.[9]

Is this false consciousness? To many Anywheres the popular hostility to large scale immigration is a classic example of people sacrificing their material interests to their cultural values.

That assumes a significant and widely spread economic benefit from current immigration. It is true that the effect on jobs and wages, even at the bottom end, is less negative than many people assume—and employment rates in 2016 were at an all time high for the British born. But mass immigration is still somewhat regressive (and would have been more so in recent years without the minimum wage) and there is not a strikingly positive economic story for the existing population on wages, employment or growth per capita either. On fiscal contribution, EU immigrants are mainly slightly positive because the vast majority are of working age and have come to work, but taking immigration as a whole in recent decades the fiscal contribution of newcomers is slightly negative.[10] (Economists are overwhelmingly pro-mass immigration but are far better at combating negative assumptions than providing a positive case, see the more detailed discussion of the economics of immigration in my book *The British Dream*.)[11]

It is a different story for employers who have been able to sharply cut their training bills in recent years, and replace the sulky, poorly educated local teenager with, say, a keen-as-mustard Latvian graduate who speaks excellent English. The public sector too has been able to cut nurse training budgets and recruit already trained nurses from Portugal or Poland. Governments and employers have been able to postpone the long overdue reform of Britain's vocational and technical training infrastructure (see chapter six).

Anywheres like to observe that it is areas of lowest immigration that are most opposed to it. That is only partly true as it seems (according to an *Economist* analysis) that it was places that had seen the highest rate of increase of immigration that were the places most likely to vote Brexit; in Boston, Lincolnshire, for example, or Stoke where the foreign born population increased 200 per cent between 2001 and 2014.[12] But, in any case, that Anywhere point misreads the social psychology of mass immigration. Xenophobia exists but more important is the psychology of recognition, or rather the lack of it. Areas of low immigration are often depressed former industrial areas or seaside towns where people feel that the national story has passed them by, as it has. Opposition to immigration there is not so much about blaming immigrants as the changing priorities of the country and its governing classes—priorities that no longer seem to include them.

Meanwhile, in areas of high immigration existing citizens doing middling and low-skilled jobs are likely to feel even more like a replaceable cog in the economic machine as they are exposed to greater competition of various kinds with outsiders. Instead of the 'one nation' they are beseeched to sign up to they will often see a political class casting aside the common sense principle of fellow citizen favouritism.

Immigration is in some ways harder to absorb in modern liberal welfare democracies than it was in the harsher climate of nineteenth century Britain when there was much less tolerance of difference. People arriving today are joining a much denser network of interdependence through the tax, welfare and public spending systems that did not exist when Jews or Huguenots arrived in earlier centuries.

Indeed, concern about ethnic diversity can be understood as a subset of a broader anxiety about free riding on the financial and emotional resources of modern citizenship. Newcomers, especially refugees and people from developing countries, often draw out more than they pay in at least in the period after arrival and do not always have the same sense of allegiance to a country's norms or its national story—an indifference that was actively encouraged by first wave multiculturalism in the 1970s and 1980s. This makes many people feel uneasy. (See the earlier discussion of Karen Stenner's latent authoritarians.)

It may also make them less generous. There are clear signs of declining support for the 'common pool' welfare that anyone can draw on (contributory welfare, by contrast, remains popular), though whether this is the result of a specifically ethnic fragmentation effect or a more general decline in social connection is hard to say.[13]

We do know that people, especially poorer people, are acutely sensitive to free-riding—hence the scrounger obsession of mass market newspapers and the mirror-image insistence by liberal pro-mass immigration advocates that immigrants make a positive economic contribution.

An Ipsos MORI poll from 2004 (to accompany my 'Too Diverse?' essay in *Prospect*) found that 45 per cent of people agreed that 'other people seem to get unfair priority over you when it comes to public services and state benefits'. And when asked which type of 'other people' they were most likely to name asylum seekers (this was soon after a period of high asylum inflows) or recent immigrants.[14]

This is not surprising. Those two groups are most obviously strangers to us, and we are less likely to identify with their position or be sure they will share our norms. But few people cited established minorities—implying that they were now regarded as part of the tapestry of the country.

The Immigration Story

How, then, with no strong economic rationale and the opposition of a clear majority of the country did we become a country of mass immigration in the last twenty years?

Having absorbed, not without friction, the post-colonial wave in the decades after the 1950s, Britain in the mid-1990s had become a multiracial society with an immigrant and settled minority population of around 4 million, or about 7 per cent.

Britain was not at that stage a mass immigration society with persistently large inflows. Today it is. About 18 per cent of today's working age population was born abroad and in the past generation Britain's immigrant and minority population (including the white non-British) has trebled to about 12 million, or over 20 per cent (25 per cent in England).[15]

Some of this is an open society success story—consider the increasingly successful minority middle class.[16] But to many people the change is simply too rapid, symbolised by the fact that many of our largest towns, including London, Birmingham and Manchester—where more than half the minority population live—are now at or close to majority–minority status.

Until the mid-1990s Britain had never had gross annual inflows of over 300,000, but since the mid-2000s the annual inflows have never been below 500,000.[17] This step change is not unique to Britain and is part of what we call globalisation. But it was not inevitable on that scale and required the active political support of the 1997–2010 Labour governments.

Labour did not intend to turn Britain into a mass immigration society but most party leaders and activists, increasingly drawn from the Anywhere liberal graduate class, felt at ease with the change. Indeed, as New Labour increasingly converged on a centre-right consensus on economics, being pro-immigration and pro-multiculturalism—'Come here and be yourself'—loomed ever larger in the centre-left political consciousness.

Several decisions were taken by Labour, all of which were reasonable in their own terms, that together created a far more open immigration regime (underpinned by the new Human Rights Act which made it harder to keep people out or deport them once here).

What were those decisions? There was the repeal of the 'primary purpose rule' that had made it tougher for some ethnic minority groups to bring in spouses. The rule was regarded as discriminatory by some South Asian groups and its abolition was a payback to loyal minority voters. Much more important, higher education was just beginning its rapid internationalisation, something actively encouraged by Labour as a means of financing a more general expansion of the university sector. With a booming economy and low unemployment there was also pressure from certain business sectors to increase work permit quotas. And when Balkan asylum seeker numbers rose sharply at the end of the 1990s there was an incentive to move people from the asylum route, with all the cost and dependency involved, to the work permit (and tax paying) route.

And then came the big one. In 2004 the former communist countries of central and eastern Europe joined the EU and Britain was the only big EU country to allow them immediate access to its labour market. It was expected that a few thousand a year would come, but in fact more than 1 million people came over the next four years. There are now 3.3 million citizens of other EU countries living in Britain, up from less than 1 million in the late 1990s, and about half of them are from central and eastern Europe.[18]

The fact that Labour took that decision to open up the labour market before it was necessary to do so is, in retrospect, one of the biggest steps on the road to the Brexit vote. The scale of arrivals was, of course, a surprise and there were economic and geo-political reasons to support the opening. Yet the lack of internal party opposition to the decision was evidence of the weakness of the Somewhere voice in the party—and in politics more generally—and the inability of the Anywhere ideology to separate out questions of racial justice from the economic and cultural impact of mass immigration.

Back in the 1970s and 1980s British politicians of left and right moved swiftly to limit Commonwealth immigration in response to democratic pressure from below—by the late 1980s net immigration was almost zero. Forty years later a new generation of politicians, especially on the left, were unable to do the same partly because their progressive politics was bound up with the inflows and, in any case, they had lost the power to control the inflows from the EU which were causing the greatest anxiety.[19]

Labour then lost the 2010 election, with its stance on immigration a decisive factor according to some analysts.[20] Gordon Brown's contempt for the immigration fears expressed by Gillian Duffy, a Rochdale Labour voter, was one of the lasting memories of the campaign and a perfect example of the mutual incomprehension of Anywheres and Somewheres. The Coalition then took power with a Conservative pledge to sharply cut annual net immigration numbers (from 250,000 to around 100,000).

The Coalition achieved short-term success, with Theresa May as Home Secretary reducing net non-EU immigration from 217,000 in

December 2010 to 143,000 in December 2013 thanks to clamping down on abuse of student visas, raising the income threshold for people wanting to bring in spouses and effectively banning low-skilled immigration from outside the EU.[21]

This dealt with the fallacy that reducing immigration had become impossible in the modern world. But the pledge to reduce net inflows to 'tens of thousands'—unwise in retrospect—was badly knocked off course by another surge from Europe starting in 2012, this time mainly young people from Spain, Portugal and Italy escaping the Eurozone crisis. Net immigration was soon back over 300,000 a year.

This is the background to the Brexit vote—one government absent-mindedly ushered in a mass immigration society without asking the voters, the next government promised to rein it in and failed to do so. And that Brexit vote has merely made more complex what was already one of the central tasks of British public policy: how to respond to the legitimate desire of a large majority to reduce immigration while minimising damage to an economy that has in some sectors become heavily dependent on migrants.

But even when, after Brexit, some sort of work-permit control is re-established for EU citizens, with more restricted access to the social state for a qualifying period, Britain's pull factor of the English language and jobs is likely to remain. Even unskilled workers from poorer EU countries, or countries further east, will still be needed in some sectors like food processing and agriculture—though investment in automation is under-developed in these areas because a reserve army of labour has been so readily available.

British workers are prepared to do tough and anti-social work if it is well paid—look at the oil rigs. But work in those sectors, like agriculture, that are most heavily immigrant dependent tends to be highly seasonal, requiring flexible 24-hour shift patterns, and is often in underpopulated areas of the country. And thanks to the margin pressure from the supermarket chains pay is as basic as the law will allow. This is not work that people with other options will willingly take.

Nonetheless the mass importation of eastern European labour after 2004 was a shock to many British people. This was in-your-face globalisation. It is one thing to lose your job because your factory has relocated to a cheaper labour country, it is quite another thing to find foreign workers, with little or no historic connection to the country, competing with you in your own country. Food manufacturing, for example, is Britain's biggest manufacturing sector, employing around 400,000 people, and more than one third of production staff are foreign born, mainly from eastern Europe, up from almost zero in 2005.

Britain is likely to remain quite a high immigration country for the foreseeable future, although after Brexit the number of low-skilled workers from the EU will eventually fall. The future direction of policy is likely to involve making a clearer distinction between permanent and short-term migrants—more than half of the annual net migration flow into Britain is short-term (students or workers) and, in the few years prior to the Brexit vote, only on average about 100,000 people a year were being granted permanent residence, in fact in the year to June 2016 it was only 67,000.[22] (Just imagine how different the politics of immigration might have been if the government's 'tens of thousands' target had been those granted permanent residence rather than net immigration.)

The lack of a clearer distinction between permanent and temporary citizens creates unnecessary resentment: people see workers from, say, Romania or Bulgaria, enjoying the full benefits of British citizenship yet unable to speak English properly and living in eastern European enclaves, apparently treating the country as a temporary economic convenience. But when someone sees a Chinese student they are unlikely to think like that. They are more likely to think there is someone who is here for a few years—to the mutual advantage of Britain and the student—who will return home soon.

In the future, temporary citizens should have more limited social and political rights—corresponding to their own transactional relationship with the country—and should leave after a few years. We can then concentrate rights, benefits and integration efforts (such as language tuition) on those who are making a full commitment to the country. There is a trade-off, as academics like Martin Ruhs and Branko Milanovic have argued, between migration and citizenship. If we want to continue with relatively high inflows we have to ring-fence the welfare state and full citizenship more jealously.

Britain became a mass immigration society, much as it became an imperial one, in a fit of absence of mind. The political class must now realise that managing that better is at the heart of what a modern state offers. And a central part of that management is managing integration of newcomers better.

What About Integration?

Enoch Powell did a double disservice to British public life and the national debate about race and integration. First, by giving voice to popular anxieties in such an extreme manner he drove too much of the argument underground for a generation. Second, with his lurid predictions of racial violence he encouraged people to set the integration bar far too low, merely avoiding 'rivers of blood' is not enough for a decent society.[23]

Outsiders can be, and often are, absorbed into long-established groups and communities over generational time—think of the many Germans with Polish surnames or Brits with Irish surnames—but it is usually easier if it happens gradually and in small numbers. This is one reason to support a return to more moderate levels of immigration.

Modern Anywhere liberalism with its stress on individual choice and autonomy has not been very adept at fashioning broad, in-group identities—creating myths of common interest and identity. Moreover, while colour-blind liberalism demands, rightly, that everyone be treated the same, that does not mean that everyone is the same. Groups exist: the idea of 'people like us', whether in class, regional or ethnic terms, is a simple reality of life. And that begs questions about how to balance individual rights with acknowledgement of group identity; about what 'communities' are; about contact, trust and familiarity across ethnic and other boundaries; about areas people feel comfortable living in and areas they don't.

When I was writing my last book, *The British Dream*, I spent time in some of the most segregated northern mill towns and regularly chatted to young Asians, usually Muslims, who had no white friends—at least until they went to college, an increasingly important place for mixing—and often the most bizarre views about British society. This is, in part, a liberal failure. It is a failure to see that as some minorities achieved a critical mass, laissez-faire liberalism (or multiculturalism as it was called in the 1970s and 1980s) made it too easy to live apart from mainstream Britain—something reinforced by the internet and satellite television. And multiculturalism, as Maajid Nawaz has pointed out, came to mean diversity between, rather than within, groups.

Anywheres often regard colonialism as Britain's original sin, like slavery in the US, and that first wave multiculturalism was part of a new British mission to show the world that difference without domination could flourish in the mother country.[24] In some ways it did offer a 'soft landing' to new arrivals from Africa or the Indian sub-continent. But by cordoning off minorities in their own districts with their own leaders and social centres and often making their progress dependent on white advocacy, white liberals were merely continuing the colonial heritage with a smiley face pasted on.

One appealing definition of a well-integrated society is one in which everyone is a potential friend. But Britain is not Singapore. We cannot even tell newcomers where to live, let alone who to be friends with. There is a trade-off between choice and integration. The more choice you give people—whether from minorities or the ethnic majority—the more ethnic clustering you are likely to see. That means the 'organic' process of 'them' becoming more like 'us' over time, as they acquire linguistic and cultural fluency, slows down or stops.

And we remain reticent about providing newcomers with a road map and clarity about what is required of them (and what they can expect from us). At the national level we have had, since the early 2000s, citizenship test and ceremonies—which proved more popular than expected—but in everyday life people are largely left alone.

The problem, as it can too often play out, has been described in an eloquent short parable by the former Dutch EU commissioner Frans Timmermans: 'Think of a newcomer, a refugee maybe, like someone asking to take part in a football match for the first time. He wants to join in, but he has no idea about the rules, so he spends the entire game in an offside position. Everyone grumbles at him, and after a couple of tries, no one passes him the ball any more. He doesn't understand what he's doing wrong and decides that the others just don't like him. He turns around and walks off. He is more excluded than before he went on the pitch; he feels unwelcome, rejected, and different. This is exactly the wretched position in which many migrants and their children (or grandchildren) have ended up in. Of course he needs to make an effort to learn the rules too, but someone needs to be there to show him what they are.'[25]

Superficially, there is more agreement on the question of integration than there is on immigration. Who can be against integration? But scratch the surface and there is deep disagreement about the extent of the integration problem, how to deal with it, and even what the goal is and why it matters. One persuasive anti-integration argument runs like this: given how important ethnicity evidently remains to both minorities and majorities (look at the extent of white flight) what is wrong with some degree of separation? Is peaceful co-existence really such a terrible thing? Where are the concrete harms from segregation so long as minorities are not held back by prejudice and discrimination?

It is hard to challenge such a view about segregation because it depends on judgments about how things are going to turn out in a few decades' time. This lack of consensus is inevitable in a liberal society. Nevertheless, most reasonable people believe at least two things about integration. First, it is a two-way process: both the host society and the incomer have to adapt, but the latter has to do so more. Second, there is, indeed, a balance to be struck between accepting that people of similar backgrounds will often want to cluster together and the desire to promote a society with a high level of trust and mutual regard across social and ethnic boundaries. And in recent years—driven mainly by high levels of immigration and the threat of jihadi terrorism—there has been a perceptible shift across the political spectrum towards the second part of that balancing act. The presumption of harm has risen, as Louise Casey's review of opportunity and integration, published in early December 2016, underlined.[26]

The actual news on integration is mixed. Different minorities bring with them different propensities to integration and move along different trajectories. There has been an assimilationist trend among some white minorities. There has been an increase in mixed race couples and children (though much less partnering out among South Asians), a gradual increase in cross-ethnic friendship with only 37 per cent of white Britons saying they have no non-white friends, some decline in residential segregation (though mainly driven by higher intra-minority mixing) and the emergence of a much larger minority middle class with some entry into the business and cultural elites (especially among British Indians and Chinese).[27]

On the negative side there is a story of 'white flight' and parallel but entirely separate lives in some places. There is the sheer indigestibility problem created by the speed/scale of recent inflows and the mixed story of central and eastern Europeans some of whom act like commuter immigrants and make no effort to mix while others are settling and integrating well. Finally, there are the extra tensions created by global jihadi terror impacting upon an already somewhat segregated Muslim minority (especially those of Pakistani, Bangladeshi and Somali descent who make up about two thirds of British Muslims).

Most Muslims do live more separate lives than other large minority groups.[28] Many of them come from traditional societies and now live in the most depressed post-industrial parts of Britain alongside a demoralised white working class whose way of life is, understandably, not something they wish to emulate. Only about one third of Muslim women work, Muslims are more likely than other minorities to speak a language other than English at home, rarely marry out, and still hold to norms that are more authoritarian, patriarchal and collectivist than the increasingly liberal, egalitarian and individualist British mainstream.[29] Moreover, British Muslim attitudes on homosexuality, blasphemy, religion in politics, even conspiracy theory accounts of 9/11, have more in common with global Muslim opinion than with the rest of modern Britain.[30]

The problem of Islamism—a radical and politicised form of the faith—is also likely to be with us for some time, partly because it provides some younger Muslims with a convenient means of combining piety with enjoyment of many of the freedoms of liberal British society. And Islamist influence encourages a relentless narrative of Muslim victimhood and Islamophobia. It is true that mainstream public opinion is, indeed, more wary of Muslims than other comparable minorities partly because of the greater daily segregation of Muslims, the unavoidable association with the jihadi violence of a small minority and the recent 'grooming' scandals in several towns involving mainly Muslim men.

It is not all bad news. Most Muslims identify strongly with Britain and share the same political concerns as the majority.[31] There is some convergence on mainstream norms over generations, with, for example, younger Muslim women more likely to support gender equality than their elders. And Bangladeshis are starting to pull away from Pakistanis in terms of educational and professional outcomes—almost the same proportion of young people from a Bangladeshi background go to Russell Group universities as do white British—thanks in part to the fact that far fewer Bangladeshis marry spouses from the sub-continent (almost half of Pakistanis still do).

Integration is in part a question of numbers. Small numbers of orthodox Jews, sectarian Sikhs or conservative Muslims will not undermine the cohesion that a decent modern society requires. But as the numbers of those living significantly apart from the mainstream grow, a minimalist approach to integration—just obey the law and pay your taxes—becomes less tenable.

And there are two trends which suggest that there is a potential long-term divergence problem. The first, deriving from Eric Kaufmann's ward-based work on the 2011 census, finds that 3.8 million or 49 per cent of non-white ethnic minorities now live in wards where the white British are a minority, in some cases quite a small minority, and that figure was only 32 per cent in 2001.[32] The second, from the work of Simon Burgess, finds that more than half of all ethnic minority school pupils in England are in schools where the white British are a minority, rising to 60 per cent for those in Year 1 (and 90 per cent for those in Year 1 in London).[33]

These two trends suggest that Britain will gradually split between one half of the country that looks like London or Slough and another half of the country that looks like Plymouth or Newcastle—a British version of America's blue and red states. Some analysts (Ludi Simpson and others at Manchester University) in effect give no special weight to the ethnic majority and conclude that integration is moving forward satisfactorily because minorities are mixing more among themselves as they follow the standard pattern of movement from the inner city to the suburbs.[34] This approach in effect rejects the idea of a dominant culture or way of life, however loosely defined.

Public opinion, including most ethnic minority opinion, does not reject the idea of a British way of life and is quite strongly integrationist, while also sensitive to minority rights and comfortable with the tendency to cluster up to a point. A majority (51 per cent) support the idea that the children of immigrants should be able to combine the culture of their parents' country with that of Britain, with 37 per cent saying they should prioritise British culture and only 2 per cent saying they should prioritise the culture of their parents (rising to just 5 per cent for minority respondents).[35]

There is no significant appetite for what is now seen as the wrong turn of laissez-faire multiculturalism of the 1970s and 1980s, when minorities were encouraged to remain immersed in their separate worlds. Indeed there is much less support now than in 1983 for the children of immigrants wearing the traditional dress of their parents' country or being taught the national history of their ancestral home.[36]

And there is persistent anxiety about lack of integration—a YouGov poll at the start of October 2016 found that 58 per cent of people thought that newcomers were not integrating well—with Leave voters (79 per cent) much more worried than Remainers (38 per cent) and older people more worried than younger.[37]

Few white British people (especially younger white British people) say they do not want someone from another race as a neighbour and only about 30 per cent of people say they would prefer to live in an area where everyone is from the same background. Different individuals, groups and generations have different comfort zones about mixing. And we have barely begun to think about how neighbourhood demography can be arranged so that people from the ethnic majority can retain a sense of ownership of an area while also accommodating minority groupings sufficiently large for them to feel at home too.

It is, however, clear from opinion surveys that people are hostile to government legislation to promote mixing. Integration in a liberal society cannot be mandated by government. That does not mean law and legislation has no role in promoting integration and reducing parallel lives. There is the basic law of the land that acts as a weak integrationist force—everything from equality and anti-discrimination legislation to laws governing spousal visas or outlawing FGM. But there are other less heavy handed ways of trying to promote everyday integration: the so-called 'nudge' techniques, the power of good examples and a robust public debate which respects minority rights but does not regard all minority practices as above criticism.

One idea that lies somewhere between simple legislation and nudging is the introduction of a legal duty on public bodies and all local and central government bodies to promote social and ethnic mixing. It would be a permanent reminder of the importance of integration lodged in the back of the mind of local officials and politicians. The duty would also be a means of spreading the best practice of councils, like Newham in East London, that no longer accept 'single identity funding' of projects that only benefit one community. Britain has many Bangladeshi mothers groups and Colombian football teams. These can be appropriate private initiatives but surely we have passed the point when the state should be funding them?

Along with the duty to promote mixing should go a requirement for the relevant local bodies to publish regular statistics on residential and school mix. Trevor Phillips, who has written in support of such a public duty in a Civitas pamphlet, places special stress on this publication of data point: 'If you are a public body and you have to tell your story to everyone, you will want it to be a good one. That is what promotes real change.'[38]

As Karen Stenner has argued (see chapter two) if the discourse of integration is only about the benefits of diversity many people, especially from the ethnic majority, will be put off. Their perfectly legitimate intuition is to worry about common norms and the sense of a single society. If we want to improve integration we cannot just preach the importance of tolerance, we have to promote interaction and a common in-group identity.

As Jonathan Haidt puts it, you can make people care less about race and group identities 'by drowning them in a sea of similarities, shared goals and mutual interdependencies'.[39] It is not talking about difference that creates integration, it is shared experiences and shared interests—joining together across class and ethnic boundaries to, for example, stop the sale of local green space to developers. This creates more powerful integration effects than 1,000 celebrations of diversity.

There is no 'one size fits all' here and integration policy will have to mean somewhat different things in different parts of the country. More than half of Britain's 300-plus local authorities are still at least 90 per cent white British. The places where the minority population is a significant factor tell three different stories. There are the 'parallel lives' places like Oldham and Bradford which still, just, have white majorities but where division is deeply entrenched. Then there are the 'super diverse' places like London and Slough and Leicester where integration has to happen between minorities because the white British are increasingly absent. And, finally, there are parts of middle Britain where minorities are just starting to grow in size and importance. These are the places where we can learn from the mistakes of the past, lean against white flight, and aim to establish schools and neighbourhoods that remain majority white but with large, well integrated, minorities.

If a large number of people come to live in a developed country like Britain from poor, traditional places in the developing world and then are largely left alone, the result is unlikely to be a well-integrated society, at least where those people settle.

But we should stop apportioning blame on the question of integration. The traditional reflex of much of liberal Britain has been to blame the racism of the ethnic majority for integration failures. Those of us (from the ethnic majority) who worry about integration should not turn that on its head and blame Muslims, and other minorities, for the failures. We need instead honest acknowledgement that integration does not happen automatically, that there are problems of segregation, and 'white flight', in some parts of Britain and we need to explore them as objectively as possible and understand the choices and human emotions behind them.

Somewhere Britain, both majority and minority, lives out the mixing story, or the lack of it, in everyday life, and notices that Anywhere Britain remains largely silent on the issue. We need to become more 'integration literate' and learn to talk about ethno-cultural differences in the same way that we talk about social class differences. In a liberal society we cannot, in most cases, legislate for mixing but a more honest public discussion can help to nudge us in a better direction.

The London Conceit

London is Anywhereville. National attachments and feelings of community tend to be weaker in big cities such as London, where there is a high population churn and where there are disproportionate numbers of recent arrivals and Anywhere people. Cost, congestion and stress makes it the least good place in Britain to live—unless you are affluent enough to carve out some protection for yourself or recently arrived from somewhere worse. If London is the future for the whole country, as some people argue, it is not a future that most people want.

It is a city that has partially outgrown its country and sometimes feels more attached to the rest of the world than to its own national hinterland. The idea that 'city states' like London are going to replace nation states does not bear close scrutiny but London is an empire-sized city attached to a medium-sized country that no longer has an empire.

It has, instead, become the apotheosis of the transactional, market society—a wonderful place to have as a bolt-hole if you are a rich foreigner, a good place to come and live and work for a few years if you are an ambitious young incomer from provincial Britain or from another country. Yet it is also the most economically, politically and ethnically polarised part of a Britain that has come to regard it with a mix of envy and wariness.

London exemplifies the emerging division between hierarchical, diverse cities and more equal, less diverse hinterlands, pinpointed by Michael Lind. In his words: 'The social liberalism of these high-end service meccas cannot disguise caste systems reminiscent of Central American republics, with extreme wealth and income stratification and a largely immigrant, menial-service class whose complexions differ from those of the free-spending oligarchs. The gap between richest and poorest in New York City is comparable to that of Swaziland.'[40]

London's population was 8.7 million in 2016, having grown at a bit less than 1 million over the last decade, mainly as a result of immigration. It is now eight times larger than the next largest city in Britain.[41] This is a ratio more commonly found in the developing world than in Europe or North America. Moreover, of the eight next largest cities in Britain only one (Bristol) has a per capita GDP higher than the national average. That makes for a very capital-centric country.

When I was growing up in London in the 1970s the capital, at least in the central zones, had a certain stuffy grandeur but looked back to imperial glory rather than to the future. That London is long gone. Peter Mandler puts it vividly: 'In recent decades it has felt as if the whole country had been turned upside down and shaken, until most of the wealth and talent had pooled in the capital.'[42]

In 2014 around 45 per cent of all advertised graduate jobs in the country were London-based.[43] And despite more public debate about 'rebalancing Britain' since the crash of 2008, the gap is getting wider. As Tim Hames, the former director general of the British Private Equity and Venture Capital Association, has pointed out: 'As far as the professional middle class is concerned London has become a form of gigantic black hole dragging everything into it. In England at least it is often London or bust.'

As Hames implies this is not a positive state of affairs for Britain or even for most people in the capital itself: 'It makes London an incredibly expensive city in which to live and work, with the property market utterly distorted by its status as an international enclave ... Moreover, it can make the rest of the country feel inconsequential. This despite the fact that cities like Aberdeen, Bristol, Cambridge, Edinburgh, Glasgow, Manchester, Newcastle and Oxford are world leaders in certain fields.'[44]

London has a high proportion of what Richard Florida calls the Creative Class—highly educated, mobile people for whom rootedness is not a high priority.[45] And it has a relatively small proportion of the middle income/middle status people who form the core of any country. Some of those people, especially those on modest incomes from the white British majority, have in recent years felt themselves squeezed out both financially and culturally between affluent professionals and the growing ethnic minority presence. This is one reason for the rapidity of white population decline in London.

As recently as 1971 the white British made up 86 per cent of the London population. In 2011 it had fallen to 45 per cent, down from 58 per cent in 2001. Nobody expected London to become a 'majority-minority' city as soon as the 2011 census. Ken Livingstone, the former London mayor, told me in an interview with *Prospect* in 2007 that London would not become a majority-minority city in my lifetime.[46] It had probably already become one as he was speaking.

White British net migration from London (around 500,000 a decade) has actually been pretty constant since the 1970s. Yet there was no white British 'return' when the city began to thrive once more in the 1980s after a long period of decline. There are a few places in outer London like Barking and Dagenham, where the speed of change suggests a strong element of hostile 'white flight' from diversity, but in general the reasons for white exit are many and complex, to do with wanting fresh air and greater space to bring up children as well as discomfort with rapidly changing neighbourhoods. Mainstream commentators are often reluctant to admit even an element of white flight. One reason for this is, I think, that they confuse white discomfort about a rapidly changing neighbourhood with white antipathy to people of different races. But if ethnic change plays no role at all in the flows, why is it that white British people of similar age and income are significantly more likely to leave London than UK-born ethnic minority citizens and are also more likely to move to whiter areas? (See Eric Kaufmann and Gareth Harris's Demos pamphlet on this issue, 'Changing Places'.)[47]

One reason for wanting to leave is the scale of churn itself, which makes stable communities increasingly rare. According to the UCL publication *Imagining the Future City: London 2062*, London's 'revolving door' saw total inflows of 7.3 million and outflows of 6.8 million in the period 2002–2011. In around one third of the thirty-three London boroughs, the equivalent of half their populations move in or out every five years. There is churn in all big cities, but not normally on this scale (at least in the developed world). There are many factors behind the churn—a large number of students, changes to family structure, the cost of living in London and, of course, the highest level of immigration the city has ever experienced.[48]

Infrastructure development—transport, schools, health—cannot, in the main, keep pace with the inflows. Liberal societies with rights and legal protections and due process are not designed for the sort of rapid infrastructure development that London requires. The very thing that attracts so many people to London (and Britain as a whole)—the stability, the rule of law, democratic due process—are the very things that make it so hard to accommodate them! It is true that transport capacity in London is expected to expand by almost 50 per cent between 2001 and 2021 but housing is a much less encouraging story. It is estimated that the city needs between 40,000 and 50,000 new homes a year to keep up with population growth, yet in 2014/15 only 18,000 homes were completed and in most years the completion rate is similarly below half of what is needed.

The result of this undersupply of new infrastructure is, of course, greater congestion and rising costs. In housing, the newest immigrants often live in conditions more associated with sprawling third world favelas. As Eric Kaufmann and Gareth Harris put it in 'Changing Places': 'Incomers are willing to trade room size and amenities for proximity to co-ethnic networks and employment.' Ian Gordon of the LSE calculates that 55 per cent of London immigrants from poor countries in the 2000s have been accommodated through an increase in persons per room.[49]

Rapid immigration has also impacted social housing, which still makes up about one quarter of London's housing stock. This is, in general, no longer available to ordinary Londoners on modest incomes but rather to the poor/unemployed or those with special needs of some kind. About one in five of the social housing stock is occupied by foreign nationals, which suggests a much higher proportion of new lets is going to newcomers.[50]

Meanwhile, a *Financial Times* investigation discovered that as a result of rapidly rising house prices in the capital members of the professional middle class—architects, engineers and academics—could no longer contemplate buying a house in whole sections of London: the City of London, Kensington, Westminster, Wandsworth, Islington, Camden and Hammersmith. In fact, in only three London boroughs is home ownership affordable to people on median incomes. Even the old upper classes feel discombobulated by changes to their neighbourhoods in places like Chelsea and Kensington as new, foreign, money pours in, according to social commentator Peter York.[51]

So, contrary to the 'greatest city in the world' boast, London is one of the least good places to live in Britain on most counts. According to the ONS, London has the highest anxiety levels and lowest life satisfaction levels of any region in the country.[52] It also has the highest crime levels in the country (though declining) and among the worst air pollution in Europe. According to an Ipsos MORI poll 85 per cent of Londoners think that England is overcrowded—higher than any other region. And according to a poll commissioned by the Yorkshire Building Society in 2013, only 13 per cent of Londoners trust their neighbour—again the lowest figure in the country and one third the level in Scotland and Wales.[53]

Of course the story is not as bleak as such a list implies—and some of those issues apply to any big first world city. London has enormous attractions too, not just economic. It has a rich public realm and much of it is free: museums, parks, the South Bank at a weekend. Its schools are the most improved in the country, especially for poorer pupils—and one reason for that is that London is home to Britain's most successful and aspirational ethnic minority communities. Its cultural life is wide and impressive. And it is, of course, a city of opportunity, albeit overwhelmingly for the affluent and the young. Indeed, it is increasingly a mono-generational city designed for people to work in for a few years and then move on, not a place to lay roots. As the UCL *Imagining the Future City* report points out, London sucks in large numbers of people in their twenties and thirties from the rest of Britain and the world and tends to expel everyone else. London loses population in all age groups except those aged 20–29.

London is, of course, one of the most economically dynamic regions in the entire developed world. It is home to many of the country's, and world's, leading companies, financial institutions and universities. But it also exhibits the drawbacks of a laissez-faire, transactional form of capitalism: economically unequal, a polarised labour market and little investment in training especially at the bottom end.

Four of its boroughs—Hackney, Tower Hamlets, Newham and Haringey—were among the twenty most deprived in England in 2010. According to the Trust for London 27 per cent of Londoners are classified as poor, which comes down to 15 per cent if housing costs are excluded.[54] And since 2009, according to the *Economist*, annual pay of a Londoner in the bottom 10 per cent has fallen by 23 per cent.[55]

There is also greater ethnic inequality in London than elsewhere in Britain: in London 55 per cent of white British adults are professionals compared to 45 per cent of minorities. In the rest of the country there is no gap, 39 per cent of the white British and the rest are in the top three occupational categories. Part of the reason is that the average white Briton in London is more affluent than whites elsewhere in the country.[56]

London pays little heed to national social contracts. London employers have no special loyalty to Londoners, let alone British citizens. London has the lowest apprenticeship figures of any region in the country: only 3 per cent of employers recruit direct from schools and youth unemployment is 17.9 per cent (and higher for many ethnic minority youths). And London's elite universities now generally admit more people from abroad than from the rest of Britain outside London.

And it has the most 'hollowed out' economy of any region— between 2008 and 2016 the number of people in professional and managerial jobs rose 19 per cent and the number in low-skill positions rose a similar 17 per cent. The number of middling jobs rose just 6.5 per cent. Thanks to high housing costs in London, low value-added activities that can move do move, and a disproportionate number of Londoners seem to work in the 'gig economy' via platforms like Uber.

Many of these factors have been exacerbated in the past twenty years by exceptionally high levels of immigration, both at the top and bottom of the labour market. At the top end a global 'war for talent' ideology takes for granted that London's top institutions must be able to attract whomever in the world they want. Of course London needs to be relatively open, and many of the people it attracts help to generate economic activity and create new jobs themselves. But when one third of all graduate jobs in London are taken by people born abroad there is also bound to be some displacement of British citizens, either in London itself or people who would have come to the capital from other parts of the country.

At the bottom end the displacement story is even clearer (and that is without even considering illegal immigration in the capital). Around 20 per cent of low-skill jobs are taken by people born abroad, and according to Ian Gordon of the LSE, wages in the bottom 20 per cent may have been depressed by at least 15 per cent in periods of peak inflow.[57] Until the big immigration surge starting in the late 1990s there were fewer people in London employed at the very bottom end of the labour market than elsewhere in the country, and they were better paid. Mass immigration has expanded the numbers at the bottom and increased the pay gap. Why would you employ a local school-leaver for a low-skill service sector job when you can hire a better motivated graduate with modest wage expectations from eastern or southern Europe?

This is not just about coffee shops. According to the Royal College of Nursing in 2013 nearly one third of new London nurses were recruited from abroad, mainly from Africa and Eastern Europe. Yet in that same year NHS London axed nearly one quarter of its training places.

A dynamic city needs immigration, especially at the top end of the labour market, where some people from abroad really do have unique skills that are vital to a company or cultural institution. But you can have too much of it, especially for the middling and poorer people of London, many from ethnic minorities, who have experienced greater pressure on public services and housing, longer commuting times, downward pressure on wages, greater competition in the job market as well as large increases in core living costs. Some 41 per cent of Londoners say they don't find their work fulfilling, a higher percentage than any other region.[58]

And any decent community needs time to absorb newcomers, time to establish the connections of familiarity and continuity that make for solid communities that together make for a great city, not just a place to make a quick buck. But despite the melting pot rhetoric the sheer scale and speed of the recent inflows into London means that it has become a more ethnically segregated city than is often realised. I detailed some of the figures on white British decline earlier, and this has left five boroughs where less than one third of the population are white British—Tower Hamlets, Newham, Harrow, Ealing and Brent.

A major recent survey by the Social Integration Commission asked people about their friendships and contacts across ethnic boundaries and found that relative to its ethnic minority population London is actually the least integrated region in the UK—London's friendship groups are least likely to reflect the ethnic mix of the places people live.[59] It also found London to be the least integrated by age and class. It is often pointed out that public housing and expensive private housing sit next door to each other in many parts of the capital, but that does not mean that the people in the different forms of housing have significant social contact. According to a YouGov poll in 2013 which asked white British people whether they felt comfortable or uncomfortable about the proportion of ethnic minority people in their neighbourhood the region with the highest answer saying uncomfortable (26 per cent) was London, no doubt because so many white British Londoners have experienced a sense of displacement in the many areas where they are now a minority.[60]

Here is the writer Zadie Smith, herself an emblem of liberal, multicultural London, reflecting on the London response to Brexit: 'I kept reading pieces by proud Londoners speaking of their multicultural, outward-looking city, so different from these narrow xenophobic places up north. It sounded right and I wanted it to be true, but the evidence of my own eyes offered a counternarrartive. For the people who truly live a multicultural life in this city are those whose children are educated in mixed environments, or who live in genuinely mixed environments, in public housing or in a handful of historically mixed neighbourhoods, and there are no longer as many of those as we like to believe ... The painful truth is that fences are being raised everywhere in London. Around school districts, around neighbourhoods, around lives.'[61]

That is not actually true of London's rich, who are increasingly ethnically mixed. Almost half of pupils at London private schools are from ethnic minorities (including white minorities), mainly British born.

And London is a relatively tolerant city—with about 90 per cent of people saying people from different backgrounds get on with one another. That does not mean, as Zadie Smith points out, that there is much common life being forged across ethnic boundaries. Walking around the centre of London one has the impression of a mixed up, colour-blind city, at ease with its ethnic diversity. And that is true of some neighbourhoods, but there is also a reality of 'sundown segregation' with many Londoners returning home to live in parallel, monocultural communities or the kind of minority ghettos revealed by the Grenfell Tower disaster. In 13 per cent of London households no one has English as their main language, and 4.1 per cent of Londoners cannot speak English well or at all. Some 40 per cent of pupils in London schools speak a language other than English at home.

Schools everywhere tend to be more segregated than the neighbourhoods that they serve and that is as true in London as anywhere else (though as just noted that does not apply to private schools). Around 60 per cent of South Asians live in majority white areas but only about one third of South Asian primary school children are in white majority schools. And, as noted in the previous section, well over half of all ethnic minority pupils in London are in schools where the white British are a minority—rising to 90 per cent for those in Year 1. Almost half of London primary school children and 41 per cent of secondary speak English as a second language.[62]

Finally, the belief that Londoners are more progressive and liberal than the 'backward shires', as commentator David Aaronovitch puts it, is only partly true. In fact, London is more politically polarised than any other part of the country. There is less hostility to immigration, reflecting the fact that more than half of the population are immigrants themselves or the children or grandchildren of immigrants—though not much less hostility, 60 percent of Londoners think that immigration is too high or much too high (compared with 75 per cent for the whole country). And the 2014 European Election results in London revealed an electorate sharply divided along ethno-cultural lines. Two out of three visible minority voters voted Labour, while two out of three white voters backed the Tories or UKIP.[63] In fact UKIP, which won 17 per cent of the vote in London, outpolled Labour by almost two to one among white voters in the capital. There is almost no difference between the proportion of white British Londoners who say that immigration strongly undermines cultural life and white British people outside London, 34.4 per cent to 34.7 per cent.[64] And 40 per cent of Londoners of all backgrounds voted Brexit.

How, then, does London get away with perpetuating such a powerful myth about itself while telling the rest of the country how dependent it is on the urban superpower? One could argue that there is a sort of 'contract with the capital' in which the rest of the country pays to raise children who then as graduates move to London where they are more productive and then pay higher taxes to repay the rest of the country. London does generate proportionally more of Britain's GDP and tax income than any other region because it has so many high earners and successful companies, but it also sucks up a disproportionate amount of public spending—the 2012 Olympics, Crossrail 2, most spending on high culture (London received public investment on transport of £2,731 per head in the past five years compared with £19 in the West Country).

And the idea that London does not need the rest of the country did not survive the financial crisis: the capital could not have supported the London-based banks without the national tax base to draw upon. (Although London is responsible for about 23 per cent of national output much of that is produced by commuters who do not live in the capital, on some estimates it only counts for about 12 per cent of per capita GDP and by that measure dominates its country economically less than Paris, Athens and Stockholm dominate theirs.)[65]

The London media, above all the *Evening Standard*, is understandably wedded to London 'boosterism' as, of course, is the mayor's office and to a lesser extent the Labour-dominated GLA. And the 'greatest city in the world' story does partly reflect the experience of affluent professionals living in pleasant parts of the capital, networking with interesting colleagues from all over the world, and with the financial cushion to buy themselves out of some of the congestion and pressure described earlier.

The voices of those in the bottom half of the income spectrum do not get heard much in the London media and many of them are in any case recent immigrants who, fresh from poorer and more chaotic places, happily endorse a London story that is partly about celebrating their arrival.

Although London is a left-wing city the 'old left' issues of pay, jobs, public services, community and public housing get drowned out by 'new left' issues of diversity and minority rights—Doreen Lawrence rather than the late Bob Crow. This makes it hard to mount a case from the left for more social and employment protection—more fellow citizen favouritism—for London's school leavers and young unemployed.

There is a bigger reason, too, why London gets away with telling itself and the rest of the country (and the world) such half-truths. The London ideology largely overlaps with, and indeed contributes to, the wider Anywhere ideology of progressive individualism that dominates the country as a whole. London's Anywhere ideology does not like immigration caps or favouritism towards long-established Londoners. It has little understanding for popular hostility to needy newcomers jumping queues in social housing or the NHS. Similarly, it cannot comprehend white ambivalence about the demographic transformation because it involves sentiments of group identity and affinity and a desire for familiarity in neighbourhoods that are not generally felt by more mobile elites, and are therefore dismissed as xenophobic. White Londoners are not supremacists or separatists but most of them do have an identity they want to retain, just like most ethnic minority Londoners.

Yet Londoners born and bred in the city, of whatever ethnic background, are thought to have no special claim on the place. As Peter Whittle of the New Culture Forum has pointed out, 'claiming Londoner status now is rather like claiming citizenship of the World.'

And the London ideology simply ignores what does not fit its worldview. It was striking how little coverage the news of London becoming a 'majority-minority' city received when it was first announced by the ONS at the end of 2012. The *Evening Standard* did not even put the news on its front page, tucking it away on page 10. And the BBC London television news had it as its seventh item. Boris Johnson's usually ubiquitous blond bob was nowhere to be seen. Official London tirelessly celebrates diversity yet its shyness about this landmark moment seemed to be an implicit recognition of how unsettling it was to many people.

According to Janan Ganesh demographic and social trends are remaking Britain in the freewheeling image of its capital city. He argued in a *Financial Times* column that Britain is becoming more urban, more diverse, more atomised, and altogether more like London. And he concluded: 'If the future this points to is a rootless, postmodern society in which nothing is sacred, then London got there long ago.' Ganesh evidently approves of the Londonisation of Britain. But a rootless, postmodern society 'in which nothing is sacred' is not, given a choice, where most people want to live.[66]

London is still living off the social capital of the past but another generation of churn on today's scale and, on current trends, it can only become an even more unpleasant place to live except for the affluent. For many of its inhabitants, both old and new, London is already an insecure, congested, transit camp. (Ben Judah's remarkable book *This is London: Life and Death in the World City* describes the netherworld of recent immigrants cut off from the mainstream in a bleak world of over-crowding and exploitation.)[67] The biggest single reason for this has been the unmanaged mass immigration of the past two decades. The challenge to London politicians is to somehow reduce those inflows and make it a more decent place for the middling majority— less 'rootless and postmodern'—without losing too much of its dynamism and vigour.

6

THE KNOWLEDGE ECONOMY
AND ECONOMIC DEMORALISATION

It was the early 1990s. I was the employment editor of the *Financial Times*, recently returned from Bonn and a front row seat reporting on German unification. I had returned full of enthusiasm for German labour practices, both the voice given to workers in larger companies and the vocational training system which gives pride and status to middling and even lower skill jobs such as working in a shop.

My editor was keen for me to write about the German labour market model, then suffering the strains of unification. But what neither he nor I seemed to grasp was that Britain was in the middle of dismantling a large part of its own vocational and technical training system. The traditional industrial apprenticeship was withering in the face of factory closures and in 1992 the thirty-five polytechnics—that had conferred prestige on higher technical qualifications—became 'new' universities, with the unavoidable downgrading of such qualifications in the rush to a mass, academic higher education system.

This was also the time when people began to talk about the knowledge economy and the expansion of professional service jobs. In fact almost every week a new report would land on my desk predicting the continued expansion of business service jobs and the virtual disappearance of low-skill employment. This was not just a passing fad, more than a decade later in 2006 in Gordon Brown's penultimate budget speech he actually predicted there would be just 600,000 low-skill jobs by 2020.

This was an extraordinary piece of wrong-headed conventional wisdom. The demand for low-skilled, and mainly low paid, jobs has in fact been increasing in recent decades, stimulated by a host of factors: Britain's flexible labour market, privatisation, the contracting out of so many jobs by big companies, the disappearance of a high wage floor in some sectors once sustained by unions and wages councils, the introduction of a more comprehensive tax credit income supplement system in 1999, the high demand for part-time work from working mothers, and, since 2004, the inflow of large numbers of eastern Europeans with a generally high work ethic and low wage expectations.

Estimates of the number of low-skill jobs, depending on the definition of low skill, range from 8 million to 13 million (25 per cent to 40 per cent of all jobs)—including, among others, retail, cleaning, hospitality, care, driving/delivery jobs, assembly line work and routine clerical and call centre work. (Some of these will be subject to automation and the onward march of the robots, even in areas like social care, but many of them will not be. And someone still has to clean the robots.)

This miscalculation was part of a bigger story of the casual way in which Britain, the first industrial nation, drifted into becoming a post-industrial one. The Thatcher revolution was focused on market structure, regulation and incentives, and just took for granted that new industries and decent jobs would spring up to replace the corporate dinosaurs of the past. Even when they did spring up they rarely did so in the places where the old industries had once flourished. In the old industrial economy there was a necessary geographical dispersal of employment in mines and ports and farms. New technologies, combined with greater economic openness, have allowed many more businesses to become less fixed to particular places, and workforces, both within and between countries.

Moreover, the grand bargain of globalisation for workers in rich countries—that many of the dirty old manufacturing jobs would be exported to developing countries but they would be re-equipped to move up the skill chain—simply did not materialise for too many of them. It was also assumed by Anywhere policymakers that once people did acquire more general skills, maybe from one of the new universities, they would be happy to move to the new jobs.

But as we saw in chapter two people are more rooted than is often assumed. Moreover, for good and ill, it is an implicit promise of the modern welfare state that you can stay put—even when your town or region loses its main industries—and support, and maybe even a job, will make its way to you (though in theory a job seeker has to be ready to apply for a job up to 90 minutes' travel time away).

Today, if you are from a university family or you are the first in your family to go, thanks in part to the rapid expansion of higher education, you are likely to be better off economically and culturally than your parents. If you have recently left school at 18 with a clutch of modest GCSEs your working life will be less structured and may feel of lower status than your parents' or grandparents'. This is the fate of too many Somewhere children in what economist Bob Rowthorn has called the 'dual economy', with about 35 to 40 per cent of people working in high productivity sectors—from the car industry to finance—and another 35 per cent working in low productivity service jobs, mainly in the private sector.

The Disappearing Middle

As we have evolved from an industrial to a post-industrial society over the past fifty years, most people in Britain have become much richer and generally now lead more comfortable, healthier and freer lives. And in the working life of the average Briton there is less drudgery and physical strain and much greater probability of a career rather than just a job.

The world of work for most people has also become more fluid and competitive. At the higher skill, knowledge economy end it is increasingly organised around Anywhere assumptions about cognitive ability, creativity and work as an expression of individual fulfillment. But, thanks to the greater ease of comparison with more prestigious careers, this has also helped to drain away much of the meaning and status that once attached to more basic jobs.

The idea of the 'dignity of labour' now sounds rather quaint: it was after all associated with pride in physical strength, the extra status of a craft skill and the respect granted a male breadwinner. All of these notions are far weaker or non-existent today. But when it was taken seriously in the days of hard (and sometimes dangerous) work in coal mines, steel mills and shipyards, there was a spill-over benefit to the way in which more mundane working class jobs were regarded too. Powerful unions also gave some workers a greater sense of control over their factories and offices. The upper and middle classes still had some fear of the working classes because of their dependence upon them.

Few people want to return to the days of 'I'm alright Jack' over-mighty unions, but there must be other ways to halt and reverse the declining status of so much non-graduate employment—one of the most potent sources of working class Somewhere disaffection with the modern liberal order.

Both the centre-left and centre-right critiques of the modern capitalist economy take too little account of human psychology. Work is not just about receiving a decent income and realising one's individual talents. There is intrinsic satisfaction from a job well done and from the teamwork that usually goes with it. But it is also about feeling valued and respected through working on behalf of others, particularly one's family, and through making a public contribution.

These latter motivations have historically been especially important to men in low status jobs (see 'What About the Family?', chapter eight). As they have declined in importance so it has become increasingly hard to motivate people, especially young men, to take basic jobs that no longer require physical strength. Hence the popularity with so many employers of that eastern European reserve army of labour in recent years.

Until quite recently the labour market in industrial societies used to be a pyramid shape with a few people at the top and many across the bottom. (As Robert Ford and Matthew Goodwin have pointed out, when Harold Wilson was elected in 1964, about half of Britain's workers were in manual work and 70 per cent of adults had no educational qualifications.)[1] With the decline of manual work and the expansion of white collar and professional jobs it then evolved into something more like a light bulb, but now looks increasingly like an hourglass, with a bulge at the top and the bottom—bulges which are as much about respect and esteem as about pay.

Middling jobs—such as high-level clerical work or skilled machine operators, jobs requiring experience rather than cognitive ability to do well—have been particularly impacted by automation and by the decline of manufacturing. For every ten middling skilled jobs that disappeared in the UK between 1996 and 2008 about 4.5 of the new jobs were high-skill and 5.5 were low-skill, according to research at Oxford University by Chris Holmes at the Oxford University Centre on Skills, Knowledge and Organisational Performance.[2] That compares with Ireland where the balance was 8 high-skill to just 2 low-skill, while in France and Germany it was about 7 high to 3 low.[3] (This hollowing out trend has been particularly noticeable in London.)

Part of this is thanks to the rapid shrinkage of the manufacturing sector, which provided a disproportionate number of middling jobs— it declined from 30 per cent of GDP in the mid-1970s to around 9 per cent today, and its share of employment has fallen to just 8 per cent (2.4 million). In the globalisation section I pointed to some of the rapid declines in employment in some industrial sectors, such as the fall from 150,000 jobs to 30,000 between 1995 and 2015 in UK medical equipment production.

There has been less of a decline in middle *income* jobs than in middle skill jobs, perhaps because of the greater income range within professional occupations. But many of the new jobs replacing those in manufacturing have been in sectors like retail where the average wage is below £9 an hour. Nearly 1 million jobs were created in British cities between 2010 and 2014 but urban wages fell by 5 per cent over the same period. There is a geographic aspect to this too—eight out of the top ten high-wage low-welfare cities are located in the South East, while nine of the bottom ten low-wage cities are in the North or the Midlands.[4] Outside the bigger cities job prospects can be even worse. Many of the peripheral towns around Manchester, Sheffield and Leeds have lost their industries but do not have the transport links to deliver their inhabitants to the newer industries in those relatively buoyant urban centres—it was only in 2015 that a direct rail link between Burnley and Manchester was finally re-established after almost fifty years. (The HS3 project is supposed to deal with this at some point in the future.)

This all helps to explain the fact that unemployment among sixteen to twenty-four year olds is more than double the national figure at 12.1 per cent—and that does not include more than 400,000 so-called Neets, young people not in employment, education or training who are economically inactive. It may also help explain why about 18 per cent of low-skill jobs are taken by people born outside the country. With the stress in mainstream culture on aspiration and success, the basic jobs that we still need to fill—cleaning, working in supermarkets, caring for the elderly—are seen by far too many people as only for 'failures and foreigners.'

When most people in the country were doing basic, low- or semi-skilled work—maybe in the same factory or office as their fathers or mothers—it made no sense to disdain it. But when, fifty years later, between a third and a half of one's generational peers are going to university or working in the better-rewarded, high productivity top 40 per cent of the economy, it becomes inevitable, perhaps, that people will start to look down on more basic jobs—especially, given Britain's 'Downton Abbey' folk memory, those that involve serving the richer and better educated.[5]

And the growing centrality of educational attainment to the allocation of high status jobs—combined with a dominant assumption about the virtues of meritocracy and upward social mobility—has made it more likely that the people in the bottom half of the income spectrum and the cognitive ability spectrum will now feel unsuccessful rather than merely unlucky or unambitious.

Increasing the pay, status and productivity of people towards the bottom end of the labour market must be one of the central priorities of any modern economic policy. Large-scale immigration has made the task harder. Whatever the benefits of economic/cultural dynamism and plugging skill gaps, the ease with which employers have been able to import trained and motivated workers has also exacerbated a traditional weakness of Britain's economy—a lack of investment in training—and helped to sustain what is called a 'low pay, low productivity equilibrium'. Brexit is an opportunity to break free of this dependence.

Status to some extent follows the money, so higher pay—in the form of the flexible living wage introduced in 2016 (at £7.20 an hour rising to £9 by 2020)—is a welcome and necessary condition of creating the jobs that people will want to do. (Though one problem with a higher minimum wage is that more people will have nobody below them on the pay/status ladder.)

Doing a job that is respected by the wider society—whether it is a high status professional job or a public service job like a nurse, policeman or soldier—makes people feel motivated, rewarded in esteem as well as money. Yet the 2015 British Social Attitudes survey found that 32 per cent of British workers did not feel their job is 'useful to society'.[6]

Even quite basic and repetitive jobs that are never going to attract much respect can at least be designed in such a way that they are more satisfying to do. It is about simple things: listening to employees, reducing the monotony with some job rotation and offering a sense of progression to those who want it and have merited it. There are employers who employ lots of people in quite basic jobs—such as food retailer Iceland and Admiral, the car insurance company—who also win prizes for creating places that are good to work. 'If people like what they do they will do it better, it's as simple as that,' says Henry Engelhardt, chief executive of Admiral.

Yet in recent years the falling relative pay for basic jobs, the overwhelming stress on mobility and educational success, the hour-glass labour market and the apartheid system created by a mass higher education system have all made it harder for the mainly Somewhere people doing routine jobs to feel valued and dignified in the modern economy. And if people think the game is stacked against them, they often just refuse to play.

Policymakers, invariably Anywhere people, have given far too little thought to how to promote aspiration and mobility while also valuing those who stay put, especially in the era of mass higher education. And despite the political rhetoric about opportunity for all, one nation and hard-working families, the great divergence in everyday life between good jobs—invariably graduate jobs—and basic jobs has barely been described, let alone addressed, by any of the main political parties.

And the selection process for these two worlds is now as brutal for every age cohort at the age of sixteen as the eleven-plus grammar school exam was in the first post-war decades. You either get decent enough GCSEs and join the 35/40 per cent who go on to do academic A levels and then usually leave home for university (or the 10 per cent who go on to some more vocational form of further education), or you become one of the 'bottom half' people destined for a job with uncertain prospects rather than a career.

In the rest of this chapter I will touch on the education story that has reinforced the state of affairs described above: the low standard of education for the bottom 20 per cent, employers' retreat from investment in training, the declining state support for technical and vocational education compared with the continuing public investment in and expansion of higher education (which has overwhelmingly favoured Anywhere children). In the final section I will touch on the well-trodden themes of inequality and job insecurity and modern British capitalism's related problems of short-termism and exceptional openness.

A Short History of Education and Training

Cognitive ability, of the exam-passing kind, has in recent decades come to overshadow all other criteria, such as character, competence or experience, as the currency of career success from school days onwards. In the 1960s and 1970s it was still possible to leave school with no or few qualifications and walk into a decently paying job and perhaps even, if ambitious, to then rise up the ranks supplementing basic education with qualifications gained at night school. Banking used to largely recruit at age sixteen from among people with O levels. Late entry into professional jobs—accountant, lawyer, engineer—was commonplace.

The decline of manufacturing and the rise of a knowledge economy in which even middle status jobs in IT or nursing or sales require a degree has placed the passing of exams at the centre of early life. That is probably an unavoidable fact of life if we do not want family connections to determine advancement even more than they do. But the particular way in which our education system has responded to this change is a fact of politics and, in particular, the political power and priorities of the Anywhere class.

Until Labour Prime Minister Jim Callaghan made his famous Ruskin College speech about educational standards in 1976 it had barely featured as a political issue. For the past forty years it has moved much closer to the centre of national life—yet many established Anywhere biases have remained in place: the dominance of elite universities, the lowly status of much technical and vocational education, the negligence towards the 'long tail' bottom 20 or 30 per cent of school leavers still in often chaotic schools.

Real spending on education has doubled in that thirty year period with a big increase under New Labour (though as a share of national income it has remained relatively constant). There has also been a big change in expectations towards the mass of pupils who, for the first time in British history, have been expected to take exams and acquire qualifications (including, for almost half the age cohort, higher educational ones). These expectations used to apply only to a minority. As recently as 1977 fewer than one third of pupils took O levels (most of the rest took the vocational CSE maths), now all pupils take the GCSEs which replaced them in 1988 and were designed for a wider ability range. In the same year only about 15 per cent of the cohort took A levels compared with 40 per cent today and only about 12 per cent went on to higher education compared with 48 per cent today.

Within schools themselves there was a step change in central government involvement from the 1980s with the creation of a national curriculum and then in the 1990s national accountability systems, notably Ofsted and exam league tables. Local authority involvement has meanwhile declined sharply as academies and free schools get funded—and managed—directly from the centre.

This upheaval and extra investment has produced some improvement in average performance at the end of secondary school, especially given that a much larger group of pupils are now being tested than thirty years ago. And as one educationalist said to me recently: 'Surely it is better for society that 80 per cent of the population get at least six out of ten than 30 per cent get nine out of ten?'

Schools that would have been regarded as average thirty years ago are now more likely to be seen as poor and most educationalists would argue that there has been an improvement in school leadership, teaching quality and consistency across schools. Nonetheless, the headline rises in GCSE and A level performance in recent decades present a distorted picture of the modest improvement in standards.

Moreover, about 17 per cent of people still leave school functionally illiterate and 22 per cent functionally innumerate (according to the Sheffield report by Sammy Rashid and Greg Brooks).[7] And this figure seems to have persisted for more than fifty years. The OECD reported in January 2016 that Britain has the lowest literary rate and the second lowest numeracy rate of the twenty-three richest countries.[8] Even allowing for the fact that cognitive ability experts assume that there is a low-IQ group of about 20 per cent in most populations (with 70 per cent hovering around the average and 10 per cent at the top)[9] it ought to be possible to eliminate much of this long tail. Several other countries, from Denmark to Singapore, manage to do so.

The upheaval in post-school education since the 1980s has been even bigger and even more tilted towards Anywhere priorities (and Anywhere children): on the one hand there was the collapse of the traditional apprenticeship system and shrinkage in the technical/vocational sector, on the other hand the channeling of people and national resources into the expansion (and internationalisation) of academic, higher education.

Britain in the 1980s took the post-industrial Anglo-Saxon route of deregulated labour markets and general, transferable skills rather than the continental model of more regulated, company-based training. This Anglo-Saxon route went with the grain of the progressive teaching methods that took hold in the 1970s and 1980s downplaying drilling and practice and the acquisition of knowledge, in favour of uncovering innate talents through learning general, analytical skills—such as 'decision making' or 'handling information critically'.

It is usually conceded that not everyone can be an Olympic champion or a brain surgeon but, nonetheless, the idea that all of us have some special talent that must be located and coaxed out has become a modern political cliché. This rather mystical notion is probably a combination of the Christian idea of the unique value of each human life with a Rousseauian idea that education is not about putting in but about releasing what is already inside. Of course, almost everyone is capable of learning and achieving something, but that does not mean that everyone is uniquely talented. Such magical thinking does little to help those of only moderate ability who benefit most from more traditional forms of learning.

In the 1960s most people left school at fifteen or sixteen and went into a job—from basic to highly skilled. Nearly half of all male school leavers used to go straight into traditional apprenticeships. As recently as the mid-1990s most young people left school at sixteen and went into paid employment. But that youth labour market has now largely disappeared. The proportion of sixteen to seventen year old pupils who also worked, even if only in a Saturday job, was 42 per cent in 1997 and is now just 18 per cent.[10] And the apprenticeship system never recovered from the de-industrialisation of the 1980s—the number of formal apprenticeships plummeted from 250,000 a year in the early 1970s to around 50,000 by 1990.[11]

Apprenticeships also went out of intellectual fashion, regarded as too job-specific and too much based on time-serving to be of much use in a more flexible era. They were actively dismantled by successive Conservative governments in the 1980s, with barely a protest from Labour. They were seen not only as old-fashioned and inflexible but also as part of a closed world of skilled white working class male privilege as apprenticeships were often acquired, like the traditional form of council house allocation, through personal networks that excluded ethnic minorities and other outsiders. Apprenticeships may, indeed, have belonged to that closed world but they were also part of a valuable bargain in which school leavers got intensive training in skills, and work habits, in return for very low wages in the short-term but with the promise of sharp increases later on when they became productive workers.

Through the 1980s and 1990s and into the 2000s employer-funded, job-specific training was increasingly replaced with state-funded generalist skills acquired from staying on longer at school or Further Education (FE) college and/or doing a three year degree at a new or traditional university.

As part of this trend the network of polytechnics, technical colleges and FE colleges was either converted into something else (in the case of the polys) or downgraded. Many of the courses providing the Higher National Certificates (HNCs) and more advanced Higher National Diplomas (HNDs)—required for the middling and higher skilled jobs of British industry and skilled trades—closed down. HNCs and HNDs are now a shadow of their former selves and are owned by a private company, Pearson. Only a few thousand of these courses are completed every year compared with more than 50,000 a year in the 1980s and most are in business studies rather than in the engineering or technical disciplines that are so desperately needed by employers. In fact there has been a sharp fall off in all the post-A level but sub-degree technical courses—so-called level 4 and 5 tertiary qualifications—funded through the Adult

Skills budget (which funds most non-university post-school education and training) plus the two year foundation degrees funded through the higher education system. There were barely 50,000 people in total on such courses in England in 2016 compared with more than 1.4 million undergraduates. Many of the people who would have been doing these technical courses a generation ago are now doing academic or possibly vocational bachelor's degrees, probably at new universities.

As the uptake of middle-level technical qualifications has plunged to an all-time low, higher education has swept all before it. This seems to have been a default position, rather than a properly worked-out strategy, flowing from the lobbying influence of the sector, its perceived success and the fact that so many Anywhere opinion formers and decision-makers had themselves experienced, and understood the benefits of, a university education. Most of them probably have no idea where their local FE college is or what goes on there. Today, around 90 per cent of all MPs are university educated and everyone in the cabinet (bar one) and the shadow cabinet (bar three).

The expansion of higher education from the early 1980s to today can be described through a few key facts: in 1984 there were 70 universities, there are now 170; 14 per cent of the age cohort went to university, is now 48 per cent (in absolute numbers, including post-graduates, that it is an increase from 900,000 to 2.3 million); the total turnover of the sector rose from £7 billion in 1984 to £33 billion today.[12]

This full-speed-ahead expansion was supported by both centre-right and centre-left and really began in earnest in 1992. In that year the then Conservative government agreed to end the two-tier higher education system established by education secretary Tony Crosland in 1965 and allowed the thirty-five polytechnics to join the elite and become fully-fledged 'new' universities, with research given equal or even higher status than teaching. Little thought appears to have been given to the decision, which was mainly the initiative of the polytechnic principals. There was a political rationale of sorts which was to prevent Labour attacks on a two-tier higher education system and an economic rationale which was to create more competition between different types of university and thereby help to keep costs down. It was waved through by the then Conservative education secretary, Ken Clarke, a Cambridge man, whose instinct and experience would have told him that more residential universities must be a step in the right direction (polys were generally not residential).

In the late 1990s the Labour government accepted the argument of advisers such as David Soskice that the conditions for German style 'organised' capitalism based on employer cooperation and proper three year apprenticeships did not exist in Britain, which should instead mimic the US and drive on to a truly mass higher education system, providing the managerial foot-soldiers for the service economy.[13] Tony Blair in his speech to the 1999 Labour conference even proposed a target of 50 per cent of the age cohort going into higher education (it was already then about 32 per cent).

The economic logic was never very clear, let alone the psychology. Where were all the sub-graduate technicians and engineers going to come from? And how were the 50 per cent not taking the approved route into higher education supposed to feel about their place in the world? As noted, there is no stigma attached to not going to university when only 15 or even 20 per cent of your age cohort do so, but it is a different story when 45 to 50 per cent do.[14] Moreover it is almost impossible to maintain the prestige of the vocational route with such high levels of university entrance, especially in the absence of separate higher vocational institutions such as polytechnics.

Nonetheless the public have certainly absorbed the message about the desirability of the road to college. Such is the complexity, uncertainty, reduced status and cost of all other post-school routes that 98 per cent of mothers interviewed for the Millenium Cohort Study said they wanted their child to go to university.

Two further developments sealed the dominance of higher education in the national mind and secured its future income. The first was the decision of the New Labour government in 1998 to introduce tuition fees (initially £1,000 a year rising to £3,000 in 2006 and then £9,000 in 2012) in order to transfer part of the cost from the taxpayer to the student beneficiary. This was a sensible idea in principle both on grounds of equity—returns to a university education, although falling as the sector expands, remain comfortably above other forms of post-school education—and in order to make universities more responsive to their student 'customers'.

At the same time, starting in earnest in the mid-1990s Britain's top universities began a systematic internationalisation of their undergraduate and post-graduate base. There had always been some international students, especially from former colonies, but this amounted to a step change. Numbers (including from the EU) rose steadily from 50,000 undergraduates in 1995 to about 230,000 in 2015, with another 200,000 post-graduates—that is about 13 per cent of undergraduates and 40 per cent of post-graduates—plateauing out after 2013 partly as a result of more restrictive opportunities for post-study work designed to clamp down on people using the student route as a permanent migration opportunity (which sharply cut numbers of poorer Indian students).

This internationalisation was not unique to Britain. US higher education has always attracted a large number of international students and other countries, particularly in the English-speaking world—Australia, New Zealand and Canada—began in the 1990s to attract large numbers of foreign students, especially from the growing middle class in the developing world, above all China and India.

This has been a largely benign aspect of globalisation. It builds on an existing British success story—the country has ten of the world's top fifty universities—in effect creating a new export industry for the country with the full fees paid by most international students helping to cross-subsidise the continuing expansion of higher education for domestic students.

But you can have too much of a good thing. Some universities have become so focused on their internationalised business plans that they have lost sight of their role in the British economy and society. They have become disconnected from what one might call the national intellectual and cultural contract. Many vice-chancellors and senior university officials and academics are children of the 1960s with Global Villager instincts. They have lobbied persistently against attempts by the government to regulate the international student route more closely and have argued that students should be removed from the net immigration numbers, despite the evidence that relatively few have been staying permanently in recent years and that, therefore, removing students would make little difference to the net figure.

Higher education has not just attracted a disproportionate amount of national policy energy—the fees debate was headline news for months—it also still attracts a hugely disproportionate per capita spend. University students have always attracted more public spending per capita (distorted somewhat by the high cost of science and medical students) but when the numbers were relatively small and spending on other forms of post-school education was also rising this seemed less unfair to the many who are never likely to take the university path.

The picture today is one of even more starkly varying funding fortunes—with the public subsidy for university study far outstripping support for vocational education or apprenticeships. Despite the increased student contribution, public spending on higher education continues to rise and it now stands at about £17 billion a year based on an estimate that less than half of tuition fees will be repaid.[15] Meanwhile, school spending has been ring-fenced from cuts, but not the Adult Skills budget which is now well below its 2002 level in real terms.[16] In fact it has fallen by 41 per cent between 2009 and 2015 and is now below £1.5 billion.[17] And too many of the courses have little value to employers and merely lead on to other courses. One consequence is that many FE colleges are in financial trouble, with one fifth in 2015 being described as financially inadequate.[18]

Higher education is now a major sector of the economy—and has played an important role in reviving post-industrial cities like Manchester, Leeds, Sheffield and Newcastle. (Indeed the inflow of money and energy from often southern-born middle class students might be regarded as one of the few bits of effective north-south rebalancing.)

At their best universities are fertile centres of economic and cultural innovation. But it is hard not to conclude that the sector has expanded far beyond any useful purpose. Universities can now expand three year degrees indefinitely and have a strong financial incentive to lower entry requirements. The graduate premium—the extra lifetime earnings a graduate can expect compared with a non-graduate—has plateaued out and may now be as little as £100,000 over a career, moreover a quarter of those graduating in 2003/4 earn no more than £20,000 a year and are mainly in non-graduate jobs.[19]

And as the Social Mobility Commission reported recently, more graduates working in non-graduate jobs is a double disadvantage for non-graduates—it is harder to find good jobs in the first place but also progression routes are harder to come by with graduates preferred to non-graduates for management positions.[20]

A swollen higher education sector and a shrunken vocational and technical sector are not producing the skills our economy needs, either for any sort of industrial revival or even to compete in the rising digital economy. British industry permanently complains about technical skill shortages and the digital sector, which now forms about 10 per cent of the economy, recently warned the House of Commons Science and Technology committee of a skills crunch and a need for another 745,000 workers with appropriate digital skills in the next couple of years.[21] Meanwhile construction is also suffering a skills shortage that could impede a renewed house building initiative; employers are struggling to fill one in three vacancies.[22] Construction apprenticeships have fallen from about 18,000 a year to less than 8,000 in the past five years alone.[23]

And the 'media studies' graduate from a new university with few obvious skills and a vague political disaffection is not just a snobbish joke. There are 133 courses at British universities for media studies students and their employment record is not encouraging—about 10 per cent of graduates are unemployed and the most common form of work after graduation is 'retail, catering and bar work'. Many such students will be the first in their families to go on to higher education but the opening up of Somewhere universities to a much broader social class intake is often just reproducing new social hierarchies inside the graduate class. One example: there has been a sharp fall-off in boarding among poorer and ethnic minority students (more than half of women from South Asian backgrounds stay at home),[24] with the proportion of boarders down from 92 per cent in 1984 to 73 per cent in 2016 and most of the drop is in the new universities.[25]

As Alison Wolf, the most trenchant critic of modern educational trends, has put it: 'In post-19 education, we are producing vanishingly small numbers of higher technician level qualifications, while massively increasing the output of generalist bachelors degrees and low level vocational qualifications. We are doing so because of the financial incentives and administrative structures that governments themselves have created, not because of labour market demand, and the imbalance looks set to worsen yet further.'[26]

In the last few years apprenticeships have come back into fashion. In 2015 the government introduced a target of 3 million apprenticeships by 2020 and an apprenticeship levy on bigger employers is due to commence in April 2017. The hope is that this will counter the training free rider problem—the reluctance to invest in training for fear that expensively trained employees will leave for another job as soon as they can—and encourage more proper apprenticeships on the German model combining workplace and classroom education.

And there has been a rapid increase in the number of pupils taking A level equivalent 'BTEC' vocational courses, thanks in part to the greater popularity of vocational qualifications at GCSE stage. The number doing BTEC courses rose to 172,000 in 2015, compared to 266,000 doing academic A levels, and a growing number of students are combining academic and vocational qualifications (and nearly a quarter of students now enter university with mainly BTEC qualifications). This is a small step in the right direction, though there are worries about the quality of some BTEC courses, grade inflation, and the fact that BTEC courses tend to attract the least able and motivated students.

Most of the recent increase in vocational training is almost entirely state funded but it cannot compensate for the steep fall in employer financed workplace training in recent years. The private sector has persistently under-invested in Stem (science, technology, engineering and mathematics) and IT skills. According to one study the average training time per worker declined by about a half between 1997 and 2012, with the greatest decline in the private sector and among the young and those in the lowest educational groups.[27] Employer funding for training also declined substantially after 2005. It is estimated by Francis Green and his co-authors, based on the Employer Skills Survey, that training funding fell by almost 15 per cent per worker 2005–2011. Over a similar period the Continual Vocational Training Survey records a more drastic cut of almost 30 per cent.[28] This provides a handsome justification for the apprenticeship levy.

'Thirty years ago the large British firms in every major town accepted the costs of apprenticeship and technical education as a kind of social overhead which they willingly paid; now it's "can't pay and won't pay" from both small and large firms,' according to the authors of 'Rebalancing the Economy', which casts a withering eye over the decline of manufacturing.[29]

This reduction in training can be partly blamed on the ability of employers, especially since 2004, to free ride on the training systems of other European countries thanks to EU freedom of movement. The idea of being a good corporate citizen is today more likely to mean having more women directors or measuring the company's carbon footprint than feeling some responsibility to train and employ British citizens. The CBI and other employer bodies, even prior to Brexit, lobbied hard for the widest possible open door for skilled workers apparently regarding themselves as having no special responsibility to British citizens.

There is another reason for the decline in employer-funded training, as Alison Wolf points out: 'If employers are being provided with an ever expanding graduate population for free, then university training has to be very bad indeed before it becomes rational to pay for an alternative ... Even if a graduate has few directly relevant skills a high level of education attests to the fact that someone will probably master job-specific skills quickly, and also has the self-discipline required to turn up to work reliably and on time, irrespective of what they studied.'[30]

The current logic seems to be to continue with the expansion of higher education. David Willetts, the former Conservative universities minister, has talked of 60 or 70 per cent of young people going through higher education (emulating Sweden)—and then allow it to recreate within its boundaries some of the graduate and even sub-graduate technical and vocational courses that used to be provided at polys and FE colleges. The new universities like Sheffield Hallam already provide a large number of vocational degrees in nursing or surveying, for example. And universities like Aston in Birmingham and Teeside in Middlesbrough in the old industrial heartlands are offering high-level engineering courses with a strong vocational element and links to local employers.

But it is not clear that this is sufficient to reboot the middle level of technical/vocational training or that universities are the right place to do it. As Alison Wolf, again, explains: 'First, universities are self-contained and separate from the workplace. They cannot ... possibly keep up with all the changes which take place in a fast-developing industry. Second, university teachers, however vocational their speciality, are making their careers as academics and researchers, not as practitioners of whatever profession, trade or calling they teach ... Research and research publications inevitably get the most attention from the ambitious and able.'[31] Indeed the modern university, especially the new universities, are increasingly a battleground between the vocational/

employment priorities of students and the academic excellence that most of the academics want to pursue.

It would be preferable to recreate elite vocational colleges, like the old polys, with strong local connections. Mass higher education in the US is based on the community colleges offering relatively cheap, and local, two year vocational courses (with the possibility of transfer to a state university). California, for example, has the same proportion of students as the UK but the majority are in local community colleges not the University of California. The system delivers the middle level skills locally where they are needed.

There is a final problem for those young people at the bottom end of the education and training system—the wild mismatch between career expectations and the grim reality of actual job opportunities for those not on track to good universities, particularly in the Midlands and the North. The egalitarian ethos—'you can be anything you want'—of modern education tends to encourage high career aspirations disconnected from any realistic means of achieving them. (Improved links between schools and local employers could help with this aspiration gap.)

A 2009 study by Westminster University found that nearly half of young people aspire to careers in just seven highly competitive fields: performing arts, professional sport, teaching, veterinary science, law, policing and medicine.[32] It is unsurprising that the National Skills Survey finds that the main reason why nearly one third of employers had recruited no young people in recent years is that no one under twenty-four had applied.[33]

The creation of a mass higher education system in the past twenty years has had an enormous and barely understood impact on British life. University has become the standard path for almost all middle class young people, above all young women, and as an increasing number of jobs—including nursing and even estate agency—have become graduate-only, large numbers from lower income backgrounds without a family history of higher education have also been pulled up into the system and then on into decent, professional jobs.

So far, so good. But, as we have seen, for those who do not get the required A levels and go to a good university, still a majority of young people, this expansion has left in its wake a twilight world of mainly lower status jobs and training opportunities—most of which carry a lower public subsidy than higher education. Many young people, especially young men, just turn their backs on the new labour market and end up working in the informal economy or not at all—18 per cent of sixteen to twenty-four year olds in the North East are Neets.

Overall employment levels have been at historic highs in recent years partly driven by higher female participation but, as we have seen, youth unemployment remains relatively high (and higher for some ethnic minority young people). The loss of a structured path into adulthood and parenthood is exacerbated by changes to the housing market which have made public housing much harder to acquire and a mortgage virtually impossible for a young person in a non-graduate job.

There is also the opportunity cost of the expensive expansion of higher education. Think of the other things that could have been done with the resources. There could have been a complete overhaul of post-sixteen education with a new network of super-FE colleges combining continuing academic education with vocational/technical training—leading either straight into work, and a British version of the German dual system of work plus college-based training, or onto higher education. There could have been a big investment in continuing adult education, in remedial education for those who have been let down by the school system and re-training for those whose industries have disappeared. (The Engineering Employers Federation in Birmingham in 2016 created apprenticeships for 350 sixteen and seventeen year olds but out of 8,500 applications could offer places to only 330 because basic education levels were so poor.)[34]

The claim of third way governments in the 1990s—especially in the more open Anglo-Saxon economies of America and Britain—was that globalisation and the export of the dirty old jobs should not be resisted and governments would help workers retrain for the higher skill new jobs in the knowledge economy and elsewhere. As already noted, this promise has simply not materialised for about a third of the population. At the lower level, the assumption that employers would invest in someone with a level 2 qualification (meaning decent GCSEs) and that progression and higher wages would follow has turned out to be false. In fact the number of jobs that do not require any qualification for entry is growing.

At the higher level, equipping people for life in the new world turned out to be: stay on at school and go on to university in a new expanded higher education sector, a less prestigious version of the elite boarding universities attended by most Anywhere politicians. But, as I have described, there is a growing divide between elite universities and the rest with too many first-in-their-family-to-go (mainly from Somewhere backgrounds) emerging with the graduate tag but ill-equipped for most highly skilled professional jobs and unwilling to take lower end ones.

And while the expansion of higher education has certainly created new opportunities for many people it has also exacerbated the fault line in British society that this book is about—those that leave and those that stay, as I discussed in chapter two. John McTernan the former New Labour adviser points out: 'Mobility comes naturally to graduates who often move away from home to university and then move again to their first job, it is part of the life-style of many middle class people. But many working class communitarians cannot see the point of it, they value their family and other networks too much—why move away from your extended family when it offers free childcare? New Labour rhetoric was on the side of change and mobility but it was off-putting to many people. We were in effect saying to many people especially in the north: stay with your community and fail, or move.'[35]

Many of the most able have always left the smaller towns and suburbs for professional advancement in the big cities. In part because of the residential university system this now happens earlier in the life-cycle and to many more people than in the past. Most other advanced countries have retained smaller elite university sectors with more middle level educational institutions, such as the community colleges in the US, and more fluid boundaries between different levels of education. In Britain it is, increasingly, university or bust.

Living Standards and Inequality

This tension between a declining market position for many employees and the political promise of some kind of respect, security and share in prosperity accounts for at least some of the Somewhere public disaffection of recent times, including the Brexit vote. And the declining status of non-graduate employment that we described earlier has been exacerbated by other economic trends: falling incomes after the financial crash, the decline in home ownership especially in the big cities, in-work poverty and that reduction in the number of middle status jobs. Although much of the political class and media has focused on inequality, sluggish social mobility and job insecurity (symbolised by zero-hours contracts) as the original sins of modern economic life all the survey evidence, both here and in the US, suggests that it is the idea that the Golden Age is behind us, rather than just ahead, and that children will not automatically live better lives than parents, that has caused most anxiety.

Thanks to the relative weakness of organised labour and Britain's flexible labour markets, the fall in economic activity caused by the financial crash led to lower incomes rather than significantly higher unemployment as was the case in most previous recessions. Real wages have been growing again in Britain since 2013 but fell by more than 10 per cent after 2007 and have not fully recovered.[36] In June 2016 there were only two regions where GDP per head had returned to its pre-crisis peak—London and the south east—and at that date as many as half of all British households had had no increase in their take-home pay since 2005—the longest period of wage stagnation since the middle of the nineteenth century.

The initial reaction to the crash was rather muted. There was no mass unemployment and the financial scandal was a system-wide one with few obvious villains (apart from the unfortunate RBS chief Fred Goodwin). There was no shift to the left—partly because of Labour's diminished appeal to so many Somewhere voters—but rather the election of two centre-right governments with a conventional attitude to deficit reduction in 2010 and 2015. But these un-radical general election results seem to have disguised a more disaffected public mood and reduced trust in 'the system'—exacerbated by the MPs expenses scandal of 2009—that came to be expressed in support for UKIP, Brexit and Corbyn's Labour in 2017. The disaffection was already there, prior to the crash, in many parts of the country—especially the former industrial Labour strongholds that never recovered from 1980s de-industrialisation—and has burst out sporadically after 2008.

It was also to be found in the so-called 'squeezed middle'—a phrase coined by the Resolution Foundation think tank in 2010—the large group who have not made it into the security of the professional class but have not dropped as low as the more persistently 'left behind' groups such as the working poor and people with few qualifications in the former industrial areas.

Despite the louder public complaints about inequality since the crash, levels of inequality have changed only a little since the late 1980s following the tax and other reforms of the Thatcher governments. Indeed, there is little evidence for many of the widely held anti-capitalist claims about sharply rising inequality and job insecurity.

It is true that relatively high levels of inequality are likely to be a greater source of disenchantment—even if inequality is actually falling—at a time of declining or static incomes and when 'we are all in this together' appeals are being made for equal sacrifice in reducing the national deficit. The greater visibility of the super rich and the attention focused on executive pay can further stir resentment—the pay of FTSE 100 chief executives in 2014 was on average 183 times greater than the average pay in those companies compared with just 69 times greater in 1999 (in the US the equivalent chief executives are paid 340 times more).[37] When Sir John Harvey Jones died in 2008 he left just £500,000 in his will. Harvey Jones, the former chairman of ICI, was one of Britain's most successful and (thanks to a television show) best-known businessmen, but he belonged to the era of relatively normal pay levels for senior executives and before the internationalisation of top jobs.

Britain remains one of the most unequal of the rich countries but income inequality has fallen since 2007, as it often does in periods of recession or slow growth, partly because bonuses and high returns fall in the financial sector and other high pay sectors while benefits and pensions rise more quickly than earnings. Indeed, according to the World Bank the UK has seen the biggest decline in inequality of any industrial country since the financial crisis.[38] Since 2007 the poorest 20 per cent of households have seen disposable incomes rise by 5 per cent while the richest 20 per cent have seen them fall by the same amount.

The income gap between all social classes has narrowed but those in the middle of the income spectrum have experienced the tightest squeeze with the middle fifth of households now closer to the bottom fifth than the top fifth—twenty years ago more than two thirds owned their own home and less than a quarter of their income came from benefits, now only half own their home and almost a third of their income comes from tax credits and benefits.[39] (Moreover, overall asset inequality has continued to rise sharply thanks in part to the rising value of housing assets and the lottery of where in the country you happen to live.)

The closing of the gap between poorer households and middling households—part of this squeezed middle story—is partly the result of more people from poorer households finding mainly low paid work, which is itself partly the result of tougher sanctions on benefit claimants. This means that more than half of the poor are in work, but it also means that the proportion of children living in a workless household fell from 20 per cent in 1994 to 12 per cent in 2015.[40]

The number of poor households—classified as those below 60 per cent of national median income (about £280 a week for a childless couple today)—has fallen from a high point of just over 25 per cent in the mid-1990s to 21 per cent today (both after housing costs).[41]

For more than twenty years the overriding aim of labour market policy has been to get people into jobs—with the carrot of in-work tax credits and the stick of squeezing benefits. Any job may, for some people, be better than none. But the growth of low skill, low wage, employment since 1979—it grew from 13 per cent of employees then to around 22 per cent in 1997, since when it has steadied at around 30 per cent—has been a dispiriting feature of the British economy. And according to the Low Pay Commission one in six private sector jobs will be minimum wage in 2020.[42]

It is well established that the decline of manufacturing has reinforced this bias against the middling job in favour of higher professional jobs and low skill basic jobs. Another 'bias against the middle' is a consequence of the sectors where Britain has its comparative advantage. Some of Britain's most successful business sectors in finance, professional services, the creative sector and so on, tend to produce rather few middle income/middle status jobs. But the highly paid professionals who dominate those sectors do generate demand for low skilled/low paid work—security/cleaning, delivery services, domestic support, restaurant/bar work. The number of hospitality jobs has increased by 16 per cent since 2000 and now accounts for 7 per cent of the workforce.[43]

But does this mean that jobs have become less secure or anti-social in some way, as is often claimed? There has been an increase in zero-hours contracts jobs from 200,000 in 2000 to 800,000 in 2015 and these can be more insecure, though they are often chosen because they suit people's circumstances, and the worst abuses—such as banning people from seeking work elsewhere—have been stopped. But the average length of job tenure has not changed much over the past decade in fact it has increased slightly from just over eight years for women and just over nine years for men. Only about one in twenty-five employees are part-time workers who would like to work longer hours. And the number of workers holding more than one job is at a twenty-five year low, according to a report in November 2016 from the Resolution Foundation.[44]

It is, however, also true that Britain's job creation success in recent years is less rosy than it looks and includes a disproportionate number of low paid and part-time jobs. An even larger proportion is accounted for by self-employment—over 80 per cent of all employment gains between 2007 and 2014 according to a report by Morgan Stanley.[45] Self-employment (4.8 million) is now only 500,000 behind public sector employment (5.3 million) but most of the rise appears to be voluntary and dominated by older people wanting pre-retirement jobs.

According to the British Social Attitudes survey stress levels have been rising sharply for people doing basic jobs—in 2005 the most stressed group at work were managers and professionals, at nearly 40 per cent, while those in routine jobs was just under 20 per cent. The managers in 2015 were still just over 40 per cent but those doing routine jobs had jumped to just under 40 per cent. And only 65 per cent of people think their job is secure.

Notwithstanding all these depressing statistics about 'bad jobs' it is also worth noting that 71 per cent of workers think they have a good job, according to that 2015 British Social Attitudes survey.[46] And Andrew Oswald of Warwick University has found no correlation at all between levels of education and job satisfaction.[47] Quite a few people in low-skill jobs have high satisfaction and some people with advanced degrees who are paid £200,000 have low satisfaction.

The disappearing middle income/middle status jobs must also be kept in perspective. Even allowing for 40 per cent of high-skill jobs and 30 per cent of low-skill jobs that still leaves 30 per cent for middling ones, and although the 'hollowing out' of skill levels is well established there seems to have been much less hollowing out of incomes, with no significant reduction in the number of people in the middle income deciles.

Short-Termism and Foreign Ownership

Finally, as this book is partly about the sometimes mixed blessings of Anywhere-favoured openness, I want to reflect briefly on how British business's relative 'short-termism' and 'financialisation' has combined with its unusual openness to foreign ownership to make it harder to grow the large, successful businesses that we need if we are to move towards a higher-wage, higher productivity economy.

The shift away from manufacturing and heavy industry starting in the 1970s has been inevitable and even desirable, but the speed has sometimes been brutal and the manner of decline has made it harder to preserve a successful core from what is left.

British manufacturing now has comparatively few large, domestically headquartered companies—many have been broken up and sold off: GEC, Lucas, TI, ICI (see below). There are now fewer than 2,000 factories employing more than 200 workers and about one third of manufacturing jobs are in foreign owned companies. Foreign ownership can be a great blessing—just think of Nissan in Sunderland—but foreign owned companies often have 'ambitions limited by their role in global supply chains ... and small UK manufacturers are routinely exposed to the sourcing decisions of overseas multinationals and the vagaries of economic decisions that are beyond their control,' as the CRESC 'Rebalancing' paper referred to earlier puts it.[48]

Of course any modern economy has to be a relatively open one—consider how when the pound fell after the Brexit vote the FTSE100 share index rose because so many of those big companies' earnings and assets are in dollars or Euros which are now more valuable in relation to sterling. (The FTSE250 rose more modestly because those second rank companies are more domestically focused.)

But that leaves the question of how open? No other developed economy has been as carefree about handing over its assets—from leading businesses in all sectors to our utilities and airports—to foreign ownership. In his book, *Britain for Sale*, Alex Brummer has described how this so often leads to not only corporate earnings but key managerial and research functions being relocated abroad.[49] France and Germany may be more open to European political integration than the UK but they are far more wary about foreign ownership of 'strategic' assets (including the food company Danone in the case of France).

Meanwhile, the rapidity of industrial decline has created so-called 'broken supply chains', meaning even successful manufacturers have to source most of the product from elsewhere. JCB, often cited as a great British success story, has seen the British content of its diggers decline from almost 100 per cent in 1979 to about one third today. Similarly Dyson vacuum cleaners outsources everything except design. Global supply chains are a common feature of today's global companies but according to CRESC British manufacturers import far more than their German counterparts.[50]

The Dyson effect can deliver dynamism, but only in a few pockets as British industry returns to a small workshop base last seen in the early stages of the industrial revolution—and such units are too small to combat weak export performance or high import penetration. It is not desirable, or possible, to recreate the manufacturing giants of the past but some scale is needed—in all sectors—to create the jobs and export earnings of the future.

Germany has far fewer start-up businesses than Britain but they have many more exporters and businesses with enough scale to ride the waves of short-term fluctuations in economic life. By contrast, Britain ranks third in the OECD for start-ups but only thirteenth for the number that go on to become significant businesses.[51]

The last Conservative government hinted that it wanted to reintroduce a public interest test for foreign takeovers, indeed for all takeovers, and the government's 2016 Autumn Statement set aside a fund worth £400 million to stop the country's flourishing technology 'unicorns' being bought by foreign rivals. This is a welcome intention but is unlikely to come to anything, and cannot compete with the Brexit devaluation which has made British companies about 15 per cent more attractive.

In any case, if the exceptional openness of the British economy to foreign ownership has contributed to the decline story the bigger share of blame must lie with that familiar bogeyman of short-termism: the narrow focus on shareholder returns and the active market in corporate control stimulated by investment banks in the City of London that often creates a disincentive to plan and invest long.

The Anglo-Saxon corporate governance model puts British businesses at a disadvantage compared with their competitors in Europe and Asia. German companies, particularly the Mittelstand of medium-sized family businesses, tend not to be quoted on the stock market. Managers can plan ahead—in developing new export markets, for example—without fear of a takeover, losing their job, or losing out on bonuses.

The greater weight that shareholders, and stock market sentiment, have in big British businesses means managers are often on a treadmill of maximising short-term earnings. As Bob Bischof, head of the German-British Forum, points out: 'Many of the best British companies sit on large cash piles. They do not spend them on product development or opening up export markets in the Far East, for fear of an adverse reaction affecting their share price. They prefer to "return cash to shareholders" through share buy-backs or look for mergers and acquisitions, rather than growing their companies organically. If all else fails, they can "bring the company into play" and sell it at a premium.'[52]

In Germany even companies that are listed on the stock market are shielded from takeovers, and usually also from their own bosses' hubristic deal-making strategies, by their supervisory boards, which include worker representatives. The German model is by no means perfect and cannot always prevent managerial empire building—consider Daimler's takeover of Chrysler—and Germany has a poor record with starting and building high-tech businesses (Britain is far superior in bio-technology). But, unlike in Britain, companies are seen as more than the possession of their shareholders. They operate in a more stable environment and are not, in general, subject to the sort of radical discontinuities that are common in Britain.

The demise of the iconic British company ICI is a good example of such a discontinuity, partly driven by the curse of stock market fashion.[53] The ICI case is not simple, and some other big chemical companies have gone through similar upheavals in the past generation. But this much is clear: at the opening of the last decade of the twentieth century ICI was Britain's largest and most venerable industrial company with research labs responsible for a host of historic breakthroughs from plastics and polythene, to new kinds of paint (Dulux was an ICI company), agrochemicals, cavity insulation for walls and more recent pharmaceutical innovations such as beta-blockers. And now it has been dismembered, with its plants and businesses either closed or sold to others, mainly foreign competitors. (It leaves a particularly large wound in the Teeside region where it once employed tens of thousands.)

Its messy conglomerate structure was not popular with the advocates of shareholder value in the 1980s and 1990s and to defend itself from a threat from takeover predator Hanson Trust it sold off its pharmaceutical arm Zeneca in 1993. The pharmaceutical division had been a loss-maker for more than two decades after the war but then in the 1960s it had its beta-blocker drug breakthrough and became ICI's most profitable arm in the 1980s and 1990s. In 1999 Zeneca merged with the Swedish drug company Astra and now much of the coveted research and development takes place in Sweden.

ICI was left with a mixed bag of businesses and, like many other global chemical companies at the time, opted to switch out of low value commodity chemicals into more profitable speciality chemicals. But when in 1997 Charles Miller Smith, the new chief executive brought in from Unilever, tried to impress the market by spending £5 billion on the speciality chemicals business of his old company it turned out to be the beginning of the end. ICI had overpaid for the Unilever company and was crippled by debt and a decade later was taken over by the Dutch group AkzoNobel. The Dutch company had also overreached itself with the ICI purchase and in 2009 was forced into another round of closures and sell-offs of what remained of ICI.

No company has a right to exist forever and if senior executives are not managing a company well the threat, and reality, of a takeover can be an important external discipline. But the fall of ICI—like that of GEC and other business giants—and the loss of many viable businesses and a valuable research infrastructure was at least in part down to the greater influence from the 1980s onwards of shareholder and stockmarket pressure and the way, in the British system, that companies themselves become commodities.

By contrast, the big three German chemical giants (BASF, Bayer and Hoechst) have also been through some big upheavals in the past thirty years but they all continue to exist and in most cases to thrive. Hoechst (now Aventis) shifted out of chemicals completely and into pharmaceuticals but both Bayer and BASF remain large diversified chemical companies. The German chemical industry as a whole is easily the largest in Europe and the world's biggest chemical exporter. BASF, based in Ludwigshafen in western Germany, is most similar to the old ICI. It is now the largest chemical company in the world with sales of €70 billion and profit of just under €7 billion, it employs 120,000 people worldwide and 53,000 of that number in Germany. How they must weep on Teeside.

The benefit of having employees represented at the highest level in large German companies—something that the May government has been thinking about for Britain too—can also be seen in the more gradual pace of de-industrialisation in the heavy industrial Ruhr region of Germany in the 1980s and 1990s compared with most of Britain's industrial regions.

The pace of de-industrialisation in Britain picked up sharply in the early 1980s as the effect of North Sea oil sent the pound rocketing and Mrs Thatcher's new free market government removed all capital controls, and in some cases sharply cut financial support to nationalised industries. (The closure of uneconomic coal mines led to the year long 1984/5 strike and the rapid subsequent rundown of the whole industry). Hundreds of thousands of industrial workers lost their jobs in the space of a few years as factory after factory closed permanently. Ambitious retraining schemes were announced for the unemployed workers but little came of them. The main cushion provided by the state was making it easy for people to claim extra disability allowances on top of unemployment benefit. Some parts of once industrial Britain remain depressed to this day, like our own version of the east German states most of which have never recovered from the economic shock of unification.

By contrast in the Ruhr area of western Germany there was relatively little conflict and retraining programmes did, sometimes, help people transfer into new industries. The Ruhr had a huge amount of public investment in physical regeneration of the old steel and coal areas and new light electronic and environmental engineering plants employed some of the former steel workers and miners. One reason that retraining programmes worked better in Germany is that they often took place within the companies that were closing plants. All large companies have to present 'social plans' when they are making workers redundant and the plans have to be approved by worker representatives. It is often cheaper to retrain a worker for another line of business than to sack him or her.

Despite all the familiar failings described above, Britons have seen a steady improvement in their conditions of life in the last seventy years—at least until the credit crunch of 2007/2008.

The standard reformist critiques of the modern capitalist economy and society in terms of inequality and job insecurity turn out to be only part of the story—and, as we have seen, often rather exaggerated.

What these critiques, and their associated policy prescriptions are missing, is a sense of the dislocation—as much psychological as income-related—created by the shift from an industrial to a knowledge-based economy. This has left many of the Somewhere people in the bottom half of the income and education spectrum feeling demoralised and disrespected.

Skilled industrial employment which once provided a kind of social and economic ballast to our society has been largely swept away. An economic system which once had a place for those of middling and even lower abilities, now favours the cognitive elites and the educationally endowed—in other words the Anywheres.

7

THE ACHIEVEMENT SOCIETY

Social mobility and meritocracy. Motherhood and apple pie. Who can possibly be against an open society in which able poorer people rise up the scale and less able richer people fall? And a society in which the connection between parents' income and class status and that of their children is not too fixed? And, following from these first two points, a society which fills its various leadership positions, politically, economically and socially, with the most suitable candidates regardless of origin?

The promotion of social mobility, as opposed to more equal incomes, as the main highway to social justice in rich democracies is now one of the least contentious issues in British politics, loudly supported by both the centre-left and centre-right. The Social Mobility Commission is a highly effective quasi-governmental think tank that keeps the issue in the public eye with regular reports on the social rigidities of British society. The 'life chances' agenda to boost the prospects of people from relatively deprived backgrounds was enthusiastically backed by David Cameron and then Theresa May.

Yet progress in this area is hard to measure and easy to discredit. The cynics always seem to be right about social mobility and meritocracy. Movements at the elite level such as the decline of state-school students at Oxbridge in the 1980s or, more recently, the political prominence of a few old Etonians, can attract all the attention while often disguising more profound shifts below the surface.

And because social mobility, in particular, is such a complex phenomenon it is hard to design effective policy measures to promote it. Everything seems either too small, such as the Office for Fair Access trying to increase the number of poorer students in elite universities and the Social Mobility Commission trying to prevent well connected young people monopolising the best internships; or, on the other hand, too big and obvious, such as improving educational standards for poorer pupils.

Social mobility and meritocracy are central to the Anywhere progressive individualist outlook but Somewheres have some cause to feel more ambivalent about them. They are based on the unspoken assumption of an achievement society, and are about ambition and success as well as about fairness. There is nothing wrong with ambition and success—indeed a successful society needs to give a high priority to both principles and the people who pursue them. But what about everyone else?

Advocates of social mobility too rarely pause to consider the effect on those who do not climb the ladder—and, as I have reminded readers several times, half of the population is always, by definition, in the bottom half of the income and cognitive ability spectrum. In a more individualistic and competitive society we are valued, at least in the public sphere, by what we achieve rather than who we are, creating a constant threat of low esteem for the less successful. This is an inevitable aspect of modern life but it sets up a tension with that more egalitarian promise of a citizen's entitlement to security and a decent life—perhaps even to recognition and esteem. ('The workers have struck for fame …', as David Bowie observed.)

As societies become more mobile and less caste or class based so do differences in cognitive ability between people become more salient. Exams and selection by talent are better than inheritance and the old-boy network. And many more people in today's Britain have opportunities that their grandparents could only have dreamt of. But with greater opportunity comes greater exposure to risk. Creating many losers may be impossible to avoid in an achievement society in which you have to earn your place rather than have it assigned to you.

Meritocracy is unassailable in principle but—as Michael Young saw in his famous parable *The Rise of the Meritocracy*—in practice it can legitimise inequality and reduce empathy for the poor. As he wrote:

'The holders of power and possessors of wealth need, in all societies, to have the assurance of the best of moral titles to their fortune. Otherwise no ruling class can rule with the unbound assurance which is the hidden spring of charisma.'[1]

Meritocracy, taken too seriously, is also humiliating and offensive to the majority. As Andrew Marr has written: 'Meritocracy suggests that those who are not at the top—struggling in the middle, or poor and powerless at the bottom—are supposed to understand that this is not their misfortune but what they, too, deserve.'[2] He was writing about the Queen, and one possible reason for the enduring popularity of the monarchy is that it stands outside the system of merit and achievement. It just is.

People on the left should be wary of the extent to which social mobility and meritocracy have become the consensus alternatives to a society with more equal starting points. And people on the right should have doubts about the extent to which, in the interests of fairness, we are forced to blunt the natural desire to promote the interests and success of one's own children. A truly meritocratic and fully mobile society would require a degree of interference in people's choices that would be hard to square with an open, liberal society.

No sensible person is against getting the best-qualified people into the right jobs nor against bright people from whatever background travelling as far as their talents will take them. But listening to the people from Anywhere talk about social mobility (as they do a great deal) it often sounds like the upwardly mobile insisting that everyone should become more or less like them. Not only is that logically impossible—the room at the top of a labour market is finite—it also presents a very narrow vision of what a good and successful life entails.

And when politicians talk about social mobility as an unqualified good they often seem not to understand the costs and trade-offs involved. Human beings are group creatures and the upwardly mobile, like the immigrant, voluntarily relinquish the security of the group for the advantages of belonging to a higher social class, or in the case of the immigrant, to a richer, more successful country. Politicians tend to look past these group attachments and describe a frictionless society of individuals moving up the social hierarchy thanks to hard work or ability.

They also pay too little attention to one of the central conundrums of societies like Britain: how can we achieve an open, mobile society—and elite—while continuing to value meaningful, in other words relatively stable, communities and without casting a shadow of failure over those who do not or cannot move up and out.

If everyone could have a higher-status career then this problem would obviously not exist, but that is not possible and in any case there are millions of basic jobs that will always need doing—in care, retail, transport, cleaning, construction and so on. Relatively open immigration is one way to fill the jobs but at the cost of an alienated indigenous working class.

The tearing down of prejudice and unjustified hierarchy also means the end of the stable, class-bound, pre-achievement society that many people found comfortable. As settled, group-based identities have given way to more individual and mobile experiences of the journey through life, the promise of greater freedom has brought with it greater responsibility for one's own destiny. Stronger class identities in the past provided some protection from feelings of personal failure—people could understand their relative lack of success as a function of their position in the social hierarchy.

Today, the loosening and reshuffling of the class system, the emergence of a larger suburban 'middle' with fuzzy boundaries, the rapid expansion of higher education and the shrinkage of the manual working class has exposed people more directly to status competition.

Only about 25 per cent of jobs in the main class categorisation are described as routine or semi-routine, although depending on how the question is asked, up to half of the population still self-identity as working class.[3]

The disappearance of a distinctive industrial working class culture of factory villages and large council estates, and a way of life that went with it, is regretted by some and welcomed by others. It was a narrow world of restricted opportunity but also of psychological protection. When almost everyone in your class at school went on to do similar basic jobs there was less reason to feel demoralised, there was comfort in numbers. Removal of that comfort must be one of the reasons behind the big increase in stress and depression in modern Britain.[4]

The pervasive assumption, if not reality, of meritocracy and upward mobility means people are more likely to compare their own lives unfavourably with those of the rich and successful in their societies rather than those just above or below them. The famous 'relative deprivation' thesis—the idea that people compare their incomes and status only with those one or two rungs up or down the ladder from them—has had its day thanks to the transparency of the networked society and the naïve egalitarianism of the education system which encourages the notion that every school child can be whatever he or she wants to be.

The same phenomenon is starting to drive global migration too. Ambitious and able young people in poor countries used to imagine how they would clamber to the top of their societies, now they are just as likely to imagine how they can escape across the oceans to the societies like ours that flaunt their attractions through the global media.

What is Actually Happening on Mobility?

We ask too much of social mobility and meritocracy while shying away from some of the hard solutions it suggests (closing down private schools? 100 per cent inheritance tax?). It has become for almost all politicians like the pious references to socialism in the Sunday speeches of the trade union leaders of the past. Unpicking the 'knot of preferment and privilege that has built up over generations' (as Clare Foges puts it) is a big task.[5] And it would be good to know that we are making at least a little progress in the right direction.

Yet the establishment consensus in recent years is that social mobility has stopped and needs to be re-started—David Cameron and Theresa May's 'life chances' agenda is partly a response to this analysis. The life chances agenda is valid, and politically necessary for Conservatives, who are still regarded as the party of the rich, but the idea of the 'end of mobility' is not true and contributes to the idea that politics doesn't change anything, that Britain is a static society run by an unchanging elite, and that huge increases in spending on education and reducing child poverty have had no effect on relative life chances.

The end of mobility thesis was established in the public mind by a 2005 LSE paper, funded and publicised by the Sutton Trust (another effective social mobility think tank) which found a decline in upward mobility between the cohort of children born in 1958 and those born in 1970. The paper attributed this fall to growing income inequality in the 1980s and the expansion of higher education being monopolised by the better off.[6]

Social mobility is not only hard to measure—and requires good data on income and occupations going back over many decades—it is also conceptually quite complex. The mobility debate overlaps with, and is often conflated with, related but distinct debates about inequality, meritocracy and access to elite jobs. When most people talk about social mobility they mean a society—assuming that ability is still more or less randomly distributed—which allows for able people from poorer backgrounds to rise up the scale and for less competent richer people to fall.

This latter sort of mobility is called 'relative mobility' or zero-sum mobility—for everyone that goes up someone comes down. But there is another kind of 'absolute mobility', or positive-sum mobility, in which people can rise into better jobs without anyone going down. That is because the economic structure can change, as it did rapidly between the 1940s and the 1970s, and continues to do more slowly today, to produce what John Goldthorpe, the leading sociologist in this field, calls more 'room at the top.'[7]

In the 1960s that meant fewer blue collar jobs and more managerial and professional jobs, many in the expanding welfare state. Back in 1950 only about 10 per cent of the population belonged to the professional and managerial class—it is now about one third depending on how you classify it.[8]

There are also two different ways of measuring these two types of mobility—measurement by income over generations and measurement by class/occupation over generations (usually using a seven-class model from 'higher managerial and professional' at the top to 'routine' at the bottom).

Although there is some overlap between these two measurements they can also give strikingly different results. The Sutton Trust study was the work of economists, which stressed the fall-off in mobility as measured by income between the 1958 cohort and the 1970 one. (For both cohorts, a father's income when a child was aged sixteen was compared with the child's earnings when aged thirty.)

But if you look at the actual figures for movement between different income groups two things strike you—first, the difference between the

1958 and 1970 cohort is rather small, surely not big enough to base a claim about a dramatic fall-off in mobility; second, the actual level of movement across the quartiles for both cohorts is high for a country that is said to be so rigid. So, for example, for the 1958ers who were born to fathers in the lowest income quartile only 31 per cent stayed in the lowest quartile and nearly 40 per cent reached the top two quartiles (22 per cent the second, and 17 per cent the first). For the 1970ers the position had deteriorated a little, with 38 per cent of those born into the bottom quartile still there at age thirty, and only 33 per cent graduating to the top two quartiles.

Both sociologists and economists agree that there has been some falling off from the high levels of mobility in the mid-twentieth century, although both record higher continuing levels of mobility—absolute and relative—than most non-experts would expect. At its height the 'total mobility' rate, using the standard seven classes classification system, was about 80 per cent—meaning only 20 per cent stayed in the class they were born into. According to a paper by Goldthorpe and Colin Mills on more recent movement, 65 per cent of sons are in a different class category to their father and most move upwards.

Most economists connect the 1980s slowdown in mobility to the sharp rise in inequality in that decade, which seems logical because as the income spectrum widens you have to get a much better paying job to move up from one quartile to another. Yet this does not show up in the sociologists' occupational analysis, perhaps because a lot of the increase in income inequality was happening within occupations, especially at the top end—a humble conveyancing solicitor versus a top City lawyer. Both forms of analysis are perfectly valid, with income acting as a useful 'sanity check' against the vagaries of occupational groups.

Moreover, lots of other things have been going on—socially and politically—in recent decades that are not necessarily picked up by these big aggregate analyses and could be affecting mobility both for better and worse. There has, for example, been a big increase in women taking higher status jobs and there are now many more female university students than male. This must have had some effect in reducing 'room at the top' for lower income men. 'Feminism has trumped egalitarianism,' the Tory thinker David Willetts concluded a few years ago.[9]

Then there is the effect of the abolition of most grammar schools in the 1960s and 1970s. The sociologists, with their stress on mobility being driven by changes to economic structure, tend to see educational institutions as merely channelers of mobility not creators of it. If grammar schools had not existed in the 1950s people would still have been selected by some mechanism for the new higher status jobs. (Before schools and then universities took over the role, big organisations from the army to large manufacturers acted as mobility 'scouts'—spotting bright people with little education and often propelling them right to the top.)

Moreover, sociologists point out that grammar schools only ever educated about 15 per cent of the age cohort and were middle-class dominated except in heavily working-class areas like South Yorkshire. (Fewer than 20 per cent of the grammar school intake were from the manual working class and once there they badly lagged their middle class peers.)

Both left and right have invested too much significance in grammar schools. It is probably true that they did help to lift a few people from close to the bottom to the very top and the loss of their rigorous, academic ethos was almost certainly a factor behind the fall off in state school representation at Oxbridge in the 1980s. But since the abolition of most grammar schools most parts of the elite have become more not less porous.

A final complicating factor may be the arrival in the latter part of the twentieth century of a more democratic, egalitarian consciousness in which all social classes came to be regarded as in some sense of equal worth, and snobbery towards the working class became illegitimate. That also meant that the old idea of 'bettering yourself' by leaving your working-class roots behind became more morally complex.

(Much has been made of the return of snobbery towards so-called 'chavs'. But the chav is just a kind of modern 'Carry On' film British caricature of the underclass ruffian—like the crafty cockney, the know-all Yorkshireman, the cautious Scotsman or the condescending toff. Few people take it seriously. More interesting is the genuine cultural ambivalence towards Essex Man and Woman who have aspired to become middle class in income while wanting to retain their working-class cultural trappings.)

THE ACHIEVEMENT SOCIETY

Making it into the Elite

Movement into and out of the elite is a somewhat different issue from social mobility in general, though they are often related. The continuing over-representation in politics and certain top professions of the 7 per cent who are educated at private schools is a fact—but that domination has been in decline in recent decades. The continuing private school stranglehold applies now to only a few niches like the senior judiciary (71 per cent), army officers (62 per cent) and leading print journalists (51 per cent).

It is worth recalling, for a bit of perspective, that sixty years ago in 1957 Anthony Eden's Conservative cabinet of eighteen were all public school educated men and ten, including Eden himself, were old Etonians. Move ahead twenty-two years to Margaret Thatcher's first cabinet in 1979 and all but two had attended public school, though the Eton count was down to six. John Major's first cabinet in 1990 was also more than two thirds public school with the Eton quota a mere two.

By contrast David Cameron's first cabinet in 2010 was the first Tory-led cabinet in which over half its members had not gone to public school, twelve out of twenty-two, and he was the sole Etonian. Theresa May's cabinet has an even lower public school representation, just five, but still with one very visible Etonian.

We should, of course, still worry about making our elite more open and representative but it is also worth recording that Britain is a less static society than many people think. Like Tory cabinets, British business has been moving in the right direction: in the late 1980s some 70 per cent of FTSE 100 chief executives were privately educated and today it is just 34 per cent (although that might be partly a function of the internationalisation of the business elite).

According to one paper on class bias in elite jobs—'Introducing the Class Ceiling: Social Mobility and Britain's Elite Occupations' by Daniel Laurison and Sam Friedman—about half of those in elite occupations now come from non professional/managerial backgrounds and the proportion has been growing slightly in recent years.[10] That is not simply a function of more 'room at the top' because the number of elite jobs grows more slowly than the bigger professional class categories—the proportion in such jobs increased from just 14 per cent to 17 per cent between 1980 and 2014.

Some of the more traditional professions such as law, medicine and finance continue to be dominated by children of higher managers and professionals, though only in the case of medicine are slightly more than half from such backgrounds (and nearly 18 per cent are directly from medical backgrounds). In almost all other higher professional jobs less than one third are from higher professional backgrounds with top jobs in IT, engineering and public administration being the most open. The paper does, however, detect some continuing cultural/social bias in the fact that those who enter elite jobs from non-higher professional backgrounds end up earning significantly less, so are presumably not reaching the very top of the tree. (Similarly, for the growing ethnic minority middle class there is evidence of clustering at the bottom of the top, see the Policy Exchange report 'Bittersweet Success' on glass ceilings for ethnic minorities.)[11]

It may indeed be the case that the longer-term trend is for high levels of social mobility—both absolute and relative—to become ever harder to achieve, particularly at the very top and in the long tail at the bottom. Social mobility has always been 'sticky' downwards—once people reach a certain level of wealth, or position, their children tend not to fall back too far; this was true even in the Soviet bloc. When, for example, the big bang swept out some of the old school tie brokers from the City they were more likely to become estate agents than binmen.

And there is today among middle-class and upper-middle class families an unprecedented focus of attention on improving or at least maintaining their own children's position—a kind of 'arms race' in everything from places in top private or state schools to the use of tutors and job internships. And as the group of hard-to-move professional families slowly expands it is likely that there will be less overall movement, at least through relative mobility.

This entrenchment of an elite upper professional class has been reinforced by another factor with the ugly name of 'assortative mating'—meaning educated and successful people marrying each other. People have always tended to marry broadly within their own class but until a generation or two ago male doctors tended to marry female nurses not female doctors, because there were so few of the latter, and businessmen married their secretaries rather than businesswomen for the same reason. Men, in other words married 'down' in educational and status terms and women tended to marry 'up'. Now with the huge increase in women entering higher education and business and the professions over the past forty years graduate professionals overwhelmingly marry other graduate professionals.

One of the consequences of double professional couples is that children from such families have double the contacts and connections that they used to have; mothers with careers can promote the interests of their children as fathers with careers have always done. And of course daughters' interests are now promoted in exactly the same way as sons'.

As Alison Wolf has pointed out in her book *The XX Factor* this shift is neatly reflected among top British politicians: 'The male prime ministers who preceded and followed Mrs Thatcher had "traditional" wives. But then there came a generational shift; and among today's party leaders and rising stars, it is all two-career, high-flying partnerships involving lawyers, designers, journalists, senior civil servants and company directors.'[12] Think of the successful professional women married to Tony Blair, Nick Clegg, Gordon Brown, Ed Miliband, David Cameron and George Osborne.

Stickiness at the top is mirrored at the bottom too with a 'long tail' of social failure—often reproduced over many generations. Social mobility not only has to take on the middle class 'arms race' but also the widely repeated statistic of relative success and failure being established by the age of three. By that age a child from a professional home is said to be almost one year ahead in vocabulary development compared with those from the poorest homes.

Technology and economic openness have wiped out many good working-class jobs and the young men and women who would once have done those jobs often don't feel able to compete in the education race, so more or less drop out in the second or third year of secondary school.

The 'hollowing out' of the labour market, as discussed in the last chapter, with fewer middle status jobs as a stepping-stone to higher status ones, must also have had an effect on mobility. John Goldthorpe, the doyen of mobility sociologists, suggests that the decline of manufacturing has not only wiped out a big band of middle status jobs but it has also reduced the 'shopfloor to boardroom' route to social mobility. You cannot start as a secretary or security guard in the City and end up as a fund manager, or at least not without leaving the company and joining at another level. Another obstacle to higher mobility from below is the requirement that many post-industrial service jobs have for 'soft skills'—the right behavioural traits and personal skills or so-called cultural capital—which tend to go with the right sort of family and upbringing.

Many of the ways that parents can help children, through networks and contacts, cannot, in a liberal society, easily be broken. And the drift towards 'credentialism'—the need for more elaborate qualifications for increasingly basic jobs—helps people at the higher and middle levels of attainment but shuts out many of those among the 40 per cent of young people who still leave school without five decent GCSEs and with fewer vocational/technical options.

Few children from the shrunken working class make it into the elite, and those whose parents reach the top tend not to fall far. But in between Britain seems to have a surprisingly high level of social churn.

Perhaps in the end mobility, like happiness, is best pursued indirectly. Goldthorpe agrees: 'I am sceptical about placing too much emphasis on mobility.'[13] This is not because he supports a rigid social order, but rather because, like Michael Young, he has an old socialist's suspicion of meritocracy and mobility, and worries about the esteem of those left behind. He would prefer, for example, to spend more money sorting out the Neets than pushing the university participation rate to 50 per cent. But there is a dilemma for mobility sceptics like Goldthorpe: a high level of social mobility risks demoralising those left behind, a low level risks demoralising those who should be rising.

There is little doubt that there are still some biases in the selection systems that decide who goes to the top universities or into the best careers. People promoting those they feel comfortable with and those who have the right 'cultural fit' is hard to root out but most big universities and companies are aware of the issue and are trying to do something about it.

Social mobility and meritocracy are never, thankfully, fully obtainable but should always be aimed at—they require a permanent state of frustration and disappointment. But so long as nearly 20 per cent of pupils leave secondary school each year barely able to read or do simple sums the government should have one very big and very simple social mobility policy: improve basic education at the bottom.

And when we think about social mobility we need to be more sensitive to widely different starting points and not always think about the sometimes huge leap to a Russell Group university. Rather than investing in pushing poorer students to university and then into low-grade graduate employment, the government would be better advised to invest more in part time further education and stepping stone para-professional jobs—such as teaching assistants or police support staff—which can give people a second chance to get on a decent career ladder.

And it would be good to hear to some good news on mobility occasionally—there is a surprising amount out there. Why did Theresa May's exceptionally un-public school Tory cabinet not receive more attention?

Somewheres are seldom against aspiration or ambition, especially for those at the bottom of the hourglass. But they are more aware than Anywheres that when success requires moving up and out it tends to cast a shadow over the lives left behind. A good society is not a collection of ladders, as the Anywheres imply. It is, ideally, a circle of mutual interest: the best and brightest still rise to the top but the contribution of all is valued.

Our market culture of individual competition is cushioned in rich welfare democracies by a political culture of equal citizenship, which acts as a constraint on the successful. At the same time in an achievement society it is easier to fail because the possibility of success has been held out to many more people. Yet we now have an achievement society in which too many people feel they cannot achieve and other roles such as housewife or breadwinner have been removed or downgraded. The social mobility agenda with the stress and anxiety it inevitably generates sometimes seems to be at war with the well-being agenda.

A concern of most Somewheres is how to retain dignity and honour in the mundane and middling while living in a world in which status, as well as wealth, is so unevenly distributed. Ambition and the pursuit of success are perfectly decent human impulses but most people know that being valued is more important than being successful.

As the writer Eamonn Callan has put it: 'We unashamedly love unremarkable cats and dogs, mediocre books, trivial jobs, ugly houses with unmemorable yards, in addition to our perfectly ordinary friends, kin and lovers ... The lover may be perfectly aware of the modest value that the beloved has in the larger scheme of things without that thought diminishing love.'

8

WHAT ABOUT THE FAMILY?

The 1960s. It is where it all began in so much of modern Britain and in so much of the Anywhere/Somewhere argument. The value shifts that took root in that decade have had an enormous impact on family life and the roles of women and men within it, and are still reverberating today.

Britain's postwar culture came to be characterised by individualism (shared with the US) which stressed personal freedom and meritocracy combined with social democracy (shared with Europe) which offered the welfare state as a partial replacement for conventional family support.

This had an initially benign expression in the rash of 1960s social reforms that, among other things, completed the 1920s political equalisation of women by providing much greater legal and economic autonomy from men and from the traditional family—easier divorce, more female-friendly employment and greater equality in the jobs market, benefits paid direct to women and later individual taxation of husband and wife. At the same time the arrival of the pill and easier abortion further separated sex from association with family and long-term commitment.

Like other aspects of 1960s liberalisation these reforms to the family, and attendant changes to welfare arrangements, also had less benign consequences. Not only did the private realm of the family decline in prestige and significance as the public realm of work and public life rose, but a significant slice of intellectual and popular culture came to associate the family with the suppression of individual freedom and female subordination.

The ambivalence about the family—a sphere of duty and unconditional attachment—went hand in hand with the decline of religion, but also with the increasing economisation of public life. As Shirley Burggraf pointed out in *The Feminine Economy and Economic Man* orthodox feminists and orthodox economists colluded in their view of the family as a place of diminished value—for the economists because it did not contribute directly to GDP, for the feminists because it prevented women from contributing their full potential in the only sphere that mattered: the male-dominated public sphere.[1]

The traditional male breadwinner family did, of course, limit women's possibilities. This was felt especially harshly by the 'Rosie the Riveter' generation who had worked in demanding and responsible jobs during the Second World War and then after the war were subject to marriage bars in most professional jobs. But the 'traditional' family was not very traditional, in fact it lasted only a few generations. It emerged in the late nineteenth century. Before then both men and women had usually worked in paid roles (though the woman often in the home) and bringing up children was an extended family task with siblings, aunts, cousins, grandparents all playing a role.

Nevertheless those housewives who for much of the twentieth century had been raising children and often holding together communities—or among the middle classes running voluntary organisations—would be surprised to learn that they had been doing nothing of value. They were working for others, expressing traditional 'female altruism'—one of society's main adhesives since the beginning of time.

Whereas the interwar women's movement had seen men and women as different and had pressed for the greater feminisation of society, the postwar movement—the so-called second wave—was uninterested in or even hostile to family life, saw men and women as not only equal but the same and saw equality in the public sphere as the main marker of progress. (The 1970s wages for housework movement was an exception.)

It is technology and economics as much as gender politics that have driven many of these changes to the most intimate relationships in British society. Thanks to the pill women have had more control over their fertility and families are smaller while the decline of heavy manual work and the growth of white collar and part-time jobs that value women's 'soft skills' have also made possible a big expansion of female self-sufficiency. And because of the wider changes in values—more individual autonomy and the greater importance attached to gender equality—there are fewer marriages, far more children born and raised outside the conventional family, and women have become much less dependent on a male breadwinner.

Middle-class women are as likely as their male counterparts to be educationally and professionally successful and thus tend to postpone child-bearing for as long as possible. And lower income women can be supported by the state if they want to have children without a permanent partner. (In 1970 the proportion of women with young children who worked full time was about 18 per cent and only about 12 per cent of women overall worked in professional jobs. Today both proportions have risen to about one third.)[2]

Many of these cultural changes and public policy reforms over the past two generations have made Britain a far better place, and not just for women. Fewer people are locked in failed marriages, women can bring up children on their own without stigma if they have to, and the public sphere of work and public life now has much greater access to the brains and talents of the female half of the population. Women without family responsibilities are now more or less completely equal to men in education and the workplace, indeed highly educated women increasingly outperform them in both.

Yet so much of the emphasis has been on greater autonomy for women, and the central importance of work outside the home, that we have lost sight of an equally important goal: how to create new forms of mutually beneficial inter-dependence between men and women in an era of equality between the sexes, and how to preserve the two-parent family, so far as possible, in an era of greater freedom.[3]

We are not doing very well on either score. There are plenty of exhausted women who are struggling to combine childrearing and paid work, most with a partner, many without. And though it is hard to detect a generalised backlash among men in response to the greater autonomy and equality of women—a 2016 Fawcett Society survey found a higher proportion of men (86 per cent) than women (81 per cent) supported equal opportunity for women[4]—there are plenty of angry men who feel discarded by the changes to family life. The internet and comments sections of newspapers buzz with male discontent. (It is not a discontent, however, that is taken seriously by the mainstream media.)

And the overall changes to the family have been little short of revolutionary in the past forty years, especially for people in the bottom half of the income spectrum. Here are some of the new realities.

The proportion of households headed by a lone parent (90 per cent of whom are women) was just 8 per cent in 1970, it is now about 25 per cent (29 per cent in England and Wales).[5] The proportion of lone parent families doubled between 1971 and 1991 and continued to rise well into the 2000s, since when it has plateaued. The early increase is associated with divorce (especially the Divorce Law Reform Act of 1969) but after 1985 there was a big increase in the number of never-married mothers or, in most cases, mothers who had experienced the breakdown of cohabiting relationships. In fact the proportion of births that took place outside marriage doubled in just sixteen years from 1985 to 2001 from 19 per cent to 40 per cent (many of them would have been to cohabiting parents).

Lone parents are not a homogeneous group but they tend to be poorer than the average. The number of lone parents in work has risen in recent years to nearly 60 per cent but it is also possible to get a decent level of welfare support staying at home. Indeed, New Labour introduced new benefits for lone parents declaring that all family forms were equally valid, reversing the hostile rhetoric of the Conservatives towards single mothers.

The prevalence of cohabitation increased rapidly in the 1980s and 1990s and the percentage of births to cohabiting couples rose from just 10 per cent in 1986 to one third in 2013.[6] Cohabitation is less stable than conventional marriage: of partnerships begun in the 2000–2004 period around one quarter were still cohabiting five years later, with 35 per cent separating and 40 per cent marrying. Cohabiting mothers, like lone mothers, tend to be poorer and younger than married ones.

Conventional two parent marriage is still the most common form of family in which to raise a child—but the proportion of children in such families has fallen from 84 per cent in 1970[7] to just over 60 per cent now with 15 per cent in cohabiting families and 23 per cent in lone parent families (if women born outside the UK were excluded the proportion born to married parents would be below 50 per cent).[8]

About one in three children of married parents will experience parental separation before they are sixteen.[9] The number of marriages ending in divorce has fallen recently but that is largely because the number of marriages has fallen from about 400,000 a year in 1973 to 250,000 now, with the number of divorces remaining at just over 100,000 a year.[10] Looking at all children in today's Britain they have about a 50:50 chance of living with both birth parents when they are sixteen years old.

Marriage is increasingly the preserve of the affluent and the educated. Nearly 80 per cent of married couples live in owner-occupied houses, half of married mothers have a degree and one quarter of married couples attend a religious service at least once a month. The proportions are all significantly lower for cohabiters.[11]

This all points to a far-reaching weakening of the married/two-parent family, especially among poorer Somewheres. Some loosening was an unavoidable, even welcome, consequence of greater equality and autonomy for women but we have far over-shot what is desirable or popular. There has been wide and deep support for more equality between the sexes—as we have seen, with little difference in attitude between men and women—but much less support for the complete abolition of the gender division of labour including the idea of the man as main (but not sole) breadwinner when children are young, as the opinion surveys make clear.

Other unintended consequences of this weakening have included a huge extra public spending bill for the state, millions of children suffering the well-documented negative consequences of not being raised in a stable two parent family, and the demoralisation of many lower income men who no longer have the existential incentive of working to provide for a family.

How do these themes connect to the larger argument of the book about the domination of Anywhere values? The post-traditional family values that emerged powerfully in the 1960s from the vanguard of left-liberal Anywhere thinking trickled down quite quickly to the whole of society. But while upper income Anywheres preached equal status for all forms of childrearing they generally continued to practice relatively orthodox family forms themselves. Conversely, lower income Somewheres talked about the central importrance of the conventional family while often practicing the new family forms.[12]

Women with well-paid professional careers can be independent of men, even when they have children, through paying for many different kinds of support. Men with respected, high status careers do not need family responsibilities to motivate them. The lower income/status Somewhere classes do not have those advantages and end up experiencing much of the damage from the change to family life: single parenthood, divorce and separation, growing up as a child with only one parent. All of the latter is much more likely to be your fate if you are in the bottom half of the income spectrum.

Women are not a single bloc any more than men are and too much of the modern equality movement, and family policy, has been dominated by the concerns of highly educated upper professional Anywhere women. They do not need a reliable, male breadwinner, but are understandably more concerned about the continuing biases at the top of the professional tree and how raising children can interfere with career progression at work. It is thanks to their influence that even a Conservative government, in order to seem modern and liberal, has expended far more time, energy and money on equality at work and childcare funding than on increasing fiscal support for family and marriage or trying to reverse the decline of the two parent family in lower income Britain.

All the main political parties have similar priorities. Here is Caroline Dinenage, a Conservative minister, addressing the UN in March 2016 on female autonomy: 'I agree with Gloria Steinem that, "nothing changes the gender equation more significantly than women's economic freedom." So we have given very high priority to maximising women's life chances in the workplace.'

And in Theresa May's first speech as prime minister she included in her list of injustices to be tackled the fact that 'if you're a woman, you will earn less than a man.' Yet there is only a small gender pay gap for men and women doing the same work, especially for those under forty (as Alison Wolf shows in her book *The XX Factor*). Indeed, since 2009 women working full time aged twenty-two to twenty-nine have been earning more than men. The gap May refers to is only generated by conflating the earnings of women of all ages, occupations and full-

time/part-time status and comparing them with the same male total—
and because many more women work part-time (43 per cent to
13 per cent for men) and are concentrated in some of the lowest paying sectors, such as cleaning and care, the average pay of women is still
nearly 20 per cent less per hour than men. And to the extent that the
gender pay gap for full time employees persists—it was 9.4 per cent
in 2015—it is mainly because men and women are concentrated in
different sectors of the labour market.[13]

Another reason for the domination of Anywhere priorities in family
policy is that the mix of feminism (in its many varieties) and individualism are quintessential 1960s liberal baby boomer values and the liberal
baby boomer generation now dominates British society and politics.
But Somewhere interests and preferences cannot usually be completely
suppressed, as we have seen in other chapters. And there is some evidence in family policy, as elsewhere, of a 'Saffy effect'—a more sceptical and selective approach to baby boomer liberalism from the next
generation (the name taken from the conservative daughter in the
television comedy *Absolutely Fabulous*). As we shall see later younger
women appear to be placing a greater value on domesticity and the
private realm, especially in lower income groups.

A final introductory observation. Anywhere liberalism has evolved
in family policy, as in some other areas, from being a generational
interest to being a class interest. In the 1960s and 1970s resistance to
authority and tradition in the family was widely shared by young people across all classes. But more recently the focus on career equality
and the downplaying of the private sphere reflects more the interests
of middle class professional women who work full-time. There is a
strong class slant in the value surveys considered later in this chapter.

More State, Less Family

In Britain and the rest of the developed world the state has hugely
increased its role in, and spending on, families in the past fifty years. This
has gone hand in hand with the big changes to family life, described
above, and a big increase in all forms of care outside the home.

The expansion of the welfare state from the 1970s onwards has
produced a raft of benefits that make it possible to be a single parent—

income support, child tax credit, housing benefit, priority on housing waiting lists—and, as noted, many of these benefits were increased when Labour came to power in 1997 (income support for a lone parent with two children under the age of eleven was a third higher at the end of 2002 than in 1997).

The state is, indeed, increasingly a welfare state. In 2014/15 welfare, including pensions (which counts for half), accounted for £258 billion, or 35 per cent of public spending—a total and a proportion that continues to rise, even during a period of austerity.[14] If you add the NHS and education to that total it would come to close to two thirds of all public spending. It is complex to calculate exactly how much of that goes today on supporting the family and by what factor it has increased over recent decades. But the Relationships Foundation has calculated that just the cost of family breakdown—the various extra costs the state has to take on to support single parents and managing the fall-out from relationship breakdown—is now £48 billion a year, up from £37bn in 2009.[15]

Some of this spending on family welfare is necessary to support lower paid and single parents and to achieve the ambition of reducing child poverty. But the way it is currently structured encourages welfare dependency (with very high financial penalties as benefits are reduced when people start work or increase their hours) and often makes it financially rational not (openly) to form a family unit at all.

Around half of lone parent households (to repeat, nine out of ten are headed by mothers) are workless, compared with less then 10 per cent of couple households.[16] About 60 per cent of single parent households receive housing benefit (most are tenants), compared with 10 per cent of couple households. But the various benefits (Job Seeker's Allowance, income support and tax credits) fall sharply for single mothers who admit to cohabiting—part of the so-called 'couple penalty'—thus creating a strong incentive not to formalise new permanent and supportive relationships. For a couple with one child the difference can be as much as £7,100 a year.

And if a couple with children admit to living together extra earnings from work are subject to a discouragingly high marginal tax rate of at least 75 per cent as tax credits and housing benefit are withdrawn, the highest such rate in the world (though the introduction of the new

Universal Credit system promises to reduce it somewhat). So tax credits by no means compensate for the fact that, unusually for rich countries, the income tax system takes no account of family responsibilities—and about 60 per cent of families with dependent children don't even receive tax credits.

Britain has also increased spending rapidly on formal childcare outside the home—it is now the second highest spender in the OECD—despite the fact that the cost to the state of subsidising pre-school childcare far outweighs tax receipts from a second earner and the overwhelming preference of most women with young children is to keep childcare as far as possible within the family. In the most recent childcare initiative the government is proposing that from September 2017 working parents of three and four year olds will receive thirty hours of free childcare a week, thirty-eight weeks a year. As the IFS put it recently: 'We still lack a proper rationale and evidence base for the more than £7 billion a year of public money that is now spent on childcare.'[17]

Most of the changes described above are reasonable, usually desirable, when taken individually, but as in other areas of public policy, the cumulative effect has produced outcomes that hardly anyone would have chosen—especially for children. And once policies and payment streams are established it becomes difficult to reverse them, even if they come to make the problem worse. Who is against supporting a struggling single mum?

A more individualistic society has led to a bigger, more intrusive state as the family and, more intangibly, the community have weakened. And one of the main reasons for that is that so much of the care work that used to be done for the old, the sick and the young within the family is now done outside it by the state-funded NHS, by state-funded carers or state subsidised child carers. Many women are now performing tasks in the public realm of the welfare state that their grandmothers would have carried out unpaid in the private realm of the family.

Much of that is a necessary development when most women now want to work outside the home, at least when their children are school age, and few families can, in any case, survive comfortably from the man's income alone.

But it is the form and the extent of work outside the home that is at issue and the behaviours and dependencies that are encouraged and discouraged by the patterns of welfare spending. In Britain's case this spending has not caused the decline of the two parent family but it has certainly reinforced it, and has in part rested on a questionable Anywhere assumption about identical male and female life goals and a shared desire for full time work outside the home even while raising children. In fact according to a British Social Attitudes survey of 2012 only 5 per cent of people (men and women) think a woman should work full-time when she has a child under school age (and only 28 per cent back full time work when the child is of school age).[18]

But thanks in part to those Anywhere assumptions, Britain has evolved one of the most family-unfriendly tax and benefit regimes in the developed world. The present system, unlike those in almost all other rich democracies, includes almost no direct support for marriage (or cohabitation) and has a particular bias against single earner couple households.

Moreover, too much spending attempts to pick up the pieces from the failure to form stable relationships rather than supporting the family unit in the first place (see that Relationships Foundation estimate of £48 billion). Of course relationships will continue to fail whatever the incentives provided by the tax and benefit system, but the level of relationship failure (both marriage and cohabitation) tends to be much higher in lower income households and it is not unreasonable to assume that arguments over money often play a role in exacerbating the situation. Almost half of pre-school children from low-income households (bottom 20 per cent) do not live with both parents compared with one in fourteen in better off households (top 20 per cent), according to Samantha Callan of the Centre for Social Justice, drawing on evidence from the Understanding Society database.[19]

Cultural and policy changes have weakened and loosened the family unit as one would expect in a more individualistic, less tradition bound society that places a high value on male-female equality, yet the family continues to be the central source of care, support and general human welfare—especially for the dependent young and old.

In the 1960s and 1970s the extended family appeared to be in decline but in recent decades grandparents have been playing an increasingly important role in childcare—nearly two thirds of grandparents help with grandchildren and spend almost ten hours a week doing so. This, incidentally, suggests that most families are less geographically mobile than is often assumed by mobile Anywheres.

It is now widely accepted that life outcomes for children are far better on average in married, two parent families than single-parent ones or even cohabiting ones[20]—though cause and effect is hard to untangle and it is often argued that the people who choose to get married are those who tend to be more affluent and successful and more conscientious parents. In any case, the short-term trauma of a break up for children and the longer term negative effects on psychological well-being and educational attainment are well documented.

The first few years of life tend to set patterns that last a lifetime and a stable, loving home is usually essential for cognitive and emotional development. This can be provided by one loving parent but is harder to achieve.

Childcare can provide a substitute for care in the home, but it is well established that spending long hours in institutionalised care has a damaging impact on very young children—unless they are from particularly deprived backgrounds or the quality of the childcare is very high.[21]

Some of this evidence is, of course, contested, and evidence for slightly older children is more positive. Yet seldom are the needs of babies and children heard in the policy argument. This is an emotional debate with powerful vested interests on the side of the status quo, while the arguments and facts I am presenting are generally at the margin of public debate supported by religious groups and mothers organisations that are seen as old-fashioned if not downright cranky.

Revising the current Anywhere-led family and welfare system will encounter resistance. But a few relatively minor changes to the tax and benefit system could help to counter the current biases against the conventional family, changes that would better reflect majority female preferences, produce more stable environments for young children to grow up in, and even save the state money.

According to Care (the Christian research body that analyses family economics) families now bear a significantly greater share of the income tax burden than they did in 1990. And although the British tax system is not more burdensome in general than that of other developed countries, it does place a particularly heavy burden on traditional one earner, two parent families on middle incomes—for a one earner family with two children in 2014 the tax burden was 25 per cent greater than the OECD average. A single earner family on a gross income of £30,000 pays a full £2,000 more in tax every year than a dual income family (with two equal earners) in part because the non-working adult in the single earner household cannot transfer their tax allowance to the worker.[22]

The UK has a mixed system, in which entitlement to means-tested benefits and tax credits is assessed on joint income while liability to income tax and National Insurance contributions is assessed on individual income. But how did we get to a situation where family responsibilities, and the extra cost of raising children, are not recognised at all in the income tax system, with means-tested tax credits introduced to compensate poorer families?

Independent taxation of husbands and wives was introduced in 1990 to give people privacy and independence in tax matters. So far so uncontroversial. It had been proposed to introduce, at the same time, a system of transferable tax allowances between married couples to replace the Married Man's Tax Allowance, introduced in the 1960s, which was 50 per cent higher than a single person's allowance. This never happened and instead a less generous Married Couples Allowance was introduced, which was gradually reduced in value by successive Tory chancellors and then finally abolished by Gordon Brown in 2000.

When the income tax system ceased to take account of family responsibilities the number of children living in poverty increased sharply. As we have seen tax credits were introduced partly to deal with this problem but this leaves those very high marginal tax rates as people try to better themselves; it also undermines the privacy point of individual taxation of husbands and wives as couples claiming tax credits have to complete a joint return.

In a two parent family with children a given amount of income has to be spread around several more people than in a single person or childless couple household. Yet the tax system does not permit the earnings (from one or both parents) to go further by allowing personal allowances—the amount you can earn before paying any tax at all, currently £11,500—to be pooled between parents of children. A non-working spouse, or a spouse who does not earn up to the £11,500 threshold, cannot transfer what is left of their allowance to the working spouse, as they can in most developed countries (or some variation of that practice).

Interestingly, this appears to have been Margaret Thatcher's one feminist policy intervention. According to Nigel Lawson, who introduced independent taxation, the transferable allowance did not happen because Margaret Thatcher 'had a pronounced lack of sympathy for mothers who stayed at home to look after their young children rather than going out to work.'[23]

And in the wider society in the 1980s and 1990s there was a big increase in cohabitation instead of marriage and a surge in the number of single parent households. This was the time when, it is said, the right was winning the economic argument but the left was winning the social and cultural argument. It came to be viewed as wrong, at least among Anywheres, to discriminate in favour of any particular form of the family. It was also assumed, as I have already noted, that men and women were not just legally and politically equal but also had the same priorities—with most women wanting to work full time even with young children and to value the public realm above the private one. There is in fact a great deal of evidence to the contrary.

What do Women Want?

British adult women now fall into three broad categories, according to social researcher Catharine Hakim: the work-centred women who give highest priority to their careers, about 15 to 20 per cent of the total (the Anywhere professional women); family-centred women whose lives are devoted to home and family, also about 15 to 20 per cent; and 'adaptive' women whose lives encompass both work and family, who make up 60 to 70 per cent of the population. The latter group tends to place the family before work when children are young and will generally choose part-time work or career breaks.[24]

As sociologist Belinda Brown puts it: 'Rather than prioritise our careers, survey after survey shows we are keen to maintain our lead role in the family and therefore we prioritise part-time work.'[25] Here are a few surveys that support this claim. A Netmums survey in 2006 of 4,000 mothers of young children found that of those working full time, only 12 per cent were entirely happy while 62 per cent of the part-timers were happy with their hours of work. And one third would have chosen to spend all the time looking after their children if they could afford it.[26] That latter figure was also repeated in a 2014 Department for Education survey of 6,393 parents which also found that 57 per cent of mothers would work fewer hours and spend more time with their children if they could afford it.[27] Similarly a Centre for Social Justice survey of 2011 found that 88 per cent of mothers with young children said the main reason for returning to work was financial pressure and a similar proportion said that more should be done to help parents who wish to stay at home.

Netmums also asked 1,300 women what modern feminism meant to them and more than two thirds said that feminism's biggest fight was now to reinstate the value of motherhood. Just under one third were concerned about increasing the number of female politicians.[28]

A British Social Attitudes (BSA) survey found that nearly half of women chose a kinship role as their primary identity, with 49 per cent of respondents giving priority to mother, wife or partner rather than an occupational or more public role.[29]

And a more recent BSA survey in 2012 found that younger women were more likely to have more traditional attitudes to the family, prioritising home and children—closer to their grandmothers than the baby boomer generation in between.[30]

This must all, of course, be seen in the context of a permanent shift away from the conventional male breadwinner model. According to the BSA survey in 1984, 41 per cent of women agreed with the proposition that 'A man's job is to earn money, a woman's job to look after the home and family', compared with just 12 per cent in 2012 (men had almost identical responses).[31] And the big shift of women into the workforce from the 1970s—initially prior to establishing a family and then alongside it—has produced a corresponding support for pro-work values: it is just normal as, in fact, it has been for thousands of years. The number of 'only housewife' women with children has fallen sharply from about half in 1970 to about 10 per cent today (and the proportion for men is just 0.6 per cent).

But what these surveys seem to show is that attachment to different male/female roles did not disappear, as Anywhere policymakers often assume, but they adapted to an era of greater equality and autonomy and opportunity for women—plus the end of the so-called family wage for men. And strong support for domesticity persists. The proportion agreeing that 'Being a housewife is just as fulfilling as working for pay' actually rose slightly from 41 per cent in 1989 to 45 per cent in 2012. And the proportion of women agreeing that 'Watching children grow up is life's greatest joy' has remained at just over 80 per cent for almost three decades.

Moreover there is overwhelming support for what is called the 'modified male breadwinner' position—the man working full-time, the woman part-time when children are young. A BSA survey of 2012 asking about the best way to organise family life found that 68 per cent of women preferred men to have the main breadwinning role with the number even higher when respondents had children. No respondents thought that fathers should take more parental leave than mothers when a child is born. And of married or cohabiting couples with pre-school children only 10 per cent of women are the only or main earner, suggesting that men are still very much playing a provider role.[32]

Another BSA survey in 2012 asked how much people agreed with the statement 'most mothers with young children prefer having a male partner who is the main family earner rather than working full-time themselves'—only 15 per cent of respondents disagreed (and only 1.6 per cent strongly).[33]

Interestingly, there is large and persistent difference between income groups, suggesting domesticity is much less popular among the affluent and educated than among working class women. In a 2006 BSA survey 67 per cent of working class women did not disagree that 'A job is alright, but most women want home and children', compared with just 44 per cent of middle class women.

Moreover, analysis of BSA surveys on these themes by Geoff Dench going back to the early 1980s suggests that the pro-work orientation of women may have peaked in the mid-1990s—just as New Labour came to power, with a raft of measures to encourage more women, including mothers of small children and single mothers, into full-time work.[34]

Yet despite all this evidence much of family policy, under both Labour and Conservatives, appears to be dominated by the assumptions of the 15 to 20 per cent of graduate Anywhere women who place career first. Belinda Brown again: 'It is, of course, important that the women who want to can derive all the status and esteem they want to from the public realm. The problem lies in their tendency to assume that the rest of us want all of that as well. And those of us who attach a higher importance to homes, children and husbands are far less visible than those of us who don't. Worse than that, women in the public realm feel they have a mandate to speak for us on account of their gender. And men with political power believe them because what they say chimes with the male world-view.'[35]

And if the majority of women still prefer a male main breadwinner then male problems in education and employment, especially those of low income males, should be much more central to thinking about families. The average woman has less interest in more women on company boards—desirable though that may be—than in having a supportive and decently earning life partner to raise children with.

Yet most recent social trends favour female advance, not male. As female employment rates have risen from about 50 per cent in the early 1970s to close to 70 per cent today, so male employment rates have fallen from over 92 per cent to 79 per cent in the same time period, with a significant increase in male inactivity. Male and female employment rates could even cross over in the next generation. There is some evidence from the US that higher rates of single parenthood are directly linked to higher male unemployment because there are more men who no longer have a family motivation to work. Single parenthood also seems to create worse outcomes for boys than girls.

Boys trail girls at almost all levels of the education system. Nearly a quarter of boys in the state school system are labeled as having special educational needs. Boys slip further behind girls every year in GCSEs and girls outperform boys in the vast majority of subjects at A level, including further maths, physics and economics—traditionally male domains.

As recently as 1980, 63 per cent of those receiving a degree were male, now one third more girls get university places and 60 per cent of those with a degree in Britain are now women.[36] Women also dominate apprenticeships. And while great efforts are made to encourage women into science and engineering almost nothing is done to try to address the huge female preponderance in teaching, especially at primary level.

Unemployment is persistently higher for men, including among graduates. Public sector employment (about 16 per cent of all jobs) is skewed towards women, with 67 per cent of the workforce female.

Women increasingly dominate in the professions, though less so at the top if they take career breaks to raise a family—a central focus of public policy and Anywhere concern. Graduate women are far more likely than non-graduate women to work full-time and though they can suffer a motherhood penalty, if they cut their hours or go part-time, it has fallen fast in recent years. Women hold half of the top professional and managerial jobs.[37] Law schools are now mostly 50/50 and medical schools are often majority female. Women are also achieving lift-off in politics symbolised by female leaders in Britain and Germany.

Meanwhile with no one to need them lower skilled men swell the ranks of the homeless and those in prison. They also have much higher rates of suicide. Most of these depressing statistics apply in particular to working class whites who more than any other group have lost their place in society and have no encouraging narrative of advance, unlike young women and ethnic minorities.

There are plenty of men who feel some resentment about these trends though the angriest are those who feel themselves victims of a pro-female bias in the family courts. Yet on the whole men have responded with equanimity to the changing position of the sexes in the past fifty years. The often predicted backlash has not materialised, though nor have the 'new men'—happily sharing domestic and care work equally with women—emerged in significant number; most surveys find that women do at least twice as much domestic work as men.

But as Geoff Dench argues in his book *Transforming Men* the greater 'freedom' men have achieved through looser or non-existent family obligations is largely illusory. He argues that men need the civilising impact of family dependents more than women do and that we ignore at our peril the old-fashioned idea that family obligations bring out the best in men. 'I found that (in 2005–2008) just having a wife or girl-friend significantly increases a man's likelihood of having a job. For professional men with interesting, well paid careers the differential is quite small: 98 per cent of male graduates aged 35 to 49 with female companions had jobs compared to 85 per cent without. But for men with no qualifications who may require a family incentive to take a low paid job the differential is much greater: 83 per cent to 50 per cent.'[38]

Supporting Partnerships in an Age of Male-Female Equality

Over the past fifty years Britain has evolved from a society with a quite rigid sexual division of labour, in which men and women occupied segregated realms, to a more flexible form of it. Most women now have a paid job, and most households need them to. But notwithstanding equal opportunity strategies geared to female economic independence most mothers still prioritise family life and prefer not to work too intensively outside the home while raising young children. Indeed most couples would have more children if they could afford to. A *Guardian* survey of 2014 found one third of couples would have more children if it weren't so expensive.[39] An *Economist* survey found the same preference for slightly larger families throughout most of Europe, including in Britain.

The Anywhere assumptions that have dominated government thinking for a generation play down these persistent differences in male and female priorities and tend to see women, even single mothers, as would-be workers who are handicapped by having children.

Moreover, in the pursuit of more equal relations between men and women Anywhere policy tends to see only individuals whereas there is in fact a family unit—and too little thought has been given to how the glue of family life still sticks everyone together, and the more general place of men in the new arrangements. If middle class women are now as financially self-sufficient as men, and many working class women are supported by the state, with benefits and priority in social housing, what is the place for the male provider?

The traditional notion of making men good citizens through family duties has largely disappeared—and anti-social behaviour of various kinds remains overwhelmingly concentrated among sixteen to twenty-four year old males. In fact the assumption of older men, too, being out of step with the times and emotionally backward, has been common in popular culture since the 1990s (consider fictional figures such as David Brent, Alan Partridge and Peter Griffin).

There is no appetite for restoring the traditional breadwinner/housewife model, but, as we have seen, most women are happy to see a male main provider as a useful support rather than an unwelcome boss. Most men, like most women, are not interested in 'patriarchal domination' but in finding the right kind of male-female mutual dependence in a more egalitarian age.

The Anywhere approach to the family is to remain neutral as to whether couples stay together or not but then compensate for family breakdown with various forms of state intervention. Somewhere common sense would prioritise making it easier for couples to stay together in the first place.

So how should the tax and benefit system be adjusted to produce that new kind of interdependence, and a new contract between the family and the state? The most important single measure, as already indicated, is to complete the work of 1990 by introducing fully transferable personal allowances between the married or cohabiting parents of children.

At a stroke this would remove the current tax penalty suffered by single earner couples. It would also go some way to compensating for the 'couple penalty' in the benefit system and help to ensure that couples would be no worse off living together than living separately (or pretending to).

The principle was, in fact, finally accepted in the 2014 Finance Act, but it only allows for the transfer of 10 per cent of an unused tax allowance of £11,500 and it only applies to married couples. There is a case for making it available to cohabiters too, so long as they can prove that they do indeed live together and have done so for more than two years. And also for restricting it only to couples with children.

Marriage advocates argue that couples are far more likely to stay together if married rather than just cohabiting—and it is true that one in eleven married couples separate before their child's fifth birthday compared with one in three unmarried couples. But there is a selection bias here: high-commitment people choose marriage and low-commitment people choose cohabitation. Nevertheless, greater financial benefit and social recognition might nudge more wavering cohabiters to take the leap into marriage, which is still somewhat harder to undo than cohabitation.

Fully transferable tax allowances between couples would be costly, about £5 billion a year (depending on who was entitled). But according to the IFS it would be far more economically progressive than the recent large increases in personal allowances and in some cases would reduce entitlement to tax credits.[40] The planned further increase in the personal allowance to £12,500 will itself cost more than £3 billion. One idea would be to make that next increase only available to couples with children. It might be simpler to just introduce a new personal allowance for all taxpayers with children under eighteen.

A further reform that would reflect more domestic Somewhere priorities against the relentless Anywhere focus on the public realm of work would be to allow mothers (or fathers) the option of spending money earmarked for childcare outside the home on care inside the home instead. Rather than spending £7 billion a year on institutionalised childcare, which forces parents to hand over their children to the care of strangers, mothers should get an allowance for looking after their own children. Several European countries have care allowances that allow mothers and fathers to choose between external daycare and family care. And despite all the current incentives only about one third of pre-school children are in institutionalised childcare.

In recent decades there has been a shift from regarding marriage as an institution for parents to raise children together in a spirit of companionship, to a more individualised conception where the emphasis is on how the emotional and physical needs of the individual are being met. This places big demands on marriage and makes it harder for partnerships to survive infidelity or for relationships to persist in some form—based on tolerance, shared goals and love for children—after separation or divorce. It is estimated that about one third of children in lone parent families never see their father three years after separation.

The state cannot force people to work harder at keeping alive marriages and partnerships when they hit turbulence but it can provide a more supportive financial framework, as described above. It could also help to make relationship education and counselling as commonplace as going to an antenatal class. As Samantha Callan has put it: 'Sustaining relationships over a longer life course is hard, especially if people expect constant emotional fulfilment. The prize lies in helping people to rekindle dormant passions and rediscover each other in the ongoing phases of life, this is where good relationship advice can help.'

The minor reforms above could strengthen two parent families and provide more mothers with the support they want without in any way rolling back the fundamentals of male/female equality. It would also be popular. The Anywhere-dominated world of family policy is likely to be wary that renewed support for conventional family forms would stigmatise other forms of family, or no family at all. But this need not be the case. Women (and men) who choose to eschew family in favour of high status careers could continue to do so, women who choose to have children on their own could continue to do so (though the benefit system, so far as possible, should not discourage them from forming new permanent relationships). And marriage should not be a condition of pooling tax allowances—evidence of having a child together and living together should suffice.

Families are central to a child's decent start in life and we ask too much of the education system to try to equalise life chances when they have already been substantially set by the age of seven. About 80 per cent of difference in educational attainment has nothing to do with school but reflects pupils' home and neighbourhood experiences. What better way to improve social mobility than by strengthening family units so more children have the support of both parents, pooling their resources and energies in the service of their children's progress?

As Belinda Brown points out, revising the assumption that men and women have the same priorities and that gender equality means encouraging men and women to behave in the same way in the public and private spheres could also, paradoxically, boost real equality.

She writes: 'It is seldom acknowledged that high rates of female employment have a negative effect on equality itself. Pushing women into the workforce leads to increased gender segregation and pay differentials. This is because the women who work are no longer those who prioritise their careers, but all of us. And as work is less important to the majority of women than our home life we choose less demanding jobs, go part-time and do not push for promotion. The result is that gender differences increase in the workforce and attempts to achieve workplace equality are set back.'[41]

Historians will argue why it is that Britain in recent years has been so unfriendly to the conventional family and that even Conservative politicians have backed ideas that only a few decades ago belonged to the counter-culture. Maybe it is a combination of our Protestant, individualist traditions—unlike the Catholicism of much of continental Europe—and an unusually powerful lobby of elite Anywhere women, and two-earner professional couples, focused on public sphere equality.

Anywhere and Somewhere women, despite their different priorities, do not always find themselves on opposite sides of the family and equality debate. There is no question that there is a continuing male bias in many areas of business and public life—too many very average men are in positions of authority that they do not deserve because of pushiness, male cultural biases and not having to experience family career-breaks. Most Somewhere women would stand alongside their Anywhere counterparts in wanting these historic biases eliminated, so far as possible, but the Somewhere worldview sees it as one part of a much bigger story of interdependence between the sexes.

The Somewhere adjustment in family policy does not want to turn the clock back on equality. But it does want to replace the narrow focus on career advancement for women at the top with a broader view of women's interests and a more benign environment for family life, what Geoff Dench calls 'equality with pluralism'.

9

A NEW SETTLEMENT

What are the limits to the Anywhere advance? Or, for that matter, the Somewhere backlash? In this final chapter I want to pull together some of the arguments, consider the balance of forces and suggest some ways a new settlement might be arrived at between the two great subterranean value blocs of modern Britain.

And I should stress subterranean. In the last few chapters I may have sometimes slipped into talking about the two value blocs as if they are conscious political entities. Far from it. They are loose, cross-class and cross-party worldviews which are perhaps fleetingly aware of common ground with others when big political choices like the EU vote have to be made.

A new balance of power will mainly mean an Anywhere-dominated political class making more space for Somewhere interests. That in turn will mean greater respect for national citizen protections on the part of business and government. But reducing immigration and making Britain more selectively open to global flows is only one part of the story. A renewal of the domestic social contract is also required—and that means, among other things, more attractive, and better supported, options for those school leavers (mainly Somewhere children) not taking the university path, along with a broader view of social mobility.

Some Anywheres believe that history is on their side and it is just a matter of sitting tight and waiting for the elderly Somewheres to die out.

There are, indeed, powerful liberalising forces at work in rich liberal democracies: affluence, education, mobility can all loosen our attachment to particular places and to each other. The *Economist* journalist Jeremy Cliffe wrote an essay after the 2015 general election titled 'Britain's Cosmopolitan Future' foretelling the 'Londonisation' of Britain—a country, he argued, increasingly shaped by its big cities full of internationally connected young people, with a rapidly expanding higher education sector and a fast growing ethnic minority population.[1]

This was a brave proposition given that more than half of voters had just backed the Conservatives or UKIP, in an apparently rather decisive vote against London-style metropolitan liberalism.

It is certainly true that some social trends, such as the expansion of higher education and greater cultural and economic fluidity, can contribute to the entrenchment of progressive individualism. But there are counter-trends too and none of Cliffe's three forces point as decisively as he thinks towards a cosmopolitan future.

First, younger people do not appear to be consistently following a more Anywhere trajectory in their preferences and priorities. The evidence of some surveys suggest that the generations moving into adulthood around the turn of the century and those, so-called Generation Z, born around that time are both more cautious and small-c conservative than the preceding baby boomers and post-baby boomer generations— though still socially liberal and content with EU membership.[2]

And what about the liberalising effect of mass higher education? On some issues graduate liberalism is pulling the rest of society with it. On many of the litmus test issues for liberalism there has been a significant narrowing of the graduate/non-graduate gap. If you look back to the early 1980s graduates were likely to be 30 or 40 percentage points more liberal than non-graduates. On both homosexuality and gender relations that gap has now shrunk to between 10 and 20 points, with the convergence in a liberal direction. (In 1985 some 65 per cent of non-graduates thought homosexuality was always wrong compared with 27 per cent of graduates. By 2013 non-graduates were down to 18 per cent compared with 7 per cent for graduates.)[3]

But on other issues gaps have remained high and stable. On support for the death penalty, for example, there is still a 30 percentage point gap. In 1989 77 per cent of non-graduates supported it compared with

45 per cent of graduates—that has fallen to 56 per cent versus 27 per cent. And in some other areas, most noticeably welfare, both graduates and non-graduates have become less liberal.

Some people argue that as higher education becomes a less elite experience the relative liberalism of graduates will diminish, diluted by more Somewhere attitudes. There is little evidence of this so far, though if the residential university experience ceases to become the norm it may become more evident. The US history suggests that the liberalising effect can weaken the more 'mass' higher education becomes, especially if it is combined with remaining in one's home town.

And the claim that larger ethnic minority populations have a liberalising effect on the rest of society just seems to be plain wrong. Or rather in the past twenty-five years as both immigration and the ethnic minority share of the population have risen sharply we have seen both a diminution of racial prejudice on the part of the ethnic majority alongside growing opposition to large-scale immigration and a steady increase in 'nostalgia for a past Britain'.

Ethnic minority citizens themselves still tend to the left politically but as minorities become more absorbed into British society there is a gradual shift towards voting along socio-economic lines. The Conservatives' share of the minority vote increased at the 2015 election (through shipped back in 2017), especially amongst the most successful and affluent minorities—above all Indians and Chinese. And there is also a narrower gap than most people realise between minority and majority opinion on wanting to reduce immigration—about 60 per cent versus 80 per cent—and on support for integration.[4]

Moreover, Cliffe overlooks the social conservatism of many minority groups. There is a wide value spectrum within and between Britain's main minority communities but almost all are more religious and more family-centred than the majority, and less likely to hold liberal views about gender relations and homosexuality—especially Muslims from South Asia. Minorities also tend to be less mobile than the white British and even though young ethnic minority Britons are more likely to go to university than their white peers they are also much more likely than whites to continue living at home, so remaining somewhat immune to liberalisation.

Future minority generations are likely to converge gradually on the more liberal consensus of mainstream Britain but may also act as a brake on that liberalism. For instance, religiosity has held relatively steady in London over the past twenty-five years due to the minority increase but has declined sharply in provincial Britain. The rapid growth in the size and visibility of minority Britain is a testament to Anywhere openness yet may end up acting as a kind of Trojan horse for Somewhere values.[5]

Anywhere values became more entrenched in the past twenty-five years partly thanks to the dominance of the baby boomer generation—symbolised by the Bill Clinton presidency in the US and the Tony Blair premiership in Britain. Big city Anywhere liberalism has been part of a so-called 'period effect'.[6]

But that period may now be over. We could be living through a global reassertion of Somewhere interests—the people from the provincial towns and the countryside—who voted for Trump and for Brexit. This is happening elsewhere too, as Francis Fukuyama recently pointed out: 'Putin remains unpopular among more educated voters in big cities such as St Petersburg and Moscow, but has a huge support base in the rest of the country. The same is true of Turkey's president Recep Tayyip Erdogan, who has an enthusiastic support base among the country's conservative lower middle class, or Hungary's Viktor Orbán, who is popular everywhere but in Budapest.'[7]

In post-Brexit Britain Anywheres will remain dominant—and after the inconclusive 2017 election may even be able to dilute or reverse Brexit—but their influence will not go on expanding indefinitely and Somewheres will not conveniently wither away. Anywhere priorities may have quite a strong life-cycle effect, strongest when people are in their twenties and thirties before they have children. As they grow older people tend to shift in a Somewhere direction, as the persistence of the authoritarianism in those British Social Attitudes surveys seems to suggest (with around two thirds of people agreeing, over a thirty year period, that 'young people do not show enough respect for traditional British values'). And as Britain as a whole gradually becomes a somewhat older society—already more than a third of the population is over fifty—there is likely to be a tilt back towards a Somewhere prioritisation of stability and order. We should also bear in mind that Somewheres tend to have larger families than Anywheres.

Pat Dade of the British Values Survey agrees that Anywheres (Pioneers in his value categorisation) will never sweep all before them.

There is an irreducible core of character types who will always prefer familiarity, stability and routine to novelty and change.

This is a key point. Much of this book has been showing how circumstances contribute to attitudes and values—mobility and education helps to shape Anywhere progressive individualism, while rootedness combined with ageing and more straitened circumstances shapes Somewhere decent populism. But as Eric Kaufmann has shown in his study of Brexit voters, referred to in chapter one, authoritarian values (hard and soft) lie partly outside of such broad experiences and have their roots in personality, parenting and maybe even in genes.[8]

Kaufmann looked at the British Election Study sample of 24,000 individuals and found a relatively weak correlation between income and likelihood to vote Remain or Brexit but a very strong one between authoritarianism and the Brexit choice, with only 20 per cent of those most opposed to the death penalty voting Brexit compared with 70 per cent of those most in favour of it. Affluent, educated people who back the death penalty voted Brexit, poorer less well educated people who oppose the death penalty voted Remain.[9]

It is not clear from Dade or Kaufmann just how many people will remain in this more authoritarian group in the future. Nonetheless, it is clear that taking all the counter-trends together the onward march of Anywheres will be slowed over the coming decades.

Cliffe and others misread the centre ground. They look at ironic, mildly anarchic, post-modern, consumerist, under forty urban Britain and see a version of Anywhere Progressive individualism. But they mistake style for substance and underestimate just how mongrel political values can be. Decent populists, even urban ones with fashionable tattoos, are more tolerant of departures from the norm than their parents or grand-parents but they still generally want there to be norms. If you look at the opinion data and listen to what people say I think it is reasonable to conclude that they prefer two parent families that take responsibility for young children and elderly parents; they want to live in stable places with a high level of trust, low level of crime and some degree of neighbourliness; they want responsible businesses that train local people rather than importing cheaper eastern Europeans; they are friendly to individual immigrants but place the interests of fellow members of the local or national club (of all colours and creeds) before outsiders.

Decent populism is more messy and inconsistent than progressive individualism, as one might expect from people who tend to think less about politics. The largest group of decent populists have reservations about the drift of modern liberalism but are not, in the main, illiberal. Or to put it the other way round, they are broadly tolerant, in a live and let live way, but do not value the same goals as liberals. Shorn of the Hard Authoritarians decent populism is a fundamentally mainstream worldview representing a large part of the centre ground of British politics.

Indeed, decent populism is staring at us out of the headlines of modern opinion surveys—as I argued in chapter two. The great liberalisation on issues of race, sexuality and gender now has large majorities at the liberal end of the spectrum—as recently as the early 1980s about 70 per cent of people thought that same-sex relationships were wrong, now almost the same percentage support gay marriage. That shift includes many decent populist Somewheres.

Yet very large majorities also reject mass immigration, place a high value on national citizenship, are hostile to much non-contributory welfare, and do not like modern multiculturalism (at least in its separatist form). It is in this overlapping majority that decent populism is to be found.

Looking back on the New Labour governments, 1997–2010, it is clear that too many decent populists felt their concerns ignored. Tony Blair's governments represented the high-water mark of the belief that globalisation and social liberalism could happily co-exist. He was in many respects a model modern politician who seemed, briefly, to speak for a broad Anywhere–Somewhere coalition, but his popular touch lost out to his Anywhere self-regard.

As New Labour approached power Somewhere anxieties, over crime for example, were respected and addressed (partly thanks to the influence of Labour pollster Philip Gould). But as Blair and his close advisers—almost all liberal baby boomer graduates—grew in confidence their overwhelmingly Anywhere worldview appeared to blinker them. They were unable or unwilling to respond to cultural concerns about immigration and over-rapid change. And even the loss of decent employment for non-graduates seemed of little interest compared to the overwhelming focus on a narrow, university-focused idea of aspiration and social mobility.

Early Blair brilliantly embodied Britain's moderate social democratic consensus in economics but his failure to grasp the importance of socio-cultural politics led to so much of his legacy unraveling—to Scottish nationalism sweeping away Labour north of the border and to Somewhere resentments about immigration and loss of voice leading us out of the EU.

Somewheres are not going Anywhere

All recent governments have been coalitions of Anywhere and Somewhere perspectives. But, as I have argued in several of the preceding chapters, Anywhere preferences and interests have been too dominant in everything from openness to globalisation and the shaping of the knowledge economy, to the dramatic expansion of higher education, and from immigration policy to family policy—even liberal interventionism in foreign policy.

But there have been trends pulling in the other direction too, partly in reaction to Anywhere overshoot. One such trend I called the 'Saffy factor' in which the children of 1960s/1970s bohemians react against the failures of their parents' 'anything goes' generation. Many social pathologies have been in decline in the last twenty years—crime, drug abuse, teenage pregnancy—partly because the proportion of younger people in the population has fallen. These pathologies were not caused by progressive individualism but it has been readier to tolerate them than today's more hard-headed social policy consensus. The 'society is to blame' reflex is still strong in parts of the public sector but it now has to compete with an ethic of personal responsibility and self-help. And in some cases, policy has simply adjusted in the light of the evidence.

The liberalisation of modern societies—and the welcome decline in discrimination—has often gone hand in hand with a more general relaxation of boundaries. This creates a particular problem for some immigrant families from more traditional societies who, as they see it, lose their children to a society that has no boundaries. It may also have helped to increase the size of the alcohol and drug dependent underclass.

Along with the decline in bad discrimination (based on race, gender and class) there has been a decline in good discrimination too—discrimination that helps to reinforce good, virtuous behaviour in everyday life. This can be traced back to the 1960s and the two separate movements that have been too closely entwined ever since. There was the rights revolution for women and minorities that represented a leap forward in human freedom and equality. But there was also a more general 'emancipatory' impulse to reject obligation and tradition that contributed to a surge in those social pathologies that we are only now recovering from thanks, in part, to the 'Saffys'.

Decent populism has also forced a few other retreats and concessions from Anywhere preferences. There has been, for example, a normalisation of the idea of national identity and attachments in recent years, even among the liberal-minded—culminating in the Danny Boyle Olympic celebration of Britain that managed, briefly, to wrap Anywheres and Somewheres in the same union flag. There has also been a much more robust and largely de-racialised debate about immigration and integration—culminating, one could argue, in the general acceptance that UKIP, although representing a sometimes intolerant (now much weakened) strand in British politics, is not actually a racist party. And the fact that reducing immigration has been at the centre of British politics in the past ten years—including some success in cutting numbers from outside the EU after 2010—is thanks to Somewheres constantly telling pollsters they think it is much too high.

Somewhere influence can be felt in other areas too, such as welfare and social policy. We all have a small stake in each others' successes and failures because in rich societies we practice risk-pooling either in compulsory insurance-based systems like France and Germany or more general tax-based, 'common pool' systems like Britain and Sweden. But in the modern state this noble idea of mutual support has, perhaps unavoidably, become smothered in bureaucratic indifference.

The demands of fiscal solidarity have risen in recent decades while the social solidarity instinct seems to have weakened. It is hard to imagine Britain now creating the 1940s welfare state. Indeed, as Britain has become more morally and ethnically diverse and individualistic there has been a growing reluctance to pay into the system and a corresponding slow down in the rate of increase in social spending. (Slightly less than half of taxpayers are actually net contributors.)[10]

Society is still in part a moral community, even if it is looser and less prescriptive than in the past. Most people rightly assume that their fellow citizens have moral agency, though clearly constrained by their background and circumstances. For that reason, Somewheres are comfortable with differentiating between the deserving and less deserving—among highly paid financiers as well as the welfare-dependent—a distinction that often makes Anywheres feel uncomfortable, especially those on the left. The point is not to abolish the distinction but to ensure that it is a fair reflection of today's less judgmental society, and not of the assumptions of fifty years ago.

But as the welfare system has expanded in recent decades, it has increasingly got out of kilter with Somewhere moral intuitions. The system has evolved from one designed to pool risk, through social insurance, to one designed to provide a safety net for poorer households through means testing.[11]

Somewheres tend towards a 'club membership' rather than a 'need' view of welfare, as preferred by many Anywheres (again, particularly those on the left). Somewheres believe welfare should go to those who have paid into the system or who deserve support because of past service or inability to help themselves.

The British welfare system is highly redistributive, even more so than the Swedish, yet it is often experienced as both profligate and miserly. Many taxpayers, especially Somewheres, feel that the current system encourages dependency in others and then provides inadequate support when they need it themselves. When people found themselves briefly dependent on it during the financial crisis they were often shocked to discover that the system they had been paying into all their lives entitled them to just £71.70 a week. Those with savings or a partner in work found their entitlements cut off after six months. Those with good work records received not a penny more than anyone else.

Recent British governments have introduced household welfare caps for the first time. They have also tried to improve work incentives by tightening access to benefits and reducing high marginal tax rates as people come off benefits (with only limited success in the case of the latter). Those measures and the broader consensus in favour of a tougher and more contribution-based social security system owes something to Somewhere preferences. The toughness has certainly been delivered in recent years in the drive to get people into jobs, but not the increase in the contributory element. In fact, the latter has continued to decline and means-testing now covers about two thirds of welfare spending compared with less than one third in 1979.

A few other areas of Somewhere influence are worth mentioning. Crime and punishment policy, for example, continues to be strongly influenced by Somewhere preferences for harsher sentencing and therefore fuller prisons. And the love affair between Somewheres and the monarchy shows no signs of weakening, an affair that has rendered any organised republican movement pointless (and so unable to take advantage of any potential future royal crisis).

There is also the policy conflict between the Department for International Development (DfID) and the Foreign Office—which is a case study in Anywhere dominance, now being gradually reversed. Most people who work for DfID believe their first duty is to the far-away needy rather than to the close at hand. They believe that the survey evidence showing more than half of the public disapproving of the large recent increases in foreign aid is just proof of their bigotry.[12]

DfID has a global, universal vision, it prides itself on not putting national interests first. In contrast with USAID, it disapproves of 'tied aid', so British taxpayers' money isn't even necessarily spent on British-manufactured products such as tents and mosquito nets. This contrasts with the Foreign Office, the role of which is to protect and advance British interests. In recent years its budget has been squeezed, and its analysts and experts sent into retirement and the private sector.

The head of the DfID office in most African countries currently has a larger budget, team, and greater resources than the High Commissioner. Moreover, the DfID representative feels free to act completely independently of the High Commission—something foreigners cannot understand. DfID reached the zenith of its power with the passing into law in 2015 of the requirement to spend 0.7 per cent of GDP on foreign aid. But there are signs that the tide is turning now. A recent government paper on foreign aid stipulates that 25 per cent of it will be spent on non-DfID departments (for example, on helping refugees to settle in the UK).

So, it has not all been one-way traffic, but Anywhere dominance is the main story. Looking back over the past twenty years it is very much easier to list significant policy initiatives that go with the grain of Anywhere thinking and interests (but note, not all the below would be opposed by most Somewheres).

Abolition of the married couples tax allowance; the Human Rights Act; the 2003 decision to open the UK labour market to central and eastern Europeans seven years before necessary; the decision not to proceed with a national ID card scheme; the 2007 decision to support entry of Romania and Bulgaria (despite EU Commission opposition); support for TTIP and further global trade opening; the decision not to intervene in significant takeover deals by foreign companies; gay marriage; the UK reaching the UN target of 0.7 per cent of GDP for foreign aid; official targets for women on boards; the annual increases in fuel duty (until recently); a referendum on proportional representation; an unbalanced devolution settlement with no recognition of English interests; universities being allowed to raise fees to £9,000 and no limit on recruitment; the sharp decline in the Adult Skills budget; the fox hunting ban; big renewable energy subsidies (now scaled back); disproportionate transport and cultural investment in London; an increase in means-testing and further reduction in contribution-based welfare; the military interventions in Iraq, Afghanistan and Libya. The list could be longer.

Giving Somewhere a Voice

Can British politics broker a new settlement between the Anywheres and the Somewheres? There is a lot at stake. If Somewhere interests are not better accommodated into the mainstream then further shocks like the Brexit vote are possible. Brexit was largely an argument between two different teams of the Anywhere-dominated political class whose argument opened a door through which Somewhere voters could charge.

The Brexit vote itself, even after the 2017 election, represents the biggest challenge to Anywhere power, and the Anywhere-dominated parties, for a generation and has already established a new balance between the two value tribes. It will make Britain a little less open and will allow for the reinforcement of national social contracts in employment and welfare. But Britain will remain by both international standards and by comparison with its own recent past a very open country, notwithstanding the hyperbolic accusations of xenophobia and bigotry from disappointed Anywheres.

There will be resistance to the shift. Some sort of stalemate is possible over the coming years, a different version of Britain in the 1960s and 1970s when neither organised labour nor the establishment were strong enough to prevail until the election of the Thatcher government in 1979.

The May government prior to the 2017 election had shown in its embrace of Brexit and some of its other actions and rhetoric that it was more open to Somewhere attitudes than any government for decades. The 2017 Conservative manifesto was one attempt to shape a new Anywhere–Somewhere settlement, though tarnished by the poor election result.

I now want to look at some of the new settlement policy ideas that any government might consider. But it should also be noted that there continue to be large areas of agreement across both class and value divides on, for example, the desirability of reducing inequality, of increasing the supply of affordable housing particularly in London and the south east, of easing the crisis in social care for the elderly—even if the agreement is largely about ends not means.

Under both the Coalition government and the subsequent Cameron Conservative government there was also a realisation that the relentless focus on upward social mobility via expanding higher education was leaving nearly half of all school leavers without good enough options. This was reflected in George Osborne's living wage policy and the apprenticeship levy. I propose a big further push to increase public prestige and state subsidy behind the two non-university routes of further technical education and apprenticeships.

Cultural differences are less easily reconciled than material ones in the two Britains, but the dividing line between the two is often fuzzy.[13] This is not a detailed policy map, and some of the ideas below have already been mentioned earlier, but here are some proposals divided into three groupings: voice, the national and society.

First, Voice. Rhetoric and policy symbolism are obviously vital in politics. Theresa May's use of the phrase 'working class' and her 'Citizens of Nowhere' reprimand to Global Villagers (both in her speech to the Conservative party conference in October 2016) were noted by both sides of the value divide. In retrospect one of the mistakes of New Labour was to celebrate change so uncritically. Of course change is ceaseless, it is one of the things that most of us do not like about human existence. Politics is about managing change, most of which emerges unintended and unshaped by human agency. People are more likely to accept it if they feel that their leaders share their cautious 'change is loss' sentiments and, more generally, if they can hear their leaders expressing sentiments that chime with their own.

As Karen Stenner and Eric Kaufmann advise on the narrower issue of rapid ethnic change: if you want people to accept it slow the pace of that change so far as possible and stress continuity and commonality between groups, not the diversity that makes people feel uneasy. This, incidentally, points to an identity paradox at the heart of Somewhere power. That power was emphatically expressed in Britain and the US in 2016 through the stirring of a semi-conscious majority identity politics yet conventional identity politics is the enemy of social solidarity and the communitarian aspirations of the Somewhere worldview.

That worldview is by no means unrepresented in our public culture. Parts of the tabloid media (including Britain's two highest circulation newspapers, the *Daily Mail* and the *Sun*) reflect it in some way. And today's politicians track opinion polls and focus groups far more closely than previous generations. But in much of mainstream politics and culture Anywhere views prevail and Somewhere values are often cruelly caricatured. (Just spend a week listening to BBC Radio 4, especially the comedy shows.) Some Anywheres had been feeling that the boot is on the other foot after the Brexit vote, thanks in part to the May government's unfavourable focus on metropolitan elites.

How can decent populism be given more outlets? Everything that falls under the loose heading of 'localism'—from increasing the power and status of local government, to regional government and mayors—can help to give people more of a sense of control and agency especially in areas of decline where a sense of failure can be contagious. The small scale and particular is what matters to most people. Politics should build up where possible from the affections that people have for their localities. (It should perhaps start with naming places with their historic and popular names. According to Maurice Glasman a Labour party survey discovered that about two thirds of the population misname the places they live, having failed to keep up with multiple local government reorganisations.)

More stress on the local means less stress on London. It also means less stress on big prestige projects and more on dealing with, say, local transport bottlenecks—a politics of small steps rather than grand gestures. I mentioned in chapter six the poor economic links between the peripheral towns around Manchester, Sheffield and Leeds, some of which have lost their industries but do not have the transport links to deliver their inhabitants quickly to those relatively buoyant urban centres. The HS3 project is supposed to deal with this at some point in the future but it is a far more important national priority than the HS2 high speed link between Manchester and London, which many people think will merely reinforce the dominance of the capital. More will be spent on London's £4.6 billion Crossrail project 2016–2021 than on all transport projects in the North in the same period.[14]

If place is central to the more rooted Somewhere worldview, it is also increasingly important to a section of Anywhere opinion through the post-material stress on the environment. Somewhere rootedness and Anywhere green sensibility is one important bridge across the great divide.

Another bridge may be a mutual interest in political reform. Compulsory voting would force political parties to focus less narrowly on swing seats and demographic groups that vote heavily. Proportional representation is a favourite subject of a sub-section of the Anywhere political class but it may also be a route to a better balance of representation between Anywhere and Somewhere interests. Legitimate populism (as well as less legitimate) that is smothered in the big parties can find an outlet in small parties like UKIP which deserve to have higher political representation in parliament and even the possibility of a role in coalition governments. As I described in chapter three, experience on the continent suggests that this usually helps to domesticate and moderate populist party views—it turns trolls into Somewhere politicians.

Next, the National. Moderate nationalism is the localism of a more globalised world, and is the means to exercise some democratic control over that process. Notwithstanding the small but slowly growing number of cosmopolitans in rich societies the loyalties that succeed national solidarity are likely to be narrower and more tribal than today's moderate nationalism, so it is well worth preserving.

The Brexit vote was in part a revolt against the erosion of national fellow citizen favouritism, symbolised by the large inflow of eastern Europeans with instant access to most of the British social state.

A NEW SETTLEMENT

Adjusting Britain's immigration system with minimum economic damage is a delicate undertaking that will take several years. In the longer run, as I argued in chapter five, we need to move to a much clearer distinction between temporary and permanent citizens, thereby allowing the welfare state and a continuing sense of national citizenship to be ring-fenced from the short-term, often more economic-instrumental, flows across the UK's borders.

But there are short-term, partly symbolic, actions that can be taken to reassure people that the country's borders are reasonably secure and we are controlling who is coming and going. This is not just a minor administrative task. In an age of greater migration flows it has become one of the central roles of government—and to increase its status and visibility we need to ostentatiously spend far more on our border functions.

We also need to return to the debate about ID cards and/or a population register. Many people who voted for Brexit have an uneasy sense that the authorities do not know how many people are here or where they are. And they are right. It is time for an overhaul of migration statistics and a much clearer oversight of movement across our borders. We do now have biometric residence permits for some non-EU temporary migrants and, after Brexit, this could be extended to all non-citizens. There is cultural resistance to the 'big brother' aspects of an ID card system for existing citizens, but there is even greater fear of social fluidity and free riding. Some sort of population register, plus a card based on a unique person number (maybe an NHS number), for connecting citizenship to entitlement would be popular and achieveable.

As many commentators have agreed we also need a better public services 'ambulance' procedure to hurry extra resources to places where large numbers of newcomers are arriving in order to reduce the sense of immigration-induced congestion (though this is a lot easier said than done).

After we have left the EU it should be possible to give people a stronger sense of the public sector belonging to all British citizens. Public sector employment, except in exceptional circumstances, should be restricted to citizens (with more stringent language and cultural fluency tests for those in customer-facing jobs). Public sector assets, above all public housing, should be reserved for citizens or those who have lived in the country for at least five years (possibly with priority for those with long-standing local roots). And public spending cuts should not apply if they lead to higher immigration, as has been the case when nurse training places are cut. (The May government quite properly removed the 6,000 annual cap on UK doctor training which should reduce the future inflow of foreign doctors, often from much poorer countries.)

In business, public procurement should, so far as possible, support local companies and employment. And, while responsible foreign ownership is often in the interests of British employees, a national interest test should apply to the acquisition of British companies and promises made in the course of a takeover battle (about employment levels, the location of Research and Development facilities and so on) should be legally enforceable.

Finally, Society. The one-sided focus on university education is now, finally, being re-thought. All school leavers should have three decent options: a place at university, at a technical college (preferably some variation on the old polytechnics), or a proper apprenticeship. And all three options should carry the same level of state support.

At present state support for education is more or less uniform up to the age of eighteen (although those who switch to a Further Education college after sixteen get somewhat lower support than those staying on at school). Thereafter it diverges significantly, with more public support going to the children of the affluent and educated. This is unjustifiable and should be changed. There should be the same level of subsidy for all eighteen to twenty-one year olds, whether on recognised apprenticeships, sub-degree technical courses or at university (medical, science and engineering students will require extra subsidy).

Today's university option is straightforward, clearly sign-posted and handsomely subsidised by the state, as a result it is sucking in more young people than is economically or socially desirable. It is true that the switch to loan funding for tuition fees and maintenance has reduced the public subsidy somewhat and shifted some of the cost on to students themselves but it is estimated that 50 per cent of students will not fully repay their loans.

By contrast, studying for an NVQ or an HND at a Further Education college does not attract the same state-supported loan package, though some courses do attract some public funding. And proper apprenticeships, combining on the job and college-based training, are now almost entirely funded by employers who therefore pay as little as they can (apprenticeships are not covered by the living wage legislation).

In future, for the technical route students should simply qualify for the same terms as university students. And apprenticeships, many of which currently pay poverty wages, should receive a wage subsidy from the state of £3,000 a year and an exemption from paying National Insurance for employers.

This reform needs to go hand in hand with more layered and subtle thinking about social mobility, which remains far too focused on the 'all or nothing' journey to a good university. The meaning of mobility will depend, to some extent, on where you start from. If you come from a workless family then getting a reasonably well-paid job with prospects is an important act of social mobility. Or if you have missed out on A levels first time round but are bright and ambitious enough to want a professional career the option to study part-time for, say, a para-legal job should be simple and adequately subsidised.

The best way to promote social mobility is to create more 'room at the top', more well-paid professional jobs—something that is not by and large in the gift of governments. But government can help to create more 'stepping stone' jobs—like teaching assistants, para-police officers—for bright people who did not go to university but want a second chance.

Family policy has been dominated by the interests of two-earner Anywhere couples and so has focused on childcare subsidies and equality at work, but the survey evidence shows that most women do not want to work, either at all or full-time, when their children are young. The restoration of a full recognition of marriage (or cohabitation) in the tax system and supporting women (or in a few cases men) to look after their own children would reduce some of the financial pressures on lower income families and might help more of them to stay together, or encourage them to form family units in the first place. It might also increase the fertility rate—given the evidence of suppressed demand for larger families—and so reduce the need for immigration to keep the workforce stable in the medium to longer run.

Finally, our state and welfare bureaucracy should more clearly enforce the basic moral rules on which there is widespread agreement—such as rewarding effort and contribution. There are many ways in which this might be done, rewarding those who strive to lead healthier lives, for example. The aims of making the welfare system more contribution based, and of reducing the marginal tax rates for people coming off benefits, are both fiendishly difficult to achieve, given all the other things that the system is trying to accomplish. But Duncan O'Leary has proposed making the current pension system a model for reforming working age welfare, with a decent floor provided by the state (not means-tested) and encouragement through the tax system to self-help.[15] Something smaller but simpler to achieve is just to reward claimants with long contribution records, of say more than ten or fifteen years, with fewer hoops to jump through (meetings to attend, forms to fill) in order to receive their benefits.

A rootless, laissez-faire, hyper-individualistic, London-like Britain does not correspond to the way most people live—or want to live. But nor do we wish to give up the wealth and opportunity created by our economically and culturally open societies.

The philosopher Isaiah Berlin said that people generally want many of the same things: security, recognition, love, meaningful work, sufficient wealth and freedom to live a good life in the many ways that can be conceived. And to achieve those things for the greatest number of people requires politics to be informed by aspects of both Anywhere freedom and Somewhere rootedness. They are always in tension but have recently got out of balance in Britain.

Yuval Levin in his book about US politics *The Fractured Republic* argues that the historical moment when it was possible to comfortably combine the two worldviews may have passed.[16] He points to the early post-war decades in the US, when the economy was booming and it was possible for the country to liberalise and become less conformist without feeling disorderly or fractured as it often does today, at least to the many millions who voted for Donald Trump. The same point could perhaps be made about Britain in the mid-1990s just before the new surge of change ushered in by New Labour.

If his pessimism proves correct we could be in for a bumpy ride. Within living memory Europe has experienced dictatorships, pogroms, mass killings and expulsions of minorities. History is unlikely to repeat itself but large-scale political violence could return to the streets of Britain and Europe.

More likely, if London-centric Anywhere interests continue to dominate, we will just gradually become a more fragmented, unpleasant and disaffected country with continuing high levels of population churn and different social and ethnic groups retreating into their parallel lives, while an increasingly shrill political class celebrates the virtues of openness from within its gated communities.

Alternatively we can give Somewhere decent populism a louder voice and use our exit from the EU to return to lower levels of immigration, place more emphasis on stability, and also renew the national social contract, especially in post-school education and employment.

If decent populist sentiments and interests are not better accommodated by our Anywhere dominated society we will experience more Brexit-style political instability and perhaps even sporadic violence if terrorists succeed in spreading panic in the most divided cities of England.

Even in our richer and more mobile society most people are rooted in families and communities, often experience change as loss and feel a hierarchy of attachments and moral obligations to others. Too often in the past generation Anywhere liberalism has looked past, or down upon, such people, but their affinities are not obstacles on the road to the good society, they are one of its foundation stones.

After the shock of 2016 a happier co-existence is possible. That means the holy grail of politics for the next generation must be the quest for a new, more stable settlement between Anywheres and Somewheres—reconciling the two halves of humanity's political soul.

NOTES

1. THE GREAT DIVIDE

1. Poll for David Goodhart by YouGov, Fieldwork 11/12 January 2011. See Peter Kellner, 'Class Politics', Progress, 20 April 2011, www.progressonline.org.uk/2011/04/20/class-politics/

2. 'Clinton, Trump supporters have starkly different views of a changing nation: 3. Views of the country and feelings about growing diversity', Pew Research Center, www.people-press.org/2016/08/18/3-views-of-the-country-and-feelings-about-growing-diversity

3. 'Tony Blair speech at Blenheim Palace', 1 October 2007, The Office of Tony Blair, www.tonyblairoffice.org/speeches/entry/tony-blair-speech-at-blenheim-palace/

4. Robert Ford and Matthew Goodwin, Revolt on the Right: Explaining Support for the Radical Right in Britain, London: Routledge, 2014.

5. Ludi Simpson and Nissa Finey, 'Understanding Society: How Mobile Are Immigrants After Arriving in the UK?', University of Essex Institute for Social and Economic Research, 2012, https://www.understandingsociety.ac.uk/d/24/Understanding-Society-Findings-2012.pdf?1355227235

6. Eric Kaufmann, 'Trump and Brexit: why it's again not the economy, stupid', LSE British Politics and Policy, 9 November 2016, http://blogs.lse.ac.uk/politicsandpolicy/trump-and-brexit-why-its-again-not-the-economy-stupid/

7. British Social Attitudes survey Libertarian-Authoritarian scale 2014.

8. 'They don't like drugs or gay marriage, and they hate tattoos: Is "Generation Z" the most conservative since WW2?', Mail Online, 15 Sepember 2016, www.dailymail.co.uk/news/article-3790614/They-don-t-like-drugs-gay-marriage-HATE-tattoos-Generation-Z-conservative-WW2.html, based on a survey of 2,000 young people by the brand consultancy Gild.

9. 'Brexit Voters: NOT the Left Behind', Fabian Society, 24 June 2016, http://www.fabians.org.uk/brexit-voters-not-the-left-behind/

10. http://unctad.org/Sections/dite_dir/docs/WIR2013/WIR13_webtab28.xls

11. Jeremy Cliffe, 'Britain's Cosmopolitan Future', a Policy Network paper, May 2015.

12. 'Michael Ignatieff on the lessons for liberals in Nick Clegg's memoir', *Financial Times*, 7 September 2016, https://www.ft.com/content/baee9688-743a-11e6-bf48-b372cdb1043a

13. Mark Leonard, 'It's no again to all things Euro: the rise of the new Eurosceptics', *New Statesman*, 28 February 2014, www.newstatesman.com/2014/02/no-again-all-things-euro

14. *Prospect*, February 2004.

15. David Goodhart, *The British Dream: Successes and Failures of Post-war Immigration*, London: Atlantic Books, 2013.

16. Robert Ford and Philip Cowley (eds), *More Sex, Lies and the Ballot Box*, London: Biteback 2015.

2. ANYWHERES AND SOMEWHERES

1. Sunder Katwala, Jill Rutter and Steve Ballinger, *Disbanding the Tribes: What the Referendum Told us about Britain (and What it Didn't)*, British Future, July 2016.

2. 'How Britain Voted', YouGov, https://yougov.co.uk/news/2016/06/27/how-britain-voted/

3. Ibid. Those who voted leave earning less than £20,000 were only 10 points ahead of those voting leave who earn over £60,000 while nearly 50 points separated those with no qualifications and those with higher degrees: Matthew Goodwin and Oliver Heath, 'Brexit vote explained; poverty, low skills and lack of opportunities', Joseph Rowntree Foundation, 31 August 2016, https://www.jrf.org.uk/report/brexit-vote-explained-poverty-low-skills-and-lack-opportunities

4. Dame Louise Casey, 'The Casey Review: A Review into Opportunity and Integration', December 2016, https://www.gov.uk/government/uploads/system/uploads/attachment_data/file/575973/The_Casey_Review_Report.pdf

5. See for example Marisa Abrajano and Zoltan Hajnal, *White Backlash: Immigration, Race and American Politics*, Princeton, NJ: Princeton University Press, 2015; also Alberto Alesina and Edward Glaeser, *Fighting Poverty in the US and Europe: A World of Difference*, Oxford: Oxford University Press, 2004.

6. Gillian Tett, 'Did Obamacare Help Trump?', *Financial Times*, 2 December

2016. See also http://www.theatlantic.com/politics/ archive/2015/03/support-for-the-affordable-care-act-breaks-down-along-racial-lines/431916/?utm_source=eb

7. Some 77 per cent wanted immigration reduced either 'a little' or 'a lot' in 2013 polling. 'Immigration: A nation divided?', British Social Attitudes Survey 31, 2014, http://bsa.natcen.ac.uk/media/38190/bsa31_immigration.pdf

8. British Socal Attitudes survey (henceforth BSA), 2013. British Social Attitudes data can be found here http://www.britsocat.com/

9. BSA 2013, http://www.britsocat.com/

10. BSA 2013.

11. http://www.worldvaluessurvey.org/

12. Christian Welzel, *Freedom Rising: Human Empowerment and the Quest for Emancipation*, Cambridge: Cambridge University Press, 2013.

13. Jonathan Haidt, *The Righteous Mind: Why Good People are Divided by Politics and Religion*, London: Penguin, 2013.

14. Thomas Sowell, *A Conflict of Visions: Ideologial Origins of Political Struggles*, New York: William Morrow & Co, 1987.

15. Jonathan Haidt, 'The Ethics of Globalism, Nationalism, and Patriotism', Centre for Humans and Nature, Sepember 2016, www.humansandnature.org/the-ethics-of-globalism-nationalism-and-patriotism

16. Karen Stenner, *The Authoritarian Dynamic*, Cambridge: Cambridge University Press, 2005.

17. Other leading British public figures I have heard, or read, expressing universalist views similar to Gus O'Donnell include Shami Chakrabati the former head of the civil liberties group Liberty, Oliver Kamm the *Times* commentator, Jonathan Portes the former senior civil servant and think tanker, Phillipe Legrain the think tanker and EU adviser, Danny Dorling and (the Australian) Peter Singer, both academics, and George Monbiot the environmental campaigner.

18. http://www.bbc.co.uk/news/uk-politics-18519395

19. Jonathan Haidt, 'When and Why Nationalism Beats Globalism', *The American Interest*, 12, 1, (2016), www.the-american-interest.com/2016/07/10/when-and-why-nationalism-beats-globalism/

20. http://www.bsa.natcen.ac.uk/media/39094/bsa33_social-class_v5.pdf

21. Daniel Finkelstein, 'Left and right are dead in our social revolution', *The Times*, 1 July 2015.

22. Mark Lilla, 'The End of Identity Liberalism', *New York Times*, 18 November 2016, http://www.nytimes.com/2016/11/20/opinion/sunday/the-end-of-identity-liberalism.html?_r=0

23. Robert Ford and Philip Cowley (editors), *More Sex, Lies and the Ballot Box*, London: Biteback 2015.

24. Nick Hillman, 'Why do students study so far from home?', *Times Higher Education*, 23 July 2015, https://www.timeshighereducation.com/features/why-do-students-study-so-far-from-home

25. Data from Higher Education Statistics Agency (HESA). 'Rise of the stay-at-home students', *The Guardian*, 12 August 2011, https://www.theguardian.com/money/2011/aug/12/stay-at-home-students; 'Do students who live at home miss out on uni life?', *The Guardian*, 4 September 2013, https://www.theguardian.com/education/mortarboard/2013/sep/04/do-students-who-live-at-home-miss-out

26. Higher Education Statistics Agency (HESA).

27. *European Sociological Review*, http://esr.oxfordjournals.org/content/early/2015/03/05/esr.jcv008.abstract

28. Ludi Simpson and Nissa Finey, 'Understanding Society: How Mobile Are Immigrants After Arriving in the UK?', University of Essex Institute for Social and Economic Research, 2012, https://www.understandingsociety.ac.uk/d/24/Understanding-Society-Findings-2012.pdf?1355227235

29. 'Understanding Society: Waves 1–6, 2009–2015', 8th Edition, http://dx.doi.org/10.5255/UKDA-SN-6614–7

30. 'Understanding Society: Waves 1–5, 2009–2014', 7th Edition. http://dx.doi.org/10.5255/UKDA-SN-6614–7

31. 'Citizenship Survey, 2010–2011', UK Data Service. SN: 7111, http://dx.doi.org/10.5255/UKDA-SN-7111–1

32. All the figures in this section can be found here http://www.britsocat.com/

33. Poll for David Goodhart by YouGov, Fieldwork 11/12 January 2011. See Peter Kellner, 'Class politics', Progress, 20 April 2011, www.progressonline.org.uk/2011/04/20/class-politics/

34. Global Trends 2014: Navigating the new', Ipsos MORI, www.ipsosglobaltrends.com/files/gts_2014_web.pdf

35. *Financial Times*, 10 September 2016.

36. http://cultural-dynamics.co.uk/viewpoints.html

37. British Social Attitudes survey, http://www.britsocat.com/

38. Another indicator of Global Villager views can be found in those BSA surveys that identify people with post-graduate qualifications—which many Global Villagers have—and whose views are almost uniformly at the extreme liberal end of the spectrum.

39. Poll for David Goodhart by YouGov, Fieldwork 11/12 January 2011. See Peter Kellner, 'Class Politics', Progress, 20 April 2011, www.progressonline.org.uk/2011/04/20/class-politics/

40. 'Nostalgia and Tradition', Ipsos MORI Global Trends 2014, www.ipsosglobaltrends.com/nostalgia-and-tradition.html

41. British Social Attitudes data from 2014 and 1986, http://www.brit-socat.com/

3. EUROPEAN POPULISM AND THE CRISIS OF THE LEFT

1. Paul Scheffer, 'Het muliculturele drama', *NRC Handelsblad*, 29 January 2000, http://retro.nrc.nl/W2/Lab/Multicultureel/scheffer.html

2. He went on to write an excellent book in 2007 about the history and dilemmas of immigration and multiculturalism in liberal societies: Paul Scheffer, *Immigrant Nations,* Cambridge: Polity Press, 2011.

3. Alain Tolhurst, 'Next up Nexit? Leader in Dutch polls ahead of their election is demanding his nation quits the EU too', *The Sun*, 12 October 2016, https://www.thesun.co.uk/news/1960403/leader-in-dutch-polls-ahead-of-their-election-is-demanding-his-nation-quits-the-eu-too/

4. Charles Leadbeater, 'The five ways the left can win back the Leavers', *New Statesman*, 8 July 2016, http://www.newstatesman.com/politics/uk/2016/07/five-ways-left-can-win-back-leavers

5. Andrew Marr, 'The Summer's over, so we're back to the battle of holding Britain together', *The Times*, 4 September 2016, www.the-times.co.uk/edition/comment/look-up-from-your-lilo-the-battle-to-hold-britain-together-is-still-raging-2cqdvrls5

6. Richard Hofstadter, 'Everyone is Talking About Populism, But No One Can Define It', in Isaiah Berlin et. al., 'To Define Populism', *Government and Opposition*, 3, 2, April 1968, pp. 137–180, http://onlinelibrary.wiley.com/doi/10.1111/j.1477–7053.1968.tb01332.x/pdf

7. This was essentially the root of the argument after the UK court ruling in early November 2016 that the Government could not start the process of leaving the EU without the approval of Parliament.

8. Krastev, Ivan, 'Between Elite and People: Europe's Black Hole', Open Democracy, 3 August 2016, https://www.opendemocracy.net/global-ization-institutions_government/europe_blackhole_3796.jsp

9. John Lloyd, 'For left-behinders, populists paint a picture of a better future', *Financial Times*, 16 August 2016, https://www.ft.com/content/bbf0f4e0–5d74–11e6-bb77-a121aa8abd95

10. Ed Conway, 'Politicians are to blame for Brexit and Trump', *The Times*, 26 August 2016, www.thetimes.co.uk/past-six-days/2016–08–26/comment/politicians-are-to-blame-for-brexit-and-trump-sx8fmc9pg

11. Cas Mudde, 'The Populist Radical Right: A Pathological Normalcy', *West European Politics*, Vol. 33, Iss. 6, 2010.

12. See Sidney Blumenthal, *The Rise of the Counter Establishment: The Conservative Ascent to Political Power*, New York: Union Square, 2008.

13. https://smithinstitutethinktank.files.wordpress.com/2015/05/who-governs-britain.pdf

14. Julian Baggini, *A Very British Populism*, Counterpoint, 2013, http://counterpoint.uk.com/publications/a-very-british-populism/

15. 'Middle-class university graduates will decide the future of the Labour Party, *New Statesman*, 14 July 2016, http://www.newstatesman.com/politics/staggers/2016/07/middle-class-university-graduates-will-decide-future-labour-party

16. Matt Singh, 'The 2.8 Million Non-Voters Who Delivered Brexit', Bloomberg, 4 July 2016, https://www.bloomberg.com/view/articles/2016-07-04/the-2-8-million-non-voters-who-delivered-brexit

17. Christopher H. Achen and Larry M. Bartels, *Democracy for Realists: Why Elections Do Not Produce Responsive Government*, Princeton, NJ: Princeton University Press, 2016.

18. Michael Lind, 'Insider Nation v. Outsider Nation', April 2016, http://thesmartset.com/insider-nation-v-outsider-nation/

19. Martin Gilens, 'Under the Influence', *Boston Review*, July 2012, http://bostonreview.net/forum/lead-essay-under-influence-martin-gilens

20. Jamie Bartlett, *Radicals*, London: William Heinemann, forthcoming 2017.

21. Ivan Krastev, 'America Hasn't Gone Crazy. It's Just More Like Europe', *New York Times*, 14 April 2016, www.nytimes.com/2016/04/15/opinion/america-hasnt-gone-crazy-its-just-more-like-europe.html

22. US income data has two different sources:
    a. Compares 1999 data to 2012 data. US Bureau of the Census, 'Real Median Household Income in the United States', retrieved from FRED, Federal Reserve Bank of St. Louis, https://fred.stlouisfed.org/series/MEHOINUSA672N
    b. John Coder and Gordon Green, 'Comparing Earnings of White Males by Education for Selected Age Cohorts', Sentier Research, October 2016, www.sentierresearch.com/StatBriefs/Sentier_Income_Trends_WorkingClassWages_1996to2014_Brief_10_05_16.pdf

23. Frank Newport, 'Fewer Americans Identify as Middle Class in Recent Years', Gallup, 28 April 2015, www.gallup.com/poll/182918/fewer-americans-identify-middle-class-recent-years-aspx

24. John Harris, 'Donald Trump supporters are not the bigots the left likes to demonise', *The Guardian*, 13 May 2016, https://www.theguardian.com/commentisfree/2016/may/13/donald-trump-supporters-bigots-left-demonise

25. Almost all counties with the highest proportion of highly educated people saw a sharp increase in support for Hillary Clinton in 2016 and vice versa for counties with the least well educated people, see http://fivethirtyeight.com/features/education-not-income-predicted-who-would-vote-for-trump/

26. See *New York Times*, 9 November 2016, for a report on how one county in Ohio, won by Obama with a 22 per cent margin in 2012, voted Trump with a six-point margin in 2016.

27. YouGov/Policy Exchange/Birkbeck survey August 2016.

28. See Jens Hainmueller and Daniel Hopkins, 'Public Attitudes Toward Immigration', *Annual Review of Political Science*, 2014.

29. http://blogs.lse.ac.uk/politicsandpolicy/trump-and-brexit-why-its-again-not-the-economy-stupid/

30. Ariel Edwards-Levy, 'Nearly half of Trump voters think Whites face a lot of discrimination', Huffington Post, 21 November 2016, http://www.huffingtonpost.com/entry/discrimination-race-religion_us_583 3761ee4b099512f845bba

31. Anne Case and Angus Deaton, 'Rising morbidity and mortality in midlife among white non-Hispanic Americans in the twenty-first century', Proceedings of the National Academy of Sciences of the United States of America, September 2015, http://www.pnas.org/content/112/49/15078.abstract

32. The experimental research consistently suggests that whites prefer more culturally similar immigrants (Western Europeans and Australians for the British). See Peter Kellner 'Why we like migrants but not immigration', YouGov, 2 March 2015, https://yougov.co.uk/news/2015/03/02/why-we-like-migrants-not-immigration/

33. Leonid Bershidsky, 'Elites must either engage populists or lose to them', Bloomberg View, 6 December 2016, https://www.bloomberg.com/view/articles/2016-12-06/elites-must-either-engage-populists-or-lose-to-them

34. Anne-Sylvaine Chassany, 'How France's National Front is winning working-class voters', *Financial Times*, 21 October 2016, https://www.ft.com/content/ad9502f4-8099-11e6-bc52-0c7211ef3198

35. Peter Kellner, 'Labour is not just the party of the working class', *The Guardian*, 31 August 2010, https://www.theguardian.com/commentisfree/2010/aug/31/labour-party-working-class; 'How Britain voted in 2015', Ipsos MORI, 26 August 2015 https://www.ipsos-mori.com/researchpublications/researcharchive/3575/How-Britain-voted-in-2015.aspx?view=wide

36. Tim Bale and Monica Poletti, ESRC Party Members Project (PMP), July 2016, https://esrcpartymembersprojectorg.files.wordpress.com/2016/07/tables-of-labour-selectorate.pdf, last accessed 8 December 2016; 'Graduates in the UK Labour Market: 2013', Office for National Statistics, 19 November 2013, https://www.ons.gov.uk/employmentandlabourmarket/peopleinwork/employmentandemployeetypes/articles/graduatesintheuklabourmarket/2013-11-19; George Arnett, 'UK

became more middle class than working class in 2000, data shows', *The Guardian*, 26 February 2016, https://www.theguardian.com/news/datablog/2016/feb/26/uk-more-middle-class-than-working-class-2000-data

37. Harvey Redgrave, an adviser to Ed Miliband on migration, wrote this in 2016: 'Miliband was conscious of the need to craft a position that spoke to the more socially conservative voters he knew he needed to woo in order to win power (generally hostile to immigration), without alienating his liberal metropolitan base (overwhelmingly pro-immigration). Every policy had to be carefully calibrated, which sometimes meant the final presentation of the position was so heavily caveated and nuanced that the public were left confused.' Harvey Redgrave, 'Migration: A Social Democratic Response', Fabian Society, 13 April 2016, http://www.fabians.org.uk/wp-content/uploads/2016/04/Redgrave_Future-Left_Migration.pdf

38. Poll for David Goodhart by YouGov, Fieldwork 11/12 January 2011. See Peter Kellner, 'Class politics', Progress, 20 April 2011, www.progressonline.org.uk/2011/04/20/class-politics/

39. Patrick Wintour, 'Middle-class voters "more leftwing" than the working-class', *The Guardian*, 26 October 2012, https://www.theguardian.com/politics/2012/oct/26/middle-class-leftwing-working-poll

4. GLOBALISATION, EUROPE AND THE PERSISTENCE OF THE NATIONAL

1. Guido Mingels, 'Global Migration? Actually, The World is Staying Home', *Spiegel Online*, 17 May 2016, www.spiegel.de/international/world/why-global-migration-statistics-do-not-add-up-a-1090736.html

2. Ibid.

3. Dani Rodrik, 'Who Needs the Nation State?', Harvard University and Centre for Economics Policy Research discussion paper, http://drodrik.scholar.harvard.edu/files/dani-rodrik/files/who-needs-the-nation-state.pdf

4. Ivan Krastev, 'Fear and loathing of a world without borders', *Financial Times*, 6 April 2016, https://ft.com/content/328f15da-fa4e-11e5-8f41-df5bda8beb40

5. Alexander Betts and Paul Collier, *Refuge: Transforming a Broken Refugee System*, London, London: Penguin, forthcoming.

6. Thomas L. Friedman, *The World is Flat: The Globalized World in the Twenty-first Century*, Penguin, 2007.

7. Pankaj Ghemawat, 'Distance Still Matters', *Harvard Business Review*, September 2001.

8. 'The World Economy Special Report', *The Economist*, 1 October 2016.

9. Some 10.7 per cent lived on less than $1.90 a day in 2013. 'Overview', The World Bank, www.worldbank.org/en/topic/poverty/overview

10. Adam Corlett, 'Examining an elephant: Globalisation and the lower middle class of the rich world' Resolution Foundation, September 2016, www.resolutionfoundation.org/app/uploads/2016/09/Examining-an-elephant.pdf

11. Ibid., p. 33.

12. Douglas Irwin, *Free Trade Under Fire*, Princeton University Press, 2009.

13. Joao Paulo Pessoa, 'International Competition and Labor Market Adjustment', CEP Discusssion Paper No. 1411, March 2016, http://cep.lse.ac.uk/pubs/download/dp1411.pdf

14. Dani Rodrik, 'Who Needs the Nation State?', Harvard University and Centre for Economics Policy Research discussion paper, http://drodrik.scholar.harvard.edu/files/dani-rodrik/files/who-needs-the-nation-state.pdf

15. Ibid.

16. Barry Eichengreen, 'Spinning Beyond Brexit', *Prospect*, November 2016.

17. Lawrence Summers, 'Voters deserve responsible nationalism not reflex globalism', *Financial Times*, 10 July 2016, https://www.ft.com/content/15598db8-4456-11e6-9b66-0712b3873ae1

18. Hugo Young, *This Blessed Plot: Britain and Europe from Churchill to Blair*, London: Macmillan,1998.

19. Brendan Simms, *Britain's Europe: A Thousand Years of Conflict and Cooperation*, London: Allen Lane, 2016.

20. David Owen, *Europe Restructured: The Eurozone Crisis and the UK Referendum*, London: Methuen, 2012. David Goodhart, 'The Path Not Taken', *Demos Quarterly*, Issue Two April 2014 http://quarterly.demos.co.uk/article/issue-2/the-path-not-taken/

21. Multiple sources:
    a. [EU working age population]
    b. [UK working-age population born in another EU country] Table 1.2, 2015 data, 'Dataset: Population of the United Kingdom by Country of Birth and Nationality', Office for National Statistics, 25 August 2016, https://www.ons.gov.uk/peoplepopulationand-community/populationandmigration/internationalmigration/data-sets/populationoftheunitedkingdombycountryofbirthandnationality
    c. [EU citizens working in low skilled jobs in UK] 'Number and pro-portion of people in employment: by country of birth, national-ity, occupation and industry, ages 16 and over, April 2015 to March 2016', Office for National Statistics, 14 July 2016, https://www.ons.gov.uk/employmentandlabourmarket/peopleinwork/employ-mentandemployeetypes/adhocs/005913numberandproportionof-

peopleinemploymentbycountryofbirthnationalityoccupationandin-dustryages16andoverapril2015tomarch2016, calculated using the Migration Advisory Committee's 2014 definition of low skilled occupations.

   d. [UK citizens abroad] 'The British in Europe—and Vice Versa', Migration Watch UK, https://www.migrationwatchuk.org/briefing-paper/354

22. Ruben Atoyan, et. al., 'Emigration and Its Economic Impact on Eastern Europe', IMF Staff Discussion Note, July 2016, https://www.imf.org/external/pubs/ft/sdn/2016/sdn1607.pdf

23. James Fontanella-Khan, 'Romanians despair that wealthy Britain is taking all their doctors', *Financial Times*, 14 January 2014, https://www.ft.com/content/f4c0b734-7c70–11e3-b514-00144feabdc0

24. United Nations Department of Economic and Social Affairs/Population Division, 'World Population Prospects: The 2015 Revision', United Nations, 2015, https://esa.un.org/unpd/wpp/Download/Standard/Population/

25. Justyna Salamońska and Ettore Recchi, 'Europe between mobility and sedentarism: Patterns of cross-border practices and their consequences for European identification', European University Institute, October 2016, http://cadmus.eui.eu/bitstream/handle/1814/43545/RSCAS_2016_50.pdf?sequence=1

26. Michael Lind, 'The Liberal Roots of Populism', *Demos Quarterly*, Issue 4, Autumn 2014, http://quarterly.demos.co.uk/article/issue-4/liberal-roots-of-populism/

27. 'National identity: Exploring Britishness', British Social Attitudes 31, 2014, http://bsa.natcen.ac.uk/media/38984/bsa31_national_identity.pdf

28. Philip Stephens, 'A return to the world of Hobbes', *Financial Times*, 27 October 2011.

29. David Miller, *Strangers in Our Midst: The Political Philosophy of Immigration*, London: Harvard University Press, 2016.

30. Naoko Shimazu, *Japan, Race and Equality: The Racial Equality Proposal of 1919*, Abingdon: Routledge, 1998.

31. Jonathan Franzen, 'Liking is for cowards. Go with what hurts', *New York Times*, 28 May 2011, http://www.nytimes.com/2011/05/29/opinion/29franzen.html

32. Richard Webber and Trevor Phillips, 'Scotland's many subcultures', *Demos Quarterly*, 18 July 2014, http://quarterly.demos.co.uk/article/issue-3/516/

33. Bonnie Honig, 'The Politics of Public Things: Neoliberalism and the Routine of Privatization', University of Helsinki, 2013, www.helsinki.fi/nofo/NoFo10HONIG.pdf

34. 'Global Citizenship A Growing Sentiment Among Citizens of Emerging Economies: Global Poll', GlobeScan, 27 April 2016, www.globescan.com/news-and-analysis/press-releases/press-releases-2016/383-global-citizenship-a-growing-sentiment-among-citizens-of-emerging-economies-global-poll.html

35. Poll for David Goodhart by YouGov, Fieldwork 11/12 January 2011.

36. 'Nextdoor Launches in Neighbourhoods Across the UK', Nextdoor, 14 September 2016, https://nextdoor.co.uk/press/20160914/

37. Trevor Philips, 'Watching the box in our ethnic boxes', http://www.integrationhub.net/watching-the-box-in-our-ethnic-boxes/

38. Janan Ganesh, 'Boxing's centre of gravity has shifted east', *Financial Times*, 16 September 2016.

5. A FOREIGN COUNTRY?

1. Kwame Anthony Appiah, *The Ethics of Identity*, Princeton, NJ: Princeton, 2005.

2. Michael Walzer, *Spheres of Justice: A Defense of Pluralism and Equality*, New York: Basic Books, 1983, chapter 2.

3. See most recently Ted Cantle and Eric Kaufmann, 'Is segregation on the increase in the UK?', www.opendemocracy.net, 2 November 2016.

4. Office for National Statistics, 'Migration Statistics Quarterly Report: August 2016', 25 August 2016, http://www.ons.gov.uk/peoplepopulationandcommunity/populationandmigration/internationalmigration/bulletins/migrationstatisticsquarterlyreport/august2016

5. For a study of how ethnic minorities view immigration, see Scott Blinder, 'UK Public Opinion Toward Migration: Determinants of Attitudes', Migration Observatory, University of Oxford, 27 May 2011.

6. Sunder Katwala, Jill Rutter and Steve Ballinger, 'What Next After Brexit?,' British Future, August 2016, http://www.britishfuture.org/wp-content/uploads/2016/09/What-next-after-Brexit.pdf

7. NatCen Social Research, 'British Social Attitudes Survey, 31st Edition', 2014.

8. Pew Research Center, 'World Publics Welcome Global Trade—But Not Immigration', 4 October 2007, http://www.pewglobal.org/2007/10/04/world-publics-welcome-global-trade-but-not-immigration/

9. NatCen Social Research, 'British Social Attitudes Survey, 33rd Edition', 2016.

10. Migration Advisory Committee, 'Analysis of the Impacts of Migration', January 2012.

11. *The British Dream: Successes and Failures of Post-war Immigration*, London: Atlantic Books, 2013.

12. 'Britain's immigration paradox', *The Economist*, 8 July 2016.

13. NatCen Social Research, 'British Social Attitudes Survey, 33rd Edition', 2016

14. 'Can We have Trust and Diversity?', Ipsos MORI, 19 January 2004, https://www.ipsos-mori.com/researchpublications/researcharchive/792/Can-We-Have-Trust-And-Diversity-8212-Topline-Results.aspx

15. ONS dataset: 'Population of the United Kingdom by Country of Birth and Nationality', https://www.ons.gov.uk/peoplepopulationandcommunity/populationandmigration/internationalmigration/datasets/populationoftheunitedkingdombycountryofbirthandnationality

16. Shamit Saggar, Richard Norrie, Michelle Bannister and David Goodhart, *Bittersweet Success? Glass ceilings for Britain's ethinc minorities at the top of business and the professions*, Policy Exchange, November 2016, https://policyexchange.org.uk/wp-content/uploads/2016/11/PEXJ5011_Bittersweet_Success_1116_WEB.pdf

17. ONS, 'Migration Statistics Quarterly Report, August 2016', http://www.ons.gov.uk/peoplepopulationandcommunity/populationandmigration/internationalmigration/bulletins/migrationstatisticsquarterlyreport/august2016

18. ONS dataset: 'Population of the United Kingdom by Country of Birth and Nationality', https://www.ons.gov.uk/peoplepopulationandcommunity/populationandmigration/internationalmigration/datasets/populationoftheunitedkingdombycountryofbirthandnationality

19. One insider told me that senior Labour figures knew that arrival estimates were too low but thought the fact that the new arrivals were white and European would mean little friction.

20. Geoffrey Evans and Yekaterina Chzhen, Explaining Voters' Defection from Labour over the 2005–10 Electoral Cycle: Leadership, Economics and the Rising Importance of Immigration', 'https://www.researchgate.net/publication/264638473_Explaining_Voters%27_Defection_from_Labour_over_the_2005–10_Electoral_Cycle_Leadership_Economics_and_the_Rising_Importance_of_Immigration

21. ONS, 'Long-Term International Migration', http://webarchive.nationalarchives.gov.uk/20160105160709/http://www.ons.gov.uk/ons/rel/migration1/long-term-international-migration/index.html

22. ONS, 'Migration Statistics Quarterly Report: August 2016', 25 August 2016 (figure refers to non-EEA nationals), http://www.ons.gov.uk/peoplepopulationandcommunity/populationandmigration/internationalmigration/bulletins/migrationstatisticsquarterlyreport/august2016

23. A community worker from Leicester recently argued to me that the city was well integrated on the grounds that it had experienced no significant race riots.

24. See Geoff Dench, *Minorities in the Open Society*, Transaction Publishers, 1986, which should be a better-known book.

25. Frans Timmermans, 'The EU can help Europeans rediscover the ties that bind us', *New Statesman*, 23 May 2016, http://www.newstatesman.com/politics/staggers/2016/05/eu-can-help-europeans-rediscover-ties-bind-us

26. Dame Louise Casey, 'The Casey Review: A Review into Opportunity and Integration', December 2016, https://www.gov.uk/government/uploads/system/uploads/attachment_data/file/575973/The_Casey_Review_Report.pdf

27. Friendship figures from YouGov, 'Why we like migrants but not immigration', 2 March 2015, https://yougov.co.uk/news/2015/03/02/why-we-like-migrants-not-immigration/

28. Integration Hub, 'Residential Patterns', www.integrationhub.net

29. Census 2011, Table DC6205EW, Economic activity by religion, by sex, by age, https://www.ons.gov.uk/census/2011census

30. ICM Unlimited survey for Channel 4 programme 'What Muslims really think', 11 April 2016.

31. 'Unsettled Belonging: A Survey of Britain's Muslim Communities', Policy Exchange, 2 December 2016, https://policyexchange.org.uk/publication/unsettled-belonging-a-survey-of-britains-muslim-communities/

32. Eric Kaufmann, 'Half Full or Half Empty? How Has Ethnic Segregation in England and Wales Changed Between 2001 and 2011', www.demos.co.uk/files/ethnicdistributione+w.pdf

33. Integration Hub, 'Education', www.integrationhub.net

34. Nissa Finney and Ludi Simpson, *Sleepwalking to segregation? Challenging Myths About Race and Migration*, Bristol: Policy Press, 2009.

35. 2012 Ipsos MORI poll for British Future, 'Mapping Integration,' David Goodhart (ed.), 2014.

36. Ipsos MORI Generations, 'Integration in Schools', www.ipsos-mori-generations.com/integration

37. YouGov, 'The Challenge Survey results', October 2016, https://d25d2506sfb94s.cloudfront.net/cumulus_uploads/document/qkp8raq0wu/TheChallenge_Results_161004_Integration_W.pdf

38. Trevor Phillips, 'Race and Faith: The Deafening Silence', Civitas, June 2016.

39. Jonathan Haidt, *The Righteous Mind: Why Good People are Divided by Politics and Religion*, London: Penguin, 2012.

40. Michael Lind, 'The Open-Borders "Liberaltarianism" of the New Urban Elite', *National Review*, 15 September 2016, http://www.nationalreview.com/article/440055/open-borders-ideology-americas-urban-elite-threat-nationalism

41. www.ukpopulation2016.com

42. Peter Mandler, 'Britain's EU Problem is a London Problem', *Dissent*, 24 June 2016.

43. Jon Kelly, 'London-centric', www.bbc.co.uk/news/resources/idt-248d9ac7–9784–4769–936a-8d3b435857a8

44. Tim Hames, 'Britain's capital punishment', *Progress*, 7 November 2013.

45. Richard Florida, *The Rise of the Creative Class: And How It's Transforming Work, Life, Community and Everyday Life*, New York: Basic Books, 2002.

46. Simon Parker, 'Interview: Ken Livingstone', *Prospect*, 29 April 2007.

47. Eric Kaufmann and Gareth Harris, 'Changing Places: Mapping the white British response to ethnic change…', Demos, 2014.

48. Sarah Bell and James Paskins (eds), *Imagining the Future City: London 2062*, London: Ubiquity Press, 2013.

49. Ian Gordon, 'Displacement and Densification: Tracing Spatial Impacts of Migration Inflows to London', LSE London/RUPS MSc seminar series, 17 February 2014.

50. Migration Watch UK, 'MW286—Who is getting local authority housing in London? Are some London councils telling the full story?', 2 January 2013, https://www.migrationwatchuk.org/briefing-paper/286

51. James Pickford, 'First time buyers in London still priced out despite Help to Buy', *Financial Times*, 11 December 2015, https://www.ft.com/content/09eed7fe-9e92–11e5-b45d-4812f209f861 and Peter York, 'The fall of the Sloane Rangers', *Prospect*, 19 February 2015, www.prospectmagazine.co.uk/magazine/the-fall-of-the-sloane-rangers-made-in-chelsea

52. ONS, Statistical bulletin: 'Personal well-being in the UK: 2015 to 2016', 7 July 2016, https://www.ons.gov.uk/peoplepopulationand-community/wellbeing/bulletins/measuringnationalwellbeing/2015to2016

53. Yorkshire Building Society, 'Yorkshire Building Society Trust Study', 2013 www.ybs.co.uk/images/media-centre/YorkshireBuildingSocietyTrustStudy.pdf

54. Hannah Aldridge, Theo Barry Born, Adam Tinson and Tom MacInnes, 'London's Poverty Profile 2015', Trust for London, 2015, p. 23.

55. 'How the other three-quarters live', *The Economist*, 17 September 2016.

56. Census 2011, DC6213EW—Occupation by ethnic group, by sex, by age, https://www.ons.gov.uk/census/2011census

57. Ian Richard Gordon, Ioannis Kaplanis, 'Accounting for big-city growth in low-paid occupations: immigration and/or service-class consumption', *Economic Geography*, 90 (1), pp. 67–90, 2014.

58. Will Dahlgreen, '37 per cent of British workers think their jobs are meaningless', YouGov, 12 August 2015, https://yougov.co.uk/news/2015/08/12/british-jobs-meaningless/

59. Social Integration Commission, 'How integrated is modern Britain?', 2014, http://socialintegrationcommission.org.uk/SIC_Report_WEB.pdf

60. YouGov, 'YouGov/ESRC, Demos and Birkbeck Survey Results', 2013, d25d2506sfb94s.cloudfront.net/cumulus_uploads/document/kf5d231qce/YG-Archive-ESRC-Demos-Birkbeck-results-300713.pdf

61. Zadie Smith, 'Fences: A Brexit Diary', *New York Review of Books*, 18 August 2016.

62. Department for Education, 'Schools, pupils and their characteristics: January 2016', 28 June 2016, https://www.gov.uk/government/statistics/schools-pupils-and-their-characteristics-january-2016

63. Trevor Phillips, Richard Webber, 'Labour's New Majority', *Demos Quarterly*, 18 July 2014, http://quarterly.demos.co.uk/article/issue-3/537/

64. British Election Study 2015, quoted in Eric Kaufmann, 'The Myth of London Exeptionalism', *Demos Quarterly*, 5 February 2015, http://quarterly.demos.co.uk/article/issue-5/ukip-in-london/

65. At 22.9 per cent of UK GVA in 2014. Daniel Harari, 'Regional and local economic growth statistics', House of Commons Library, 30 August 2016.

66. Janan Ganesh, 'A censorious creed that gnaws away at the Conservative vote', *Financial Times*, 11 August 2014.

67. Ben Judah, *This is London: Life and Death in the World City*, London: Picador, 2016.

6. THE KNOWLEDGE ECONOMY AND ECONOMIC DEMORALISATION

1. Robert Ford and Matthew J. Goodwin, *Revolt on the Right: Explaining Support for the Radical Right in Britain*, Abingdon: Routledge, 2014.

2. 'UK economy shows shift to low-skilled jobs, research finds', *Financial Times*, 19 January 2015, http://www.ft.com/cms/s/0/6a8544ae-9d9e-11e4-8ea3-00144feabdc0.html#axzz4JBcFfD2o

3. The Institute for Fiscal Studies has also calculated that over the past twenty years the proportion of middle skill jobs has fallen from 36 per cent to just below 30 per cent, while over the same period (1993 to 2013) the low skill proportion rose from about 28 per cent to 31 per cent. See Figure 1 in Katie Schmuecker, 'Future of the UK Labour Market', Joseph Rowntree Foundation, February 2014, https://www.jrf.org.uk/report/future-uk-labour-market

4. http://www.centreforcities.org/press/nearly-a-million-new-jobs-created-in-british-cities-since-2010-but-average-salary-drops-by-1300-per-city-resident/

5. See Theodore Dalrymple's observation about the erosion of the distinction between service to others and servitude to others: Theodore Dalrymple, 'Why Britain (and Europe) depends on migrants', *The Spectator*, 26 March 2016, http://www.spectator.co.uk/2016/03/why-britain-and-europe-depends-on-migrants/

6. A YouGov poll found 37 per cent of workers, around 11.5 million people, felt their job is not making a meaningful contribution to society. Tom W. Smith, 'Job satisfaction in the United States', University of Chicago, 17 April 2007, www-news.uchicago.edu/releases/07/pdf/070417.jobs.pdf and 'Work', British Social Attitudes 33, 2016, http://bsa.natcen.ac.uk/media/39061/bsa33_work.pdf

7. Sammy Rashid and Greg Brooks, 'The levels of attainment in literacy and numeracy of 13- to 19-year-olds in England, 1948–2009', University of Sheffield, 2010.

8. Brendan Cole, 'Young people in England have "lowest literacy levels" in developed world says OECD', International Business Times, http://www.ibtimes.co.uk/young-people-england-have-lowest-literacy-levels-developed-world-says-oecd-1540711

9. See the work of behavioural geneticists such as Robert Plomin and Rosalind Arden.

10. 'The death of the Saturday job: the decline in earning and learning amongst young people in the UK', UK Commission for Employment and Skills, 16 June 2015, https://gov.uk/government/publications/the-death-of-the-saturday-job-the-decline-in-earning-and-learning-amongst-young-people-in-the-uk.

11. http://www.trainingzone.co.uk/deliver/training/a-history-of-apprenticeships-pt2

12. 'List of UK universities by date of foundation', Wikipedia, https://en.wikipedia.org/wiki/List_of_UK_universities_by_date_of_foundation; 'Higher education providers', Higher Education Statistics Agency, https://www.hesa.ac.uk/support/providers; Haroon Chowdry et. al., 'Widening Participation in Higher Education: Analysis using Linked Administrative Data, IFS Working Paper W10/04, Institute for Fiscal Studies, May 2010, https://www.ifs.org.uk/wps/wp1004.pdf; 'Students in Higher Education 2014/15', Higher Education Statistics Agency, 11 February 2016, https://www.hesa.ac.uk/data-and-analysis/publications/students-2014–15; and 'Finances', Higher Education Statistics Agency, https://www.hesa.ac.uk/data-and-analysis/providers/finances

13. Conversation with the author.

14. The boot is on the other foot. Many older people from working class backgrounds who went to university have vivid memories of being despised and even physically attacked by some, among the large majority, who took the expected route into local jobs.

15. This includes £4 billion in research grants, plus about £13 billion in tertiary education expenditure. 'Public Expenditure: Statistical Analyses 2015', HM Treasury, July 2015, p. 83, https://www.gov.uk/government/uploads/system/uploads/attachment_data/file/446716/50600_PESA_2015_PRINT.pdf; Shiv Malik, 'Student fees policy likely to cost more than the system it replaced', *The Guardian*, 21 March 2014, https://www.theguardian.com/education/2014/mar/21/student-fees-policy-costing-more

16. Alison Wolf, 'Heading for the precipice: Can further and higher education funding policies be sustained?', King's College London, June 2015, www.kcl.ac.uk/sspp/policy-institute/publications/issuesand-ideas-alison-wolf-digital.pdf,

17. 'Adult skills funding: what happened in the last Parliament?', Full Fact, 22 March 2016, https://fullfact.org/economy/adult-skills-funding-what-happened-last-parliament/

18. Sally Weale, 'Colleges face deterioration without urgent funding, warn MPs', *The Guardian*, 16 December 2015, https://www.theguardian.com/education/2015/dec/16/colleges-further-education-funding-government

19. Alison Wolf with Gerard Dominguez-Reig and Peter Sellen, 'Remaking Tertiary Education: Can we create a system that is fair and fit for purpose?', Education Policy Institute, King's College London, November 2016, http://epi.org.uk/wp-content/uploads/2016/11/remaking-tertiary-education-web.pdf

20. The Chartered Institute of Personnel and Development estimates that 35 per cent of all bank and post office clerks have degrees, ten times the percentage in 1979; 44 per cent of police officers entering the force at the rank of sergeant or below are graduates, up from 2 per cent in 1979; the number of newly employed teaching assistants with a degree is 37 per cent up from 6 per cent in 1979. 'Alternative pathways into the labour market', Chartered Institute of Personnel and Development (CIPD), 11 October 2016, https://www.cipd.co.uk/knowledge/work/trends/alternative-labour-market-pathways

21. House of Commons Science and Technology Committee, 'Digital skills crisis', Second Report of Session 2016–17, House of Commons, 7 June 2016, www.publications.parliament.uk/pa/cm201617/cmselect/cmsctech/270/270.pdf

22. Sally Percy, 'Vacancies left unfilled as skills shortage bites', *The*

Telegraph, 29 January 2016, www.telegraph.co.uk/sponsored/education/uk-productivity/12128866/skills-shortage.html

23. This is partly the result of the stop-start nature of the building industry, especially following the financial crash, which makes it appear less attractive as a long-term career investment. 'How can the Construction Industry react to falling apprenticeship numbers?' UK Construction Online, 16 July 2015, www.ukconstructionmedia.co.uk/features/how-can-the-construction-industry-react-to-falling-apprenticeship-numbers/

24. Priya Khambhaita and Kalwant Bhopal, 'Home or away? The significance of ethnicity, class and attainment in the housing choices of female university students', *Race Ethnicity and Education*, 18, 4, (2015), pp. 535–566, https://dx.doi.org/10.1080/13613324.2012.759927 and Lucy Tobin, 'Rise of the stay-at-home students', *The Guardian*, https://www.theguardian.com/money/2011/aug/12/stay-at-home-students

25. Roughly 38 per cent of students at Million+ universities are domiciled less than ten miles away from their university, compared to only 14 per cent at Russell Group universities. Nick Hillman, 'Why do students study so far from home?', *Times Higher Education*, 23 July 2015, https://www.timeshighereducation.com/features/why-do-students-study-so-far-from-home

26. Alison Wolf, 'Heading for the Precipice: Can Further and Higher Education Policies be Sustained?', The Policy Institute at King's, June 2015, http://www.kcl.ac.uk/sspp/policy-institute/publications/Issuesandideas-alison-wolf-digital.pdf

27. Francis Green et al, 'What has been Happening to the Training of Workers in Britain?', http://discoversociety.org/wp-content/uploads/2013/09/43.-Green-et-al.pdf

28. 'Continuing Vocational Training Survey—CVTS4', BIS Research Paper Number 102, Department for Business, Innovation and Skills, February 2013, https://www.gov.uk/government/uploads/system/uploads/attachment_data/file/81645/bis-13–587-continual-vocational-training-survey-cvts4.pdf

29. Julie Froud et al, 'Rebalanching the Economy (Or Buyer's Remorse', CRESC Working Paper Series, No. 87, January, 2011, https://www.searchlock.com/search?q=cresc+rebalancing+the+economy

30. Alison Wolf, 'Heading for the Precipice: Can Further and Higher Education Policies be Sustained?', The Policy Institute at King's, June 2015, http://www.kcl.ac.uk/sspp/policy-institute/publications/Issuesandideas-alison-wolf-digital.pdf

31. Ibid.

32. A bigger study by the Education and Employers Taskforce of 10,000 thirteen to eighteen year olds found that over half had career ambitions in just three broad areas—culture, media and sports; health; business and public service professionals. Fewer than 1 per cent of young people showed an interest in seven occupational areas that together recruit millions of workers. Graeme Atherton et. al., 'How Young People Formulate their Views about the Future', Research Report DCSF-RR152, University of Westminster, Oct. 2009, https://core.ac.uk/download/pdf/4160330.pdf

33. Anthony Mann et al, 'Nothing in common: The career aspirations of young Britons mapped against projected labour market demand (2010–2020)', http://www.educationandemployers.org/wp-content/uploads/2014/06/nothing_in_common_final.pdf

34. Philip Inman, 'Don't teach Brexit schoolkids about Tennyson: teach them maths', *The Observer*, 20 November 2016, https://www.the-guardian.com/politics/2016/nov/20/brexit-dont-teach-schoolkids-tennyson-teach-them-maths-gcse

35. David Goodhart, 'Exploring the cultural challenges to social democracy', Policy Network, 2011, http://www.policy-network.net/publications_download.aspx?ID=7374

36. Real hourly wages are around 25 per cent lower than they would have been if wage growth had continued at the rate observed during 2000–2007. Stefano Scarpetta, 'Editorial: Back in work, but still out of pocket', OECD Employment Outlook 2016, OECD 2016, https://www.oecd.org/els/emp/Employment-Outlook-2016-Editorial.pdf,

37. 'FTSE chiefs earn 183 times average salary of UK workers', *Financial Times*, 17 August 2015, https://www.ft.com/content/b3d0225e-4416-11e5-af2f-4d6e0e5eda22

38. Shawn Donnan, 'Inequality decreased after global financial crisis', *Financial Times*, 2 October 2016, https://www.ft.com/content/5aae6948-88a2-11e6-8cb7-e7ada1d123b1

39. Chris Belfield et. al., 'Living standards, poverty and inequality in the UK: 2016', Institute for Fiscal Studies, 19 July 2016, https://www.ifs.org.uk/publications/8371

40. 'Working and workless households: 2015', Office for National Statistics, 6 October 2015, https://www.ons.gov.uk/employmentand-labourmarket/peopleinwork/employmentandemployeetypes/bulletins/workingandworklesshouseholds/2015–10–06/pdf

41. Jonathan Cribb et. al., 'Living Standards, Poverty and Inequality in the UK: 2013', IFS Report R81, Institute for Fiscal Studies, http://www.ifs.org.uk/comms/r81.pdf and 'Households below average income: 1994/95 to 2014/15', Department for Work and Pensions, 28 June

2016, https://www.gov.uk/government/statistics/households-below-average-income-199495-to-201415

42. 'National Minimum Wage: Low Pay Commission Report Spring 2016', Gov.uk, March 2016, https://www.gov.uk/government/uploads/system/uploads/attachment_data/file/571631/LPC_spring_report_2016.pdf

43. Cameron Tait, 'March of the Waiters', Fabian Society, 29 October 2016, www.fabians.org.uk/march-of-the-waiters/

44. Adam Corlett and David Finch, 'Double take: workers with multiple jobs and reforms to National Insurance', Resolution Foundation, November 2016, www.resolutionfoundation.org/app/uploads/2016/11/Double-take.pdf

45. Jonathan Ashworth et. al., 'The UK's self-employment phenomenon: why the labour market isn't so strong after all', Morgan Stanley Research, 2014.

46. 'Work', British Social Attitudes 33, 2016, http://bsa.natcen.ac.uk/media/39061/bsa33_work.pdf

47. Jonathan Gardner and Andrew Oswald, 'How does education affect mental well-being and job satisfaction?', Warwick University, June 2002, www2.warwick.ac.uk/fac/soc/economics/staff/ajoswald/reveducationgardneroswaldjune2002.pdf

48. Julie Froud et al, 'Rebalanching the Economy (Or Buyer's Remorse', CRESC Working Paper Series, No. 87, January, 2011, https://www.searchlock.com/search?q=cresc+rebalancing+the+economy

49. Alex Brummer, Britain For Sale: British Companies in Foreign Hands, The Hidden Threat to Our Economy, London: Random House, 2013.

50. Julie Froud et al, 'Rebalanching the Economy (Or Buyer's Remorse', CRESC Working Paper Series, No. 87, January, 2011, https://www.searchlock.com/search?q=cresc+rebalancing+the+economy

51. Theresa May, 'The new role for business in a fairer Britain', Financial Times, 21 November 2016, https://www.ft.com/content/12a839d4-af18-11e6-a37c-f4a01f1b0fa1

52. Bob Bischof, 'Tackling the UK's export malaise', Reaction, 20 September 2016, http://reaction.life/tackling-uks-export-malaise/

53. See Geoff Owen, From Empire to Europe: The Decline and Revival of British Industry since the Second World War, London: HarperCollins, 2000.

7. THE ACHIEVEMENT SOCIETY

1. Michael Young, The Rise of the Meritocracy, 1870–2033: An Essay on Education and Equality, London: Penguin, 1961.

2. Andrew Marr, 'The Queen at 90', The Sunday Times, 17 April 2016, www.thesundaytimes.co.uk/sto/newsreview/article1687659.ece

3. Some 22 per cent of those employed were working in semi-routine or routine jobs from July to September 2016. 'EMP11: Employment by socio-economic classification', Office for National Statistics, 16 November 2016, https://www.ons.gov.uk/employmentandlabourmarket/peopleinwork/employmentandemployeetypes/datasets/employmentbysocioeconomicclassificationemp11. In 2015, 23 per cent of those asked if they thought of themselves as belonging to any particular class said they were working class. This rose to 60 per cent when given an option of working class or middle class from which to choose. This included nearly half of those working in managerial or professional jobs. 'Social class', British Social Attitudes 33, 2016, www.bsa.natcen.ac.uk/media/39094/bsa33_social-class_v5.pdf

4. A YouGov poll in 2015 found that 29 per cent of people always or often feel stressed, 24 per cent always or often feel anxious and 17 per cent always or often feel depressed. Suicide is the biggest killer of men under forty-five. There were 4,623 male suicides in 2014. 'Nearly one in three people are regularly stressed, survey for Mental Health Awareness Week reveals', Mental Health Foundation, 10 May 2015, https://www.mentalhealth.org.uk/news/nearly-one-three-people-are-regularly-stressed-survey-mental-health-awareness-week-reveals   and Jamie Doward '"Let's reach out to men to halt shocking suicide rate"', *The Observer*, 31 October 2015, https://www.theguardian.com/society/2015/oct/31/social-media-campaign-male-suicide

5. Clare Foges, 'How to create a level playing field for young people to be inspired', *Evening Standard*, 11 August 2016, http://www.standard.co.uk/comment/comment/clare-foges-how-to-create-a-level-playing-field-for-young-people-to-be-inspired-a3317626.html

6. Jo Blanden, Paul Gregg and Stephen Machin, 'Intergenerational Mobility in Europe and North America', Centre for Economic Performance, http://cep.lse.ac.uk/about/news/IntergenerationalMobility.pdf

7. John H. Goldthorpe, 'Understanding—and Misunderstanding—Social Mobility in Britain: The Entry of the Economists, the Confusion of Politicians and the Limits of Educational Policy', University of Oxford, 2012, https://www.spi.ox.ac.uk/fileadmin/documents/PDF/Goldthorpe_Social_Mob_paper_01.pdf

8. In July to September 2016, 42.5 per cent of those in employment were working in jobs classified as higher managerial and professional, or lower managerial and professional. 'EMP11: Employment by socio-economic classification', Office for National Statistics, 16 November 2016, https://www.ons.gov.uk/employmentandlabourmarket/peopleinwork/employmentandemployeetypes/datasets/employmentbysocioeconomicclassificationemp11

9. Rosa Prince, 'David Willets: feminism has held back working men', *The Telegraph*, 1 April 2011, www.telegraph.co.uk/education/educationnews/8420098/David-Willets-feminism-has-held-back-working-men.html

10. Daniel Laurison and Sam Friedman, 'Introducing the Class Ceiling: Social Mobility and Britain's Elite Occupations', http://www.lse.ac.uk/sociology/pdf/Working-Paper_Introducing-the-Class-Ceiling.pdf

11. Shamit Saggar, Richard Norrie, Michelle Bannister and David Goodhart, 'Bittersweet Success? Glass Ceilings for Britain's Ethnic Minorities at the Top of Business and the Professions', Policy Exchange, November 2016, https://policyexchange.org.uk/wp-content/uploads/2016/11/PEXJ5011_Bittersweet_Success_1116_WEB.pdf

12. Alison Wolf, *The XX Factor: How Working Women are Creating a New Society*, New York: Crown Publishing, 2013.

13. David Goodhart, 'They're wrong—social mobility is not going downhill', *The Sunday Times*, 26 July 2009, http://www.timesonline.co.uk/tol/news/politics/article6727099.ece

8. WHAT ABOUT THE FAMILY?

1. Shirley Burggraf, *The Feminine Economy and Economic Man: Reviving The Role Of Family In The Postindustrial Age*, New York: Basic Books, 1998.

2. Institute for Employment Studies, 'Report Summary: Women in the Labour Market, Two Decades of Change and Continuity', http://www.employment-studies.co.uk/report-summaries/report-summary-women-labour-market-two-decades-change-and-continuity

3. 'Women and Work: The Facts', Business in the Community, http://gender.bitc.org.uk/all-resources/factsheets/women-and-work-facts

4. Jemima Olchawski, 'Sex Equality: State of the Nation', http://www.fawcettsociety.org.uk/wp-content/uploads/2016/01/Sex-equality-state-of-the-nation-230116.pdf

5. Centre for Population Change, 'The Changing Demography of Lone Parenthood in the UK', p. 4 http://www.cpc.ac.uk/publications/cpc_working_papers/pdf/2014_WP48_The_changing_demography_of_lone_parenthood_Berrington.pdf

6. Ann Berrington and Juliet Stone, 'Cohabitation trends and patterns in the UK', http://www.cpc.ac.uk/publications/Cohabitation%20trends%20and%20patterns%20in%20the%20UK.pdf

7. American College of Pediatricians, 'The Impact of Family Structure on the Health of Children—Effects of Divorce', November 2014, www.acpeds.org/wordpress/wp-content/uploads/11.26.14_Impact-of-Family-Structure.pdf

8. Some 63 per cent of dependent children were living in a married couple family in 2016. 'Families and households in the UK: 2016', Office for National Statistics, 4 November 2016, https://www.ons.gov.uk/peoplepopulationandcommunity/birthsdeathsandmarriages/families/bulletins/familiesandhouseholds/2016

9. One Plus One, 'Children Affected by Separation', http://www.oneplusone.org.uk/content_topic/breaking-up/limiting-the-effects-of-separation-on-children/

10. John Bingham and Ashley Kirk, 'Divorce rate at lowest level in 40 years after cohabitation revolution', *The Telegraph*, 23 November 2015, www.telegraph.co.uk/news/uknews/12011714/Divorce-rate-at-lowest-level-in-40-years-after-cohabitation-revolution.html

11. Ann Berrington and Juliet Stone, 'Cohabitation trends and patterns in the UK', ESRC Centre for Population Change, February 2015, www.cpc.ac.uk/publications/Cohabitation%20trends%20and%20patterns%20in%20the%20UK.pdf

12. This is the point made by Charles Murray in *Coming Apart*, his book about white America and the patterns of behaviour in the two imaginary towns Belmont and Fishtown. Charles Murray, *Coming Apart: The State of White America, 1960–2010*, Crown, 2013.

13. Equal Pay Portal, 'United Kingdom Data on the Gender Pay Gap', http://www.equalpayportal.co.uk/statistics/

14. Office for National Statistics, 'How is the Welfare budget spent?', http://visual.ons.gov.uk/welfare-spending/

15. Relationships Foundation, 'Counting the Cost of Family Failure', http://knowledgebank.oneplusone.org.uk/wp-content/uploads/2016/03/Counting-the-Cost-of-Family-Failure-2016-Update.pdf

16. Office for National Statistics, 'Working and Workless Households: 2015', http://www.ons.gov.uk/employmentandlabourmarket/peopleinwork/employmentandemployeetypes/bulletins/workingandworklesshouseholds/2015–10–06#households

17. Paul Johnson, 'IFS Budget Analysis 2014: Introductory Remarks', https://www.ifs.org.uk/budgets/budget2014/opening_remarks.pdf

18. British Social Attitudes 30, 'Gender Roles, An incomplete revolution?', http://www.bsa.natcen.ac.uk/media/38457/bsa30_gender_roles_final.pdf

19. Samantha Callan, 'The state of the nation report: Fractured families', http://www.centreforsocialjustice.org.uk/core/wp-content/uploads/2016/08/BreakdownB_family_breakdown.pdf

20. Focus on the Family, 'Marriage: Talking Points', http://www.focusonthefamily.com/socialissues/marriage/marriage/marriage-talking-points. See also the reports by Norman Denis and George Erdos based on the 1958 National Cohort study, John Ermisch et al in the *Journal of*

the Royal Statistical Society 2004, the 2009 review of the evidence by Ann Mooney et al of the Institute of Education and a huge amount of evidence from the US.

21. Marco Francesconi and James J. Heckman, 'Child Development and Parental Investment,' *Economic Journal*, 126, October 2016, http://onlinelibrary.wiley.com/doi/10.1111/ecoj.12388/abstract

22. Alistair Pearson and David Binder, 'The Taxation of Families 'https://www.care.org.uk/sites/default/files/Care_The-Taxation-of-Families-International-Comparisons-2012.pdf

23. Don Draper and Leonard Beighton 'Independent taxation: 25 years on', Care Research paper, Christian Action Research and Education (Care), September 2013.

24. Catharine Hakim, 'Competing family models, competing social policies', http://www.catherinehakim.org/wp-content/uploads/2011/07/AIFSarticle.pdf

25. Belinda Brown, 'Family-friendly feminism', http://quarterly.demos.co.uk/article/issue-4/family-friendly-feminism/

26. Ann Fennell, 'Who cares about the family?', http://www.landisfree.co.uk/who-cares-about-the-family-by-ann-fennell/

27. Tom Huskinson et al, 'Childcare and early years survey of parents 2014–2015', https://www.gov.uk/government/uploads/system/uploads/attachment_data/file/516924/SFR09-2016_Childcare_and_Early_Years_Parents_Survey_2014-15_report.pdf.pdf

28. 'Rise of the modern FeMEnist—Latest Netmums Survey Results', Netmums, Oct. 2012, www.netmums.com/coffeehouse/general-coffeehouse-chat-514/news-current-affairs-12/836486-rise-modern-femenist-latest-netmums-survey-results-all.html

29. Geoff Dench, *What Women Want: Evidence from British Social Attitudes*, England: Hera Trust, 2010.

30. Brown, Belinda, 'Family-friendly feminism', *Demos Quarterly*, http://quarterly.demos.co.uk/article/issue-4/family-friendly-feminism/

31. British Social Attitudes 30, 'Gender Roles, An incomplete revolution?', http://www.bsa.natcen.ac.uk/media/38457/bsa30_gender_roles_final.pdf

32. Ibid.

33. British Social Attitudes Information System, http://www.britsocat.com/

34. This may be especially true of younger women. Nearly one third of eighteen to thirty-nine year olds agreed with the statements 'A preschool child is likely to suffer if his mother goes out to work' and 'A job is alright but what most women want is a home and children'— up from, respectively, 22 per cent and 15 per cent in 2002. Similarly

a survey for the Young Woman's Trust found 37 per cent of young women saying women were better suited for caring for children than having a paid job. Geoff Dench, *What Women Want: Evidence from British Social Attitudes*, England: Hera Trust, 2010.

35. Belinda Brown, 'Family-friendly feminism', http://quarterly.demos.co.uk/article/issue-4/family-friendly-feminism/

36. Business in the Community, 'Women and Work: The Facts', http://gender.bitc.org.uk/all-resources/factsheets/women-and-work-facts

37. Office for National Statistics, 'Women in the labour market 2013', http://www.ons.gov.uk/employmentandlabourmarket/peopleinwork/employmentandemployeetypes/articles/womeninthelabourmarket/2013–09–25

38. Geoff Dench, *Transforming Men: Changing Patterns of Dependency and Dominance in Gender Relations*, Transaction Publishers, 1998.

39. Amelia Hill, 'Cash-strapped parents choosing to have only one baby', *The Guardian*, October 2014, https://www.theguardian.com/lifeandstyle/2014/oct/31/one-child-families-costs-expensive-survey

40. David Binder, 'David Binder: Why we need a fully transferable tax allowance in the budget', Conservative Home, 11 March 2014, www.conservativehome.com/platform/2014/03/david-binder-the-ever-increasing-tax-burdens-on-one-earner-couples-with-children.html

41. Belinda Brown, 'Family-friendly feminism', http://quarterly.demos.co.uk/article/issue-4/family-friendly-feminism/

9. A NEW SETTLEMENT

1. Jeremy Cliffe, 'Britain's Cosmopolitan Future', Policy Network, May 2015, http://www.policy-network.net/publications/4905/Britains-Cosmopolitan-Future

2. Will Jennings et al, 'Thatcher's Children, Blair's Babies', *British Journal of Political Science*, forthcoming.

3. British Social Attitudes data can be found here: http://www.britsocat.com/, see www.britsocat.com/BodyTwoCol_rpt.aspx?control=CCESDMarginals&MapID=HOMOSEX&SeriesID=12

4. 'Immigration Policy and Black and Minority Ethnic Voters', Migration Watch UK, 25 March 2015, https://www.migrationwatch.org/briefing-paper/357

5. British Jews are perhaps a special case, with, like most minorities, a mix of Anywhere and Somewhere priorities. 'Rootless cosmopolitans' was Stalin's dismissive epithet but most Jews living today in Israel or the west are happy to no longer be cursed with rootlessness. Most British Jews are better educated and probably more internationally

connected than the average citizen, so in some respects Anywheres. But they are also strongly clustered residentially and a recent history of persecution gives them a special interest in social stability, meaning strong Somewhere intuitions too. Moreover the fastest growing section of the community is the ultra-Somewhere Haredim.

6. In chapter one I explained that students of public opinion look at changes to attitudes in three different ways: is it a cohort effect mainly impacting on one group, such as young people?; is it a temporary life-cycle effect that will change as people age?; or is it a period effect that impacts almost the whole society?

7. Francis Fukuyama, 'US against the world?', *Financial Times*, 12 November 2016.

8. Eric Kaufmann, 'Trump and Brexit: why it's again not the economy, stupid', LSE British Politics and Policy, 9 November 2016, http://blogs.lse.ac.uk/politicsandpolicy/trump-and-brexit-why-its-again-not-the-economy-stupid/

9. 'Brexit Voters: NOT the Left Behind', Fabian Society, 24 June 2016, http://www.fabians.org.uk/brexit-voters-not-the-left-behind/

10. Matthew Holehouse, 'More than half of homes take more than they contribute', *The Telegraph*, 26 June 2014, www.telegraph.co.uk/finance/personalfinance/tax/10929370/More-than-half-of-homes-take-more-than-they-contribute.html

11. See Duncan O'Leary, 'Making Welfare Popular', *Demos Quarterly*, 31 July 2015, http://quarterly.demos.co.uk/article/issue-6/making-welfare-more-like-pensions/

12. That view would have been reinforced by the UKIP election poster in 2015 in parts of Kent and Essex that consisted simply of a picture of David Cameron with a quote from him celebrating as his greatest achievement in office raising the foreign aid budget to 0.7 per cent of GDP.

13. Will Jennings and Gerry Stoker, 'The Bifurcation of Politics: Two Englands', Vol. 86, Issue 3, July–September, 2016, *Political Quarterly*, http://onlinelibrary.wiley.com/doi/10.1111/1467–923X.12228/abstract

14. 'Transport Secretary urged to close £1,600 per person London-North spending gap', IPPR North, 8 August 2016, http://www.ippr.org/news-and-media/press-releases/transport-secretary-urged-to-close-1-600-per-person-london-north-spending-gap

15. Duncan O'Leary, 'Making Welfare Popular', *Demos Quarterly*, 31 July 2015, http://quarterly.demos.co.uk/article/issue-6/making-welfare-more-like-pensions/

16. Yural Levin, *The Fractured Republic: Renewing America's Social Contract in the Age of Individualism*, New York: Basic Books, 2016.

SELECT BIBLIOGRAPHY

Baggini, Julian, *A Very British Populism*, London: Counterpoint, 2013.

Bowen, Innes, *Medina in Birmingham, Najaf in Brent: Inside British Islam*, London: Hurst, 2014.

Brown, Belinda, 'Family-friendly Feminism', *Demos Quarterly*, Issue 4, Autumn 2014.

Brummer, Alex, *Britain for Sale: British Companies in Foreign Hands, The Hidden Threat to our Economy*, London: Random House, 2013.

Cliffe, Jeremy, *Britain's Cosmopolitan Future: How the Country is Changing and Why its Politicians Must Respond*, London: Policy Network, 2015.

Dench, Geoff, *Transforming Men: Changing Patterns of Dependency and Dominance in Gender Relations*, New Brunswick and London: Transaction Publishers, 1998.

———— (ed.), *The Rise and Rise of Meritocracy*, Oxford and London: Blackwell Publishing and Political Quarterly, 2006.

————, *Minorities in the Open Society*, New Brunswick and London: Transaction Publishers, 2003.

————, *What Women Want: Evidence from British Social Attitudes*, London: Hera Trust, 2010.

Fawcett, Edmund, *Liberalism: The Life of an Idea*, Princeton and Oxford: Princeton University Press, 2014.

Ford, Robert and Matthew Goodwin, *Revolt on the Right: Explaining Support for the Radical Right in Britain*, London: Routledge, 2014.

Gilens, Martin, 'Under the Influence', *Boston Review*, July 2012.

Goodhart, David, 'Too Diverse?', *Prospect*, February 2004.

————, *The British Dream: Successes and Failures of Post-War Immigration*, London: Atlantic Books, 2013.

————, 'A Postliberal Future?', *Demos Quarterly*, Issue 1, Winter 2013/2014.

————, 'The Path not Taken', *Demos Quarterly*, Issue 2, Spring 2014.

————, 'London: all that glistens…', *Demos Quarterly*, Issue 4, Autumn 2014.

————, 'Racism: Less is More', *Political Quarterly*, July–September 2014.

Haidt, Jonathan, *The Righteous Mind: Why Good People are Divided by Politics and Religion*, London: Allen Lane, 2012.

————, 'When and Why Nationalism Beats Globalism', *The American Interest*, July 2016.

Hansen, Randall, *Citizenship and Immigration in Post-War Britain*, Oxford: Oxford University Press, 2000.

Judah, Ben, *This is London: Life and Death in the World City*, London: Picador, 2016.

Katwala, Sunder, Jill Rutter and Steve Ballinger, 'What Next After Brexit: Immigration and Integration in Post-Referendum Britain', London: British Future, 2016.

Kaufmann, Eric and Gareth Harris, 'Changing Places: Mapping the white British response to ethnic change…', London: Demos, 2014.

Krastev, Ivan, *Populism Today*, Aspen Institute, 2007.

Lasch, Christopher, *The Revolt of the Elites and the Betrayal of Democracy*, New York: W.W. Norton & Company, 1995.

Lind, Michael, 'The Rubes and the Elites', *Salon*, 2008.

————, 'The Coming Realignment', *The Breakthrough*, April 2014.

————, 'The Liberal Roots of Populism', *Demos Quarterly*, Issue 4, Autumn 2014.

————, 'Why Both Sides Are Wrong About Trade', *Politico*, April 2015.

Miller, David, *Strangers in our Midst: The Political Philosophy of Immigration*, Cambridge, MA and London: Harvard University Press, 2016.

Mudde, Cas, *The Populist Radical Right: A Pathological Normalcy*, Malmo University, 2008.

Murray, Charles, *Coming Apart: The State of White America 1960–2010*, New York: Crown Forum, 2012.

O'Leary, Duncan, 'Making Welfare Popular', *Demos Quarterly*, Issue 6, Summer 2015.

Orgad, Liav, *The Cultural Defense of Nations: A Liberal Theory of Majority Rights*, Oxford: Oxford University Press, 2015.

Owen, David, *Europe Restructured: The Eurozone Crisis and its Aftermath*, York: Methuen, 2012.

Owen, Geoff, *From Empire to Europe: The Decline and Revival of British Industry Since the Second World War*, London: Harper Collins, 1999.

Peal, Robert, *Progressively Worse: The Burden of Bad Ideas in British Schools*, London: Civitas, 2014.

Phillips, Trevor, *Race and Faith: The Deafening Silence*, London: Civitas, 2016.

Putnam, Robert, 'E Pluribus Unum: Diversity and Community in the Twenty-first Century, The 2006 Johan Skytte Prize Lecture', *Scandinavian Political*

SELECT BIBLIOGRAPHY

Studies, Volume 30, Issue 2, 15 June 2007, http://onlinelibrary.wiley.com/doi/10.1111/j.1467-9477.2007.00176.x/abstract

Rodrik, Dani, 'Who Needs the Nation State?', Harvard University and Centre for Economics Policy Research discussion paper.

Rowthorn, Robert, 'The Costs and Benefits of Large-Scale Immigration', London: Civitas, 2015.

Scheffer, Paul, *Immigrant Nations*, Cambridge: Polity Press, 2011.

Scruton, Roger, *News from Somewhere: On Settling*, London: Bloomsbury, 2004.

Siedentop, Larry, *Democracy in Europe*, London: Penguin, 2011.

Simms, Brendan, *Britain's Europe: A Thousand Years of Conflict and Cooperation*, London: Allen Lane, 2016.

Sowell, Thomas, *A Conflict of Visions*, New York: William Morrow & Co, 1987.

Stenner, Karen, *The Authoritarian Dynamic*, Cambridge: Cambridge University Press, 2005.

Williams, Joan, *White Working Class: Overcoming Class Cluelessness in America*, Boston: Harvard Business Review Press, 2017.

Williams, Karel et al., 'Rebalancing the Economy (or Buyer's Remorse)', Centre for Research on Socio-Cultural Change, 2011.

Wolf, Alison, *The XX Factor: How Working Women are Creating a New Society*, London: Profile Books, 2013.

Young, Michael, *The Rise of the Meritocracy*, London: Thames & Hudson, 1958.

INDEX

1960s liberalism: 6

Aaronovitch, David: 142

Achen, Christopher: *Democracy for Realists*, 61

Afghanistan: Civil War (1992–5), 82; Operation Enduring Freedom (2001–14), 225

Akesson, Jimmie: defection from Moderate Party, 70

AkzoNobel: 175

Algeria: 104

Alternative für Deutschland: 53, 70, 73

American Dream: 65

anti-Semitism: 57

Anywheres: 10, 12–13, 15, 17–18, 20–1, 41–3, 45, 51, 74, 114–15, 118, 149, 177, 197, 202, 205, 207, 210, 215, 228; characteristics of, 4–5, 17, 24–5, 34–5, 37, 46, 123; conflict with Somewheres, 23, 79, 81, 193, 215; education levels of, 156, 158, 198; employment of, 11; European, 103; family dynamics of, 211–14; liberals, 27–8; mobile, 203; political ideologies of, 63–4, 76, 81–2, 109–10,

112, 120, 213, 224, 232–3; political representation/voting patterns of, 13, 17, 26–7, 36, 62, 69, 75, 78, 91–2, 153, 167, 218–19, 221, 227; potential coalition with Somewheres, 220, 222, 225–6, 233; progressive individualism, 11, 60, 180, 219; view of migrant integration, 134

Apple, Inc.: product lines of, 86

Appiah, Kwame Anthony: 117

assortative mating: 188

Aston University: 164

austerity: 98, 200

Australia: 4, 160

Austria: 56, 69–70

authoritarianism: 8, 12, 30, 33, 44, 57; concept of, 57; hard, 45

Baggini, Julian: observations of British class system, 59

Bangladesh: 130

Bank of England: personnel of, 86

Bartels, Larry: *Democracy for Realists*, 61

Bartlett, Jamie: *Radicals*, 64

Basel Accords: 85

BASF: 176

INDEX

Bayer: 176

Belgium: 73, 75, 101; Brussels, 53, 89, 93, 95, 98

Berlusconi, Silvio: 65

birther movement: 68

Bischof, Bob: head of German-British Forum, 174

Blair, Tony: 10, 76, 159, 189; administration of, 218; foreign policy of, 96; speeches of, 3, 7, 49; support for Bulgarian and Romanian EU accession, 26; unravelling of legacy, 221

Bloomsbury Group: 34

Bogdanor, Vernon: concept of 'exam-passing classes', 3

Boyle, Danny: Summer Olympics opening ceremony (2012), 111, 222

Branson, Richard: 11

Brexit (EU Referendum)(2016): 1–2, 19, 27, 81, 89, 93, 99–100, 125, 233; negotiations, 103; polling prior to voting, 30, 64; Remainers, 2, 19–20, 52–3, 132; sociological implications of, 4–7, 13, 53–4, 118, 126, 167–8, 225; Stronger In campaign, 61; Vote Leave campaign, 42, 53, 72, 91, 132; voting pattern in, 7–9, 19–20, 23, 26, 36, 52, 55–6, 60, 71, 74, 215, 218

British Broadcasting Corporation (BBC): 112, 145; *Newsnight*, 60; personnel of, 15; Radio 4, 31, 227; *Today*, 60

British Empire: 107

British National Party: European election performance of (2009), 119; supporters of, 38

British Future: 19

British Private Equity and Venture

Capital Association: personnel of, 135

British Social Attitudes (BSA) surveys: 153; authoritarian-libertarian scale, 44–5; findings of, 38–9, 44, 106–7, 120, 202, 206–7, 218; immigration survey (2013), 44; personnel of, 218–19

British Values Survey: establishment of (1973), 43; groups in, 43

Brooks, Greg: Sheffield report, 155

Brown, Belinda: 205, 207–8

Brown, Gordon: 106; abolition of Married Couples Allowance, 204; budget of (2006), 147–8; political rhetoric of, 16–17

Brummer, Alex: *Britain for Sale*, 173

Bulgaria: 26; accession to EU, 225 (2007); migrants from, 126; population levels of, 102

Burgess, Simon: 131

Burggraf, Shirley: *Feminine Economy and Economic Man, The*, 194

Cahn, Andrew: 98

Callaghan, Jim: Ruskin College speech (1976), 154

Callan, Eamonn: 191

Callan, Samantha: 202, 212

Cambridge University: 35, 179, 186; faculty of, 37; students of, 158–9

Cameron, David: 71, 103, 179, 183, 189; administration of, 226; cabinet of, 187

Canada: 160; mass immigration in, 119

capital: 9, 100; cultural, 190; human, 34; liberalisation of controls, 97; social, 110

capitalism: 7, 11; organised, 159

INDEX

Care (Christian Action Research & Education): 203

Carswell, Douglas: 13

Case, Anne: 67

Casey, Louise: review of opportunity and integration, 129

Catholicism: 15, 213; original sin, 57

Cautres, Bruno: 72

Center for Humans and Nature: 30

Centre for Social Justice: 206; personnel of, 202

chauvinism: 33; decline in prevalence of, 39; violent, 106

China, People's Republic of: 10, 95, 104, 160; accession to WTO (2001), 88; manufacturing sector of, 86; steel industry of, 87

Chirac, Jacques: electoral victory of (2002), 49

Christianity: 33, 69, 83, 156

citizenship: 68, 121–2; democratic, 7; global, 114; legislation, 103; national, 5; relationship with migration, 126; shared, 113; temporary, 126

Clarke, Charles: British Home Secretary, 84

Clarke, Ken: education reforms of, 158–9

Clegg, Nick: 11, 13, 189

Cliffe, Jeremy: 10–11; 'Britain's Cosmopolitan Future' 216; observations of social conservatism, 217

Clinton, Bill: 29, 76; administration of, 218

Clinton, Hillary: electoral defeat of (2016), 67–8

Coalition Government (UK) (2010–16): 13, 54, 226; cabinet members of, 16; immigration policies of, 124–5

Cold War: end of, 83, 92, 95, 98

Collier, Paul: 110; view of potential reform of UNHCR, 84

colonialism: 87; European, 105

communism: 58

Communist Party of France: 72

Confederation of British Industry (CBI): 164

confirmation bias: concept of, 30

Conservative Party (Tories)(UK): 19, 207; dismantling of apprenticeship system by, 157; ideology of, 76, 196; members of, 31, 164, 187; Party Conference (2016), 226; Red Toryism, 63; supporters of, 24, 35, 77, 143, 216–17

conservatism: 4, 9; cultural, 58; social, 217; Somewhere, 7–8; working-class, 8

Corbyn, Jeremy: elected as leader of Labour Party, 20, 53, 59, 75, 78

Cowley, Philip: 35

Crosland, Tony: Secretary of Education, 36; two-tier higher education system proposed by, 158

Crossrail 2: 228; spending on, 143

Czech Republic: 69, 73

D66: supporters of, 76

Dade, Pat: 43–4, 219; role in establishment of British Values Survey, 43, 218–19

Daily Mail: 227; reader base of, 4

Danish Peoples' Party: 55, 69–70, 73; ideology of, 73

Darwin, Charles: 28

death penalty: 44; support for, 39, 216–17

Deaton, Angus: 67

deference, end of: 63
Delors, Jacques: 96, 103–4;
    President of European
    Commission, 94
Democratic Party: ideology of, 62,
    65; shortcomings of engagement
    strategies of, 66–7
Demos: 137
Dench, Geoff: 207; concept of
    'quality with pluralism', 214;
    Transforming Men, 209
Denmark: 69, 71, 99; education
    levels in, 156
Diana, Princess of Wales: death of
    (1997), 107
double liberalism: 1, 11, 63
Duffy, Gillian: 124
Dyson: 173; Dyson effect, 173

Economist: 10, 210, 216
Eden, Anthony: administration of,
    187
Eichengreen, Barry: 91
Elias, Norbert: 119
Employer Skills Survey: 163
Engineering Employers Federation:
    166
Englishness: 111
Erdogan, Recep Tayyip: 218
Essex Man/Woman: 186
Estonia: population levels of, 102
Eton College: 179, 187
Euro (currency): 100–1; accession
    of countries to, 98–9
European Commission: 26, 97
European Convention on Human
    Rights: 83–4
European Court of Justice (ECJ):
    103
European Economic Community
    (EEC): 92; British accession
    to (1973), 93; Treaty of Rome
    (1957), 101

European Exchange Rate
    Mechanism (ERM): 97–8
European Parliament: elections
    (2009), 71–2; elections (2014),
    72
European Union (EU): 10, 25,
    53, 76, 89, 92–4, 99–100, 120,
    124, 160, 215, 221–2, 229,
    233; Amsterdam Treaty (1997),
    94; Common Agricultural
    Policy, 92, 96; establishment
    of (1957), 91–2; freedom of
    movement principles, 100–1,
    163–4; Humanitarian Protection
    Directive (2004), 83; integra-
    tion, 50, 98–9, 173; Lisbon
    Treaty (2009), 94; Maastricht
    Treaty (1992), 94, 96, 103;
    members states of, 16, 31, 55,
    71, 216; personnel of, 128;
    Schengen Agreement (1985),
    94–5, 99, 117; Single European
    Act (1986), 94; Treaty of Nice
    (2000), 94
Euroscepticism: 69
Eurozone Crisis (2008–): 92, 99
Evening Standard: 143–5

Facebook: 86
family culture: 196–7; childcare,
    202–3; cohabitation, 196, 211;
    divorce figures, 196–7; gen-
    der roles, 206–13; legislation
    impacting, 195–6; lone parents,
    196; married couples tax allow-
    ance, 225; relationship with state
    intrusion, 200–2; tax burdens,
    203–4; tax credit systems, 202,
    204–5, 225
Farage, Nigel: 11; leader of UKIP,
    72; political rhetoric of, 20
Fawcett Society: surveys conducted
    by, 195–6

federalism: 69

feminism: 185, 199, 205; gender pay gap, 198–9; orthodox, 194

Fidesz: 69, 71, 73

Fillon, François: 73

Financial Times: 91, 108, 115, 138, 145, 147

Finkelstein, Daniel: 34

Five Star Movement: 53, 55, 64, 70, 73

Florida, Richard: concept of 'Creative Class', 136

Foges, Clare: 183

food sector: 17, 102, 125, 126

Ford, Robert: 35, 150

foreign ownership: 172–74, 230

Fortuyn, Pim: assassination of (2002), 50, 69

France: 69, 75, 94–6, 101, 173; agricultural sector of, 96; compulsory insurance system of, 222; Paris, 104, 143; high-skill/low-skill job disappearance in, 151; Revolution (1789–99), 106

Frank, Thomas: concept of 'liberalism of the rich', 62

Franzen, Jonathan: 110

free trade agreements: opposition to, 62

Freedom Party: 69; electoral defeat of (2016), 70; ideology of, 73; supporters of, 70

French Colonial Empire (1534–1980): 107

Friedman, Sam: 'Introducing the Class Ceiling: Social Mobility and Britain's Elite Occupations', 187

Friedman, Thomas: *World is Flat, The*, 85

Front National (FN): 53, 69, 72–3; European electoral performance

of (2014), 72; founding of (1973), 72; supporters of, 72

Gallup: polls conducted by, 65

Ganesh, Janan: 115, 145

gay marriage: 5, 76; opposition to, 46–7; support for, 26, 220

General Electric Company (GEC) plc: 172, 175

German-British Forum: members of, 174

Germany: 70, 73, 86, 94, 96, 100–1, 173–4, 209; automobile industry of, 96; chemical industry of, 176; compulsory insurance system of, 222; education sector of, 166; high-skill/low-skill job disappearance in, 151; labour market of, 147; Leipzig, 58; Ludwigshafen, 176; Reunification (1990), 96, 147, 176; Ruhr, 176–7

Ghemawat, Prof Pankaj: 85–6

Gilens, Martin: study of American public policy and public preferences, 61–2

Glasman, Maurice: 227

Global Financial Crisis (2007–9): 56, 169–70, 177; Credit Crunch (2007–8), 98, 177

Global Villagers: 31–2, 44–5, 160, 226; characteristics of, 46; political representation of, 75; political views of, 109, 112

globalisation: 9–10, 50–2, 81–2, 85, 87–8, 90–1, 105–6, 148; economic, 9; global trade development, 86–7; growth of, 85–6; hyperglobalisation, 88–9; relationship with nation states, 85–6; sane, 90

Golden Dawn: 74; growth of, 105

Goldman Sachs: personnel of, 31
Goldthorpe, John: 184–5, 189–90
Goodhart, David: 12
Goodwin, Fred: 168
Goodwin, Matthew: 150
Gordon, Ian: 137–8, 140
Gould, Philip: 220
Gove, Michael: 64, 91
great liberalisation: 39–40, 47;
    effect of, 40
Greater London Authority (GLA):
    143
Greece: 53, 56, 69, 74, 99, 105;
    Athens, 143; government of, 98
Green, Francis: 163
Green Party (UK): supporters of,
    38
Group of Twenty (G20): 89
Guardian: 14, 210

Habsburg Empire (Austro-
    Hungarian Empire): collapse of
    (1918), 107
Haidt, Jonathan: 11, 30, 33, 133;
    Righteous Mind, The, 28–9
Hakim, Catharine: 205
Hall, Stuart: 14–15
Hames, Tim: 135–6
Hampstead/Hartlepool alliance: 75
Hanson Trust: subsidiaries of, 175
Hard Authoritarian: 43–7, 51, 119,
    220; characteristics of, 24–5;
    political views of, 109
Harris, Gareth: 137; 'Changing
    Places', 137
Harvard University: faculty of, 57
Heath, Edward: foreign policy of,
    96
Higgins, Les: role in establishment
    of British Values Survey, 43
High Speed 2 (HS2): 228
High Speed 3 (HS3): aims of, 151,
    228

Hitler, Adolf: 94
Hoescht: 176
Hofstadter, Richard: 'Everyone is
    Talking About Populism, But No
    One Can Define It' (1967), 54
Holmes, Chris: 151
homophobia: observations in BSA
    surveys, 39; societal views of,
    39–40, 216
Honig, Bonnie: concept of 'objects
    of public love', 111
Huguenots: 121
Huhne, Chris: 16, 32
human rights: 5, 10, 55, 113;
    courts, 113; legislation, 5, 83–4,
    109, 112; rhetoric, 112–13
Hungary: 53, 64, 69, 71, 73–4, 99,
    218; Budapest, 218

Ignatieff, Michael: leader of Liberal
    Party (Canada), 13
Imperial Chemical Industries (ICI):
    172, 174–5; personnel of, 169;
    subsidiaries of, 175
Inbetweeners: 4, 25, 46, 109;
    political views of, 109
India: 104
Inglehart, Ronald: theories of value
    change, 27
Insider Nation: concept of, 61, 64;
    evidence of, 61–2
Institute for Fiscal Studies (IFS):
    201; findings of, 211–12
International Monetary Fund
    (IMF): 86–7, 102
interracial marriage: societal views
    of, 40
India: 10, 160
Ipsos MORI: polls conducted by,
    42, 122
Iraq: 84; Operation Iraqi Freedom
    (2003–11), 82

Islam: 50; Ahmadiyya, 84; conservative, 131; Halal, 68; hostility to, 73; Qur'an, 50
Islamism: 130
Islamophobia: 130
Italy: 55, 64, 69–70, 73, 96; migrants from, 125

Jamaica: 14
Japan: 86; request for League of Nations racial equality protocol (1919), 109
Jews/Judaism: 121, 259; orthodox, 131; persecution of, 17
jingoism: 8
Jobbik: 53, 64, 74
Johnson, Boris: 145
Jones, Sir John Harvey: death of (2008), 169
Jordan, Hashemite Kingdom of: government of, 84
Jospin, Lionel: defeat in final round of French presidential elections (2002), 49
Judah, Ben: *This is London: Life and Death in the World City*, 145

Kaufmann, Eric: 8–9, 131, 219, 227; 'Changing Places', 137
Kellner, Peter: 78
King, Mervyn: Governor of Bank of England, 86
Kinnock, Neil: 98
knowledge economy: 147, 149, 154, 166, 221
Kohl, Helmut: 94
Kotleba: 74
Krastev, Ivan: 55, 65, 82–3

labour: 9, 89–90, 149; eastern European, 125–6; gender division of, 197; hourglass labour market, 150, 191; living wage, 26, 152; market, 95, 101–2, 124, 140, 147–8, 150–2, 156–7, 181, 225
Labour Party (Denmark): 77
Labour Party (Netherlands): 50; supporters of, 76
Labour Party (UK): 2, 23, 53, 57, 72, 123, 157, 159, 207; Blue Labour, 63; electoral performance of (2015), 75; European election performance (2014), 72; expansion of welfare state under, 199–200; members of, 14, 20, 36, 59, 61, 77–8, 84; Momentum, 53; New Labour, 33, 75, 107, 123, 155, 159, 167, 196, 207, 220, 226, 232; Party Conference (2005), 7; social media presence of, 79; supporters of, 17, 35, 75, 77, 143, 221; voting patterns in Brexit vote, 19
Lakner, Christoph: concept of elephant curve, 87
Lamy, Pascal: 97
Latvia: adoption of Euro, 98–9; migrants from, 25–6
Laurison, Daniel: 'Introducing the Class Ceiling: Social Mobility and Britain's Elite Occupations', 187
Law and Justice Party: 69, 71, 73
Lawson, Nigel: 205
Le Pen, Jean-Marie: victory in final round of French presidential elections (2002), 49, 69
Le Pen, Marine: 53; electoral strategies of, 73
Leadbeater, Charles: 53
League of Nations: protocols of, 109
left-behinders: 20

Lega Nord: 69

Levin, Yuval: *Fractured Republic, The*, 232

liberal democracy: 2, 31, 55

Liberal Democrats: 23, 53–4; members of, 16; supporters of, 38, 78

Liberal Party (Canada): members of, 13

liberalism: 4–5, 12–13, 29–31, 55, 76, 119, 127–8, 199, 233; Anywhere, 27–8; baby boomer, 6; double, 1, 63; economic, 11; graduate, 216–17; meritocratic, 34; metropolitan, 216; orthodox, 13–14; Pioneer, 44; social, 4, 11

libertarianism: 8, 11, 22, 39, 44

Libya: 84; Civil War (2011), 225

Lilla, Mark: 35

Lind, Michael: 105, 135

Livingstone, Ken: 136

Lloyd, John: 56

London School of Economics (LSE): 54, 137–8, 140, 183

Low Pay Commission: findings of, 170

Lucas Industries plc: 172

male breadwinner: 149, 194, 195, 198, 206, 207

Manchester University: faculty of, 131

Mandelson, Peter: British Home Secretary, 61; family of, 61

Mandler, Peter: 135

Marr, Andrew: 53, 181

Marshall Plan (1948): 92

mass immigration: 14, 55, 104–5, 118–19, 121–4, 126–7, 140, 228–9; accompanied infrastructure development, 137–9; brain-drain issue, 102; debate of issue, 81–2; freedom of movement debates, 100–3; housing levels issue, 138–9; impact on wages, 152; integration, 129–32, 140–2; non-EU, 124–5; opposition to, 16–17, 120, 220

May, Theresa: 63, 179, 183, 198–9; administration of, 173, 176, 187, 191, 230; British Home Secretary, 124–5; 'Citizens of Nowhere' speech (2016), 31; political rhetoric of, 15, 31, 226

McCain, John: electoral defeat of (2008), 68

meritocracy: 152, 179–80, 190; critiques of, 180–1; perceptions of, 182–3

Merkel, Angela: reaction to refugee crisis (2015), 71

Mexico: borders of, 21

migration flows: global rates, 82, 87; non-refugee, 82

Milanovic, Branko: 126; concept of elephant curve, 87

Miliband, Ed: 78, 189

Mill, John Stuart: 'harm principle' of, 11–12

Millennium Cohort Study: 159

Miller, David: concept of 'weak cosmopolitanism', 109

Mills, Colin: 185

Mitterand, François: 94, 97

mobility: 8, 11, 20, 23, 36, 37, 38, 153, 167, 219; capital: 86, 88; geographical, 4, 6; social, 6, 33, 58, 152, 168, 179, 180, 182, 183–191, 213, 215, 220, 226, 231

Moderate Party: members of, 70

Monnet, Jean: 94–5, 97, 103–4

Morgan Stanley: 171

Mudde, Cas: observations of populism, 57
multiculturalism: 14, 50, 141–2; conceptualisation of, 106; laissez-faire, 132

narodniki: 54
national identity: 14, 38, 41, 111–12; conceptualisations of, 45; indifference to, 41, 46, 106, 114; polling on, 41
nationalism: 38, 46–7, 105; chauvinistic, 107, 120; civic, 23, 53; extreme, 104; moderate, 228; modern, 112; post-, 8, 105–6, 112; Scottish, 221
nativism: 57
Neave, Guy: 36
net migration: 126; White British, 136
Netherlands: 13–14, 50, 69, 73, 75, 99–100; Amsterdam, 49, 51; immigrant/minority population of, 50–1; Moroccan population of, 50–1
Netmums: surveys conducted by, 205–6
New Culture Forum: members of, 144
New Jerusalem: 105
New Society/Opinion Research Centre: polling conducted by, 33
New Zealand: 160
Nextdoor: 114
non-governmental organizations (NGOs): 21; refugee, 82
Norris, Pippa: 57
North American Free Trade Agreement (NAFTA): 91; opposition to, 62
North Atlantic Treaty Organization (NATO): 85, 92; personnel of, 84

Norway: 69
Nuttall, Paul: leader of UKIP, 72;

Obama, Barack: 67; approval ratings of, 60; electoral victory of (2012), 68; healthcare policies of, 22–3; target of birther movement, 68
O'Donnell, Gus: background of, 15–16; British Cabinet Secretary, 15
O'Leary, Duncan: 232
Open University: Centre for Research on Socio-Cultural Change (CRESC), 172–3
Operation Iraqi Freedom (2003–11): political impact of, 56
Orbán, Victor: 69, 218
Organisation for Economic Co-operation and Development (OECD): 201, 204; report on education levels (2016), 155–6; start-ups ranking, 173
Orwell, George: *Nineteen Eighty-Four*, 108–9
Osborne, George: 189; economic policies of, 4, 226
Oswald, Andrew: 171
Ottoman Empire: collapse of (1923), 107
outsider nation: concept of, 61, 64
Owen, David: 99
Oxford University: 15, 35, 179, 186; Centre on Skills, Knowledge and Organisational Performance, 151; faculty of, 31, 151; Nuffield College, 32

Pakistan: persecution of Ahmadiyya Muslims in, 84
Parris, Matthew: 115
Parsons, Talcott: concept of 'achieved' identities, 115

Party of Freedom (PVV): 69; ideology of, 73; supporters of, 50, 76

Paxman, Jeremy: 42

Pearson: ownership of Higher National Certificates (HNCs)/ Higher National Diplomas (HNDs), 157

Pegida: ideology of, 73

Pessoa, Joao Paulo: 88

Phalange: 74

Phillips, Trevor: 133

Pioneers: characteristics of, 43–4

Plaid Cymru: supporters of, 38

Podemos: 53, 64

Poland: 56, 69, 73; migrants from, 25–6, 121

Policy Exchange: 'Bittersweet Success', 188

political elites: media representation of, 63–4

populism: 1, 5, 13–14, 49–52, 55–6, 60, 64, 67, 69–74, 81; American, 54, 65; British, 63; decent, 6, 55, 71, 73, 219–20, 222, 227, 233; definitions of, 54; European, 49, 53, 65, 68–9, 74; left-wing, 54, 56; opposition to, 74; right-wing, 33, 51, 54

Populists: 54

Portillo, Michael: 31

Portugal: migrants from, 121, 125

post-industrialism: 6

post-nationalism: 105

poverty: 83, 168; child, 183–4, 200, 204; extreme, 87; reduction of, 78, 200; wages, 231

Powell, Enoch: 'Rivers of Blood' speech (1968), 127

Professionalisation of politics: 59

Progress Party: 69

progressive individualism: 5

Progressive Party: founding of (1912), 54

proportional representation: support for, 228

Prospect: 14, 91, 136

Prospectors: characteristics of, 43

Protestantism: 8, 213

Putin, Vladimir: 218

Putnam, Robert: 22; theory of social capital, 110

racism: 32, 73–4, 134; observations in BSA surveys, 39; societal views of, 39; violent, 127

Rashid, Sammy: Sheffield report, 155

Reagan, Ronald: 58, 63; approval ratings of, 60

Recchi, Ettore: 104

Refugee Crisis (2015–): 83–4; charitable efforts targeting, 21–2; government funds provided to aid, 83; political reactions to, 71

Relationships Foundation: 202

Republic of Ireland: 99; high-skill/ low-skill job disappearance in, 151; property bubble in, 98

Republican Party: ideology of, 62, 65; members of, 68

Resolution Foundation: 87–8; concept of 'squeezed middle', 168–9; reports of, 171

Ricardo, David: trade theory of, 101

Robinson, Eric: 36

Rodrik, Dani: 82, 89; concept of 'hyperglobalisation', 88; theory of 'sane globalisation', 90

Romania: 26; accession to EU, 225 (2007); migrants from, 102, 126

Romney, Mitt: electoral defeat of (2012), 68

Roosevelt, Theodore: leader of Progressive Party, 54

Rousseau, Jean-Jacques: 156

Rowthorn, Bob: 149

Royal Bank of Scotland (RBS): personnel of, 168

Royal College of Nursing: 140

Rudd, Amber: foreign worker list conflict (2016), 17

Ruhs, Martin: 126

Russell Group: 55; culture of, 37; student demographics of, 130–1, 191

Russian Federation: 2, 92; Moscow, 218; St Petersburg, 218

Rwanda: Genocide (1994), 82

Saffy factor: concept of, 199, 221–2

Scheffer, Paul: 85; 'Multicultural Tragedy, The' (2000), 49–50

Schumann, Robert: 94

Sciences Po: personnel of, 104

Scottish National Party (SNP): 1, 23, 54, 112; electoral performance of (2015), 75; ideology of, 53

Second World War (1939–45): 105, 194; Holocaust, 109

Security and identity issues: 41, 78, 81

Settlers: characteristics of, 43

Sikhism: 131

Singapore: 101, 128; education levels in, 156

Slovakia: 69, 73–4

Slovenia: adoption of Euro, 98–9

Smer: 69, 73

Smith, Zadie: 141–2

Social Democratic Party: supporters of, 75–6

social mobility: 6, 33, 58, 179–80, 183, 187, 189–91, 220; absolute mobility, 184, 188; relative mobility, 184; slow, 168; upward, 152

Social Mobility Commission: 161, 179–80

socialism: 49, 72, 183, 190

Somewheres: 3–5, 12–13, 17–18, 20, 41–3, 45, 115, 177, 180, 191, 214, 223, 228; characteristics of, 5–6, 2, 32; conflict with Anywheres, 23, 79, 81, 193, 215; conservatism, 7–8; employment of, 11; European, 103; immigration of, 106; moral institutions, 223–4; political representation/voting patterns of, 13–14, 24–6, 36, 53–5, 77–9, 124, 227; political views of, 71, 76, 109, 112, 119, 199, 218, 224–6, 232; potential coalition with Anywheres, 220, 222, 225–6, 233; view of migrant integration, 134

Sorrell, Martin: 31

Soskice, David: 159

South Korea: 86

Soviet Union (USSR): 92, 188; collapse of (1991), 82, 107

Sowell, Thomas: 30; *A Conflict of Visions*, 29

Spain: 53, 56, 64, 74; government of, 98; migrants from, 125; property bubble in, 98

Steinem, Gloria: 198

Stenner, Karen: 30, 44, 122, 133, 227; *Authoritarian Dynamic, The*, 30–1

Stephens, Philip: 108

Sun, The: 227

Sutherland, Peter: 31–2

Sutton Trust: end of mobility thesis, 183–5

Swaziland: 135

Sweden: 56, 70, 100; general elections (2014), 70; Stockholm, 143; taxation system of, 222

Sweden Democrats: 70; electoral performance of (2014), 70; ideology of, 73

Switzerland: 37

Syria: Civil War (2009–), 82, 84

Syriza: 53, 69

Taiwan: 86

Teeside University: 164

terrorism: jihadi, 71, 74, 129

Thatcher, Margaret: 58, 63, 95, 189, 205; administration of, 169; economic policies of, 176

Third Reich (1933–45): 104; persecution of Jews in, 17

Times Education Supplement: 37

Timmermans, Frans: EU Commissioner, 128

Thompson, Mark: Director-General of BBC, 15

trade theory: principles of, 101

Transatlantic Trade and Investment Partnership (TTIP): 89; support for, 225

Trump, Donald: 50, 62, 74, 85; electoral victory of (2016), 1–3, 5–7, 13, 27, 30, 64–8, 81, 232; political rhetoric of, 14, 22–3, 51, 54, 66–7; supporters of, 56, 67

Tube Investments (TI): 172

Turkey: 218

Twitter: use for political activism, 79

Uber: 140

UK Independence Party (UKIP): 53, 55, 63–4, 69, 71–3, 228; electoral performance of (2015), 75; European election performance (2009), 71–2; members of, 13; origins of, 72; supporters of, 24, 35, 38, 72, 75, 143, 168, 216, 222

ultimatum game: 52

Understanding Society: surveys conducted by, 37–8, 202

unemployment: 101–2; gender divide of, 208–9; not in employment, education or training (Neets), 151–2, 190; youth, 139, 151–2, 166

Unilever: 175

United Kingdom (UK): 1–3, 8, 11–12, 21, 27–8, 31, 33, 41, 44, 59–60, 69, 73, 75, 81, 83, 91, 111–12, 147, 165, 173, 180, 193–5, 199, 204, 217, 227; Aberdeen, 136; accession to EEC (1973), 93; Adult Skills budget of, 161, 225; apprenticeship system of, 154, 157, 162–3, 166; Birmingham, 7, 123, 166; Boston, 121; Bradford, 133, 136; Bristol, 136; British Indian population of, 77; Burnley, 151; Cambridge, 136; City of London, 95, 106, 174; class system in, 58–9, 75, 123, 135–6, 149–52, 172, 182–3, 186, 195; Dagenham, 136; Department for Education, 206; Department for International Development (DfID), 224; Divorce Law Reform Act (1969), 196; economy of, 152, 170; Edinburgh, 54, 136; education sector of, 35, 147, 154–8; ethnic Chinese population of, 77; EU citizens in, 101; Finance Act (2014), 211; Foreign and Commonwealth Office (FCO), 224; Glasgow, 136; high-skill/low-skill job disappearance in, 150–1; higher education sector of, 35–7, 47, 159–62, 164–7, 179, 208, 230–1; Home Office, 17; House of Commons, 162; general election in (2015), 60; House of Lords, 31; Human Rights Act, 123, 225; income inequality levels in, 169–70, 172, 177, 184–5; labour market of, 16, 26, 124, 140–1, 148, 150–1, 152, 225; Leicester, 133; Leeds, 161; London, 3–4, 7, 10–11, 18–19, 24, 26, 34, 37, 59, 79, 101, 114–15, 119, 123, 131, 133–45, 151, 168, 216, 218, 226, 228, 232–3; Manchester, 123, 136, 151, 161, 228; manufacturing sector of, 17, 88; mass immigration in, 122–4, 126–7, 228–9; Muslim immigration in, 41–2, 44; Muslim population of, 127, 130; National Health Service (NHS), 72, 91, 111, 120, 140, 144, 200–1, 229; National Insurance system of, 204; Newcastle, 131, 136, 161; Northern Ireland, 38; Office for Fair Access, 180; Office for Standards in Education, Children's Services and Skills (Ofsted), 155; Office of National Statistics (ONS), 138, 144–5; Oldham, 133; Olympic Games (2012), 111, 143, 222; Oxford, 136; Parliamentary expenses scandal (2009), 56, 168; Plymouth, 131; public sector employment in, 171, 208–9, 229–30; regional identities in, 3–4, 186; Rochdale, 124; Scotland, 110, 138; Scottish independence referendum (2014), 53, 110; self-employment levels in, 171; Sheffield, 161; Slough, 131, 133; social mobility rate in, 58, 184–5, 187; start-ups in, 173–4; Stoke, 121; Sunderland, 52, 172; Supreme Court, 66; taxation system of, 222; Treasury, 16; UK Border Agency, 108; vocational education in, 163; voting patterns for Brexit vote, 7–9, 19–20, 23, 26, 36, 52; wage levels in, 168; Wales, 138; welfare state in, 199–203, 223–4, 231–2; Westminster, 54, 58, 60; youth unemployment in, 151–2

United Nations (UN): 102, 198; Conference on Trade and Development (UNCTAD), 10; Declaration of Human Rights (1948), 109; Geneva Convention (1951), 82–4; High Commission for Refugees (UNHCR), 82, 84; Security Council, 99

United States of America (USA): 1–2, 6–7, 22–3, 36–7, 51, 57, 60, 74, 86, 89, 94, 128, 168, 193, 208, 227; 9/11 Attacks, 130; Agency for International Development (USAID), 224; Asian population of, 68; borders of, 21; Chinese Exclusion Act (1882), 54; class identity in, 65–6; Congress, 67; Constitution of, 57; education system of, 166; higher education sector of, 167; Hispanic population of, 67–8, 85; House of Representatives, 67; immigration debate in, 67–8; Ivy League, 36, 61; New York, 135; political divisions in, 65; Senate, 67

University College London (UCL): *Imagining the Future City: London 2061*, 137, 139
University of California: 165
University of Kent: 36
University of Sussex: 36
University of Warwick: 36; faculty of, 171

Vietnam War (1955–75): 29
Visegrad Group: 69, 73, 99
Vlaams Belang: ideology of, 73

wages for housework: 194
Walzer, Michael: 117–18
War on Drugs: 62
WEIRD (Western, Educated, Industrialised, Rich and Democratic): 27
Welzel, Christian: *Freedom Rising*, 27
Westminster University: 165
white flight: 129, 134, 136
white identity politics: 9, 67
white supremacy: 8, 68, 73–4
Whittle, Peter: 144
Wilders, Geert: 50, 76
Willetts, David: 164, 185
Wilson, Harold: electoral victory of (1964), 150

Wolf, Prof Alison: 162, 164–5; *XX Factor, The*, 189, 198
working class: 2–4, 6, 51–2, 59, 61, 65; conservatism, 8 political representation/views of, 8, 52, 58, 63, 70, 72; progressives, 78–9; voting patterns of, 15, 52, 75–6; white, 19, 68
World Bank: 84
World Trade Organisation (WTO): 10, 85, 89–90, 97; accession of China to (2001), 88
World Values Survey: 27

xenophobia: 2, 14, 50–1, 57, 71, 119, 121, 141, 144, 225

York, Peter: 138
York University: 36
YouGov: personnel of, 78; polls conducted by, 16–17, 42, 66, 79, 114, 132, 141
Young, Hugo: 93
Young, Michael: 119, 190; *Rise of the Meritocracy, The*, 180–1
Yugoslav Wars (1991–2001): 97
Yugoslavia: 97

Zeman, Milos: President of Czech Republic, 73

ALLEN LANE
an imprint of
PENGUIN BOOKS

Also Published

Jonathan Losos, *Improbable Destinies: How Predictable is Evolution?*

Chris D. Thomas, *Inheritors of the Earth: How Nature Is Thriving in an Age of Extinction*

Chris Patten, *First Confession: A Sort of Memoir*

James Delbourgo, *Collecting the World: The Life and Curiosity of Hans Sloane*

Naomi Klein, *No Is Not Enough: Defeating the New Shock Politics*

Ulrich Raulff, *Farewell to the Horse: The Final Century of Our Relationship*

Slavoj Žižek, *The Courage of Hopelessness: Chronicles of a Year of Acting Dangerously*

Patricia Lockwood, *Priestdaddy: A Memoir*

Ian Johnson, *The Souls of China: The Return of Religion After Mao*

Stephen Alford, *London's Triumph: Merchant Adventurers and the Tudor City*

Hugo Mercier and Dan Sperber, *The Enigma of Reason: A New Theory of Human Understanding*

Stuart Hall, *Familiar Stranger: A Life Between Two Islands*

Allen Ginsberg, *The Best Minds of My Generation: A Literary History of the Beats*

Sayeeda Warsi, *The Enemy Within: A Tale of Muslim Britain*

Alexander Betts and Paul Collier, *Refuge: Transforming a Broken Refugee System*

Robert Bickers, *Out of China: How the Chinese Ended the Era of Western Domination*

Erica Benner, *Be Like the Fox: Machiavelli's Lifelong Quest for Freedom*

William D. Cohan, *Why Wall Street Matters*

David Horspool, *Oliver Cromwell: The Protector*

Daniel C. Dennett, *From Bacteria to Bach and Back: The Evolution of Minds*

Derek Thompson, *Hit Makers: How Things Become Popular*

Harriet Harman, *A Woman's Work*

Wendell Berry, *The World-Ending Fire: The Essential Wendell Berry*

Daniel Levin, *Nothing but a Circus: Misadventures among the Powerful*

Stephen Church, *Henry III: A Simple and God-Fearing King*

Pankaj Mishra, *Age of Anger: A History of the Present*

Graeme Wood, *The Way of the Strangers: Encounters with the Islamic State*

Michael Lewis, *The Undoing Project: A Friendship that Changed the World*

John Romer, *A History of Ancient Egypt, Volume 2: From the Great Pyramid to the Fall of the Middle Kingdom*

Andy King, *Edward I: A New King Arthur?*

Thomas L. Friedman, *Thank You for Being Late: An Optimist's Guide to Thriving in the Age of Accelerations*

John Edwards, *Mary I: The Daughter of Time*

Grayson Perry, *The Descent of Man*

Deyan Sudjic, *The Language of Cities*

Norman Ohler, *Blitzed: Drugs in Nazi Germany*

Carlo Rovelli, *Reality Is Not What It Seems: The Journey to Quantum Gravity*

Catherine Merridale, *Lenin on the Train*

Susan Greenfield, *A Day in the Life of the Brain: The Neuroscience of Consciousness from Dawn Till Dusk*

Christopher Given-Wilson, *Edward II: The Terrors of Kingship*

Emma Jane Kirby, *The Optician of Lampedusa*

Minoo Dinshaw, *Outlandish Knight: The Byzantine Life of Steven Runciman*

Candice Millard, *Hero of the Empire: The Making of Winston Churchill*

Christopher de Hamel, *Meetings with Remarkable Manuscripts*

Brian Cox and Jeff Forshaw, *Universal: A Guide to the Cosmos*

Ryan Avent, *The Wealth of Humans: Work and Its Absence in the Twenty-first Century*

Jodie Archer and Matthew L. Jockers, *The Bestseller Code*

Cathy O'Neil, *Weapons of Math Destruction: How Big Data Increases Inequality and Threatens Democracy*

Peter Wadhams, *A Farewell to Ice: A Report from the Arctic*

Richard J. Evans, *The Pursuit of Power: Europe, 1815-1914*

Anthony Gottlieb, *The Dream of Enlightenment: The Rise of Modern Philosophy*

Marc Morris, *William I: England's Conqueror*

Gareth Stedman Jones, *Karl Marx: Greatness and Illusion*

J.C.H. King, *Blood and Land: The Story of Native North America*

Robert Gerwarth, *The Vanquished: Why the First World War Failed to End, 1917-1923*

Joseph Stiglitz, *The Euro: And Its Threat to Europe*

John Bradshaw and Sarah Ellis, *The Trainable Cat: How to Make Life Happier for You and Your Cat*

A J Pollard, *Edward IV: The Summer King*

Erri de Luca, *The Day Before Happiness*

Diarmaid MacCulloch, *All Things Made New: Writings on the Reformation*

Daniel Beer, *The House of the Dead: Siberian Exile Under the Tsars*

Tom Holland, *Athelstan: The Making of England*

Christopher Goscha, *The Penguin History of Modern Vietnam*

Mark Singer, *Trump and Me*

Roger Scruton, *The Ring of Truth: The Wisdom of Wagner's Ring of the Nibelung*

Ruchir Sharma, *The Rise and Fall of Nations: Ten Rules of Change in the Post-Crisis World*